INSIDE IRAN
WOMEN'S LIVES

JANE HOWARD

MAGE PUBLISHERS
WASHINGTON, D.C.
2002

LIBRARY OF CONGRESS CATALOGING-IN-PUBLICATION DATA

Howard, Jane Mary, 1959-
Inside Iran,: Women's Lives / Jane Howard
p. com.
Includes biographical references and index.
1. Women--Iran--Social conditions.
2. Women--Employment--Iran.
3. Women--Education--Iran.
I. Title.
HQ1735.2.H68 2002 / 305.42'0955--dc21

ISBN 0-934211-71-X

MAGE BOOKS ARE AVAILABLE THROUGH BOOKSTORES
OR DIRECTLY FROM THE PUBLISHER.
VISIT MAGE ON THE WEB AT http://www.mage.com
OR CALL 1-800-962-0922 OR 202-342-1642
TO ORDER BOOKS OR TO RECEIVE OUR CURRENT CATALOG.

CONTENTS

In memory of my father

Prologue

I arrived at Tehran's Mehrabad airport with rather a lot of hand luggage—a baby, a toddler, two cameras, a computer, my jewelry and a baby carriage. I was feeling extremely hot and bothered, having donned the compulsory headscarf and coat to cover up according to Islamic law. The KLM crew had been helpful enough, sympathizing when I told them I would be living in Tehran for several years. The only notable moment on the flight had been when a crew member whispered in my ear, "Didn't you have a beer?" I explained guiltily that I had hidden the can under the seat where it would not get knocked over by the children. Apparently "alcoholic" rubbish had to go into a separate bag, as it could not be dumped on the soil of the Islamic Republic of Iran.

However, when I asked the stewardess if someone could give me a hand getting down the steps, she said tartly: "I'm sorry, we can't help with hand luggage." When I asked her how she thought I could manage with two sleeping children and numerous bags, her jaw dropped and she apologized profusely. "I didn't recognize you now you've covered up—it makes everyone look the same, you know." She helped me down the aisle, then stopped in embarrassment at the door. "I'm afraid I'm not allowed to come down the steps with you. It's company policy that we don't leave the plane, or else we would have to cover up, too. We don't even stay overnight."

She found a helpful passenger, but when I got to the terminal, I realized that I had left the baby carriage behind in the confusion. I was immediately surrounded by Iranians trying to help. The security guard radioed the plane. "Yes, we found it, and we've sent it with another passenger," was the answer. They did not say which passenger. I searched the arrivals hall, getting hotter and hotter. It turned up on the baggage carousel.

My husband, Laurens, met me on the other side of passport control. It was his job with the United Nations that had brought us to Iran. He had warned me not to expect a kiss. Public displays of affection are frowned on, even between man and wife. For men and women who are not related, a kiss in public can lead to a flogging.

What kind of a country had I come to? The Iranians in the arrivals hall could not have been more helpful, but their lives are hemmed in by Islamic rules and revolutionary regulations. I wanted to find out more, to find out what everyday life was really like for women in Iran. During my time in Iran I got to know women at home, women at work, women who were happy, women who were sad. The more women I met, the more I heard them insist: "The headscarf is the least of our problems."

1

All the President's Women

I was invited to dinner with the wife of the president of Iran, and I was wondering what to wear. It was December 1997 and I was living in Tehran, where my husband was posted with the UN. The wives and daughters of the ruling elite would be there, as well as the relatives of the late Ayatollah Khomeini, leader of the 1979 revolution. These are women whom the outside world has only seen veiled in black, with a triangle for a face. These shadowy figures are at the heart of Iran's Islamic regime, held up as models of womanhood, yet for the most part, anonymous and hidden. I wondered, not for the first time, what these women wore under their *chadors,* the black sheets that cover the most traditional and Islamic Iranian women. I also wondered how they felt about the revolution two decades ago, which ordered women to cover up, shun the West and devote themselves to their homes.

As I fingered the invitation, decorated with an intricate floral border, I thought that perhaps I should finally invest in a chador. But this was to be a women-only dinner, so I knew that it would be exempt from *hejab,* the strict rules of covering up under Islamic law. I couldn't imagine arriving clutching a chador with one hand or with gritted teeth, like the women I saw struggling back from the bazaar with their hands full of shopping bags and squirming toddlers. I knew I didn't really need a chador. Living in northern Tehran, most foreigners and many Iranians conform to the law with a long coat and headscarf. Since moving to Iran, I had accumulated four of the unlined overcoats known as *manteau*s or *rupush*es. I had bought them in different colors, in a vain quest for a garment that would feel cool and light in 105°F heat. But in the end, like everyone else, I often wore black. It seemed easier not to stand out in the crowd.

I put on black velvet trousers and a silk shirt and covered up with a long thin black coat with large gilt buttons and padded shoulders. I was careful not to wear open-toed sandals (considered immodest) and made sure I had black socks on. It is not unusual to be stopped in the street and berated for wearing see-through stockings, or, worse still, none at all. These days, foreigners who break the law—euphemistically known as "the Islamic Dress Code"—usually get away with a scolding, but Iranian women, especially young ones, can be interrogated for hours or even days at special centers for "the Prevention of Vice and Enjoining of Virtue." Some two decades after the revolution, women still live in fear of a flogging for showing more than a couple of inches of hair in violation of religious tradition and the "Islamic Penal Code." The sentence has been gradually reduced and now generally entails a fine, but the fear remains.

I set off for the dinner with Evelien von der Schulenburg, wife of the most senior UN official in Iran. We drove to one of the Shah's former palaces in a leafy area at the foot of the mountains, where the deposed ruler used to entertain in grand style. Big gates opened and we swept into an imposing 1950s-style building set in a large park. We walked up the steps, then pushed our way through a curtain hanging inside the entrance to frustrate male curiosity (the word *hejab* originally meant "curtain" in Arabic). Inside was a row of female Foreign Ministry officials, surprisingly difficult to recognize without their usual strict Islamic dress. They urged us to take off our scarves and coats.

Then we were taken through to meet our hostess, Zohreh Sadeghi, the wife of President Khatami (like all Iranian women, she uses her own name) and her two daughters, Leila and Narges. Dressed in a dark suit, she welcomed us warmly but shyly. The daughters, smart and poised, spoke more English. Most of the guests seemed to have dressed as if for a smart lunch.

We were ushered into a large anteroom furnished around the edges with the formal, French-style gilt furniture loved by Iranians. We sat and nibbled pistachio nuts, dates, dried fruit and sweetmeats, and watched the other guests arrive. The dinner was being held in honor of dignitaries present at the summit of the Organization of the Islamic Conference.

More than fifty heads of state and their spouses were at the conference. The wife of the prime minister of Malaysia, Dr. Siti Hasmah Mohamed Ali, looked exotic in vivid oriental silk. The wife of the UN Secretary-General, Nane Annan, looked sophisticated in black. The ambassador of Sierra Leone, Alari Cole, the only female diplomat to head a mission in Tehran, appeared in a brightly colored national dress. Not everyone looked as stunning. One Iranian wore a synthetic-looking suit with a peach-colored jacket and a black skirt. Strange matching handkerchiefs dangled down around her hips from the hem of her top. As she walked, I noticed that her black stockings were not tights but knee-highs. One had slipped and was exposing her leg. Several women did not take off their headscarves.

"Where in the world is *she* from," I said to Evelien, suddenly. We both gasped at her grand entrance. She was tall, leggy, with dyed blonde hair. She was wearing a long, black velvet gown covered in sequins and split up to the thigh. She walked confidently across the room, straight up to us and introduced herself. "Hello, I'm Faezeh Hashemi," she said. The daughter of the former president Rafsanjani, and one of the most famous women in Iran, hers was the most daring outfit of the evening.

"Do you mind if I touch it," laughed Evelien, leaning over to feel the texture of the dress.

Looking rather distracted, and having some difficulty with English, Faezeh, as she is known, brightened when I asked her how preparations were going for the Islamic Countries' Women's Games, due to start just after the summit ended. She offered to send us an invitation to the opening ceremony. I was unable to attend but later heard how colorful figures on Rollerblades whizzed round the arena at top speed, reenacting an Iranian legend about a woman warrior. After distinguishing herself in battle, the fighter is revealed to be a woman when her hair falls down.[1] The skaters, in fact, were men. "They couldn't have women letting their hair down," Faezeh told me later, "so they had to put wigs on the male skaters."

When the dinner was served, waitresses in strict navy-blue uniforms brought out endless qualities of food. The lavish seven or eight course meal included Iranian caviar, chicken in walnut and pomegranate sauce, chicken with tangy red *zereshk* (barberries), and the ubiquitous kabab. But it was disappointingly bland compared to the sophisticated home cooking I had already encountered in Iranian homes.

Faezeh Hashemi did not stay long at the dinner. She was too busy with her latest project. She's passionate about sports, politics and a host of other causes. Women's sports were almost banned after the revolution, when mullahs suggested that it was more appropriate for women to keep fit in their own homes, away from prying eyes. But Faezeh has used her connections to campaign for better sports facilities for women and their right to compete in the international arena. She was rumored to have won

---

1. The story of Gordafarid, a woman fighter, is taken from the epic poem the *Shahnameh,* by the tenth-century poet Ferdowsi. Gordafarid dons armor and takes on Sohrab, one of the greatest heroes of the day. When Sohrab discovers she is a woman, he is embarrassed and lets her back into her fortress, as he does not want the soldiers to find out.

*A lone pilgrim kisses the grill at the tomb
of Ayatollah Khomeini, located south of Tehran.*

*Faezeh Hashemi, daughter of the former president Rafsanjani,
is one of the best-known women in Iran.*

the biggest number of votes of any single candidate in the 1996 parliamentary elections although officially she came in second. However, four years later she failed to win re-election, losing her parliamentary seat when the popularity of her father waned. She sees herself as a champion of women's rights, publicly defending the right of women to wear blue jeans and sneakers underneath the veil. Some months after our first meeting, she launched into publishing and started up a newspaper, *Zan,* or "Woman." It did not set out to cover women's issues alone, but also to provide support to the relatively liberal government of President Khatami, who was elected in a landslide in 1997. *Zan* did not survive for long. It was closed down in a vicious power struggle between a growing band of reformers and conservatives who saw themselves as guardians of the revolution and defenders of Islam.

Faezeh's mother—a solid-looking, warm, lively woman—was also at the dinner. As a family, they seemed an unconventional. Her sister, Fatemeh, was also there, dressed in a smart, scarlet suit. She has also been active in defending women's rights, within Islamic limits. In the 1990s, Fatemeh headed an office in the Foreign Ministry set up to try to improve the image of Iranian women abroad. Outsiders are surprised to find that Iran sees itself as a defender of women's rights. It tries to distance itself from ultra-conservative regimes such as the one in Saudi Arabia or the one then in power in neighboring Afghanistan. In both these countries, women have had to contend with being banned from working or driving, let alone entering politics. Fatemeh complained to me later that Western observers blamed Islam for a host of iniquities, which could mostly be laid at the door of tradition. "In Islamic countries, people's customs, traditions and superstitions are mixed up with Islamic laws, and the result you are presented with is not just Islam," she said. "We believe that if you could follow pure Islam, it could meet the needs and aspirations of women in the whole world."

This is the Islamic feminist point of view, which states that Islam affords all the protection a woman is likely to need. While Fatemeh agreed that women's rights in Iran have room for improvement, she found no difficulty with the statute that permits a girl to be married at the age of nine whereas a boy must wait until fifteen. "I personally think a difference of five to six years is appropriate because girls mature earlier, become wiser, earlier than boys, even in physical terms," she said. "Girls grow up sooner." She and her sister also defended the system of arranged or "assisted" marriages, where the parents choose marriage partners for their children. Fatemeh and Faezeh married two brothers from the same family. The matchmaking took place in unusual surroundings: "My husband's father and my father were in the same cell in jail together and that was the grounds for their acquaintance," she said.[2] "In Iran, the tradition is different from what happens in the West. In fact, I was courted."

None of the women at the party saw any contradiction between their belief in tradition and their right to work and take part in public life. The fact that they were not covered up, presenting the strictly anonymous official image, did not make them any less of a puzzle to me. The evening intensified my desire to find out more about the lives of other women in Iran.

* * *

To most outsiders, Iran remains a mystery. It is Middle Eastern, but not Arab. It has a grim, dark image of revolution and terror, yet travelers report warm, hospitable people who love to meet foreigners. Women cannot travel abroad without their husband's permission, yet more girls than boys go to university. Iran defies description, and visiting journalists, even the most committed, tend to find what they expect to find and seek no further. Few of them travel outside the big cities of Tehran, Isfahan and Shiraz, and few grasp the geographical complexities and vastness of the country.

Iran is cut off from its neighbors by the Caspian Sea and the Persian Gulf to the north and south, and by ranges of mountains and deserts to the east and west. Yet it has always served as an important trading route. This applies equally to the days of the Silk Road and to the time of the Great Game in the nineteenth century, when Britain and Russia vied with each other over control of Iran and access to the Persian Gulf, Afghanistan and India. Living in Tehran, in the high plateau in the middle, it is easy to enjoy a pleasant, dry climate in spite of chronic pollution and twelve million inhabitants. Although on the edge of a great salt desert, Tehran is always green and fresh, with plenty of surface water coursing down from the melting snow of the Alborz Mountains. I learned to ski (suitably covered, with long coat flapping) at a resort only an hour's drive to the north, whereas to the south you can put an off-road vehicle through its paces on sand dunes and dried out riverbeds.

Iran's population of more than sixty million is now mostly concentrated in cities. The migration from villages to towns is probably the most significant feature of twentieth century life and is undoubtedly where the roots

---

2. Both fathers were clergymen who were active in opposing the Shah. They were jailed for activities such as distributing the speeches of Ayatollah Khomeini and organizing opposition circles.

of the revolution lie. Yet many still live a traditional, rural life and more than a million Iranians describe themselves as nomads. They live in tents, and move from pasture to pasture in isolated mountain areas. In spite of repeated attempts to get them to settle, they continue to eke out a living rearing sheep and goats. Women of the various tribes produce some of the world's most sought-after carpets and handicrafts. Forced to settle, they miss the independence and status of the traditional life. I was shocked to hear of some of the problems of suicide and depression they encounter.

The sheer size of the country is difficult to convey. *A Travel Guide to Iran* points out that from one corner of Iran to the other is approximately the same as the distance from Paris to Athens. A visit to Baluchestan, on the border with Pakistan and Afghanistan, gave me an idea of the scale of things. The flight from Tehran, much of it over completely empty desert and scrub, took around two hours. The bus journey would take nearer to twenty-two. From the regional capital to Mount Taftan, a smoldering volcano on the border where I visited a cluster of villages, there were few signs of human habitation on the road. No wonder girls still have difficulty traveling to school in this region. Yet in the north, the Caspian Sea provinces are densely populated and highly cultivated. Women work in water up to their knees in flooded rice paddies and pick tea in plantations of emerald-green bushes. The green of the north is startling, indeed some areas of *jangal*, or mountain forest, have subtropical flora all of their own.

The central desert area, the Dasht-e Kavir, is disappointingly empty apart from spectacular dried up salt lakes. But at regular intervals there are impressive remains of old caravanserais, fortified staging posts built along the ancient Silk Road. The towns around the edge of the desert, such as Yazd, Kerman and Kashan, are highly sophisticated commercial and cultural centers. Cities such as Isfahan and Shiraz are the most popular tourist destinations nowadays, with their stunning mosques, decorated palaces and beautiful gardens dating back to the glittering Safavid dynasty of the sixteenth to eighteenth centuries.

To the west are the borders with Iraq, Turkey, Armenia and Azerbaijan. When I arrived in Tehran, I found I could make myself understood at the local grocer's shop by recalling a few words of Turkish. Around a quarter of Iran's population speak Turkish, not just in the western provinces, but also in the cities. The western Zagros Mountains are home to the Kurds, who have their own language and, unlike the vast majority of Iranians, are Sunni, not Shiite Muslims.

The south is another country again, or several countries. Around the southern port of Bandar Abbas, you see many dark faces, and you may hear music with African rhythms, a legacy of trade with Zanzibar. Some women wear a *borqa*, a rigid face mask with a slit for the eyes, more common on the other, Arab, side of the Gulf.[3] Near the border with Iraq, a large number of villages are Arabic speaking and bear the scars of the long Iran-Iraq war. Saddam Hussein invaded in 1980 in an attempt to take control of the Iranian oil fields of Khuzestan. The conflict ground on for eight years with massive loss of life estimated at up to one million dead. The war undoubtedly allowed the leaders of the 1979 revolution to consolidate their hold on power as the people accepted all kinds of emergency measures and privations as being in the national interest. Talking to some Iranians who remember that period as if it were yesterday, it sometimes feels as if the war had an equal or even greater impact on them than the revolution itself. In one house near the southwestern city of Ahwaz, an empty ammunition box was still being used for storage. Many homes display photos of young men lost in the fighting. And when I interviewed residents of this area as part of an oral English exam, they told me anecdotes about bombs dropping and palm trees burning. About the revolution they had much less to say, although this may have been due to natural caution.

A striking ethnic mix mirrors Iran's geographical diversity. Turks, Arabs, Kurds, Armenians live alongside nomadic groups such as the Bakhtiari, Qashqa'i, Lurs and Turkmen—each with distinct ethnic origins. There are so many different languages that when children begin school, only a minority of them have Persian, also known as *Farsi*, as their mother tongue. When a Ministry of Education official explained this to me, I asked her to repeat it more slowly—I could scarcely believe it.

Not surprisingly, one of the key unifying factors is religion. Iran remains an overwhelmingly Islamic country, with various religious minorities such as the Christian Armenians, Jews and the Zoroastrians, who follow an ancient, pre-Islamic faith. Some are officially recognized, and tolerated, but other faiths exist underground. Having worked as a BBC correspondent in neighboring Turkey, where religion is kept carefully out of government, I always found it fascinating to observe the differences. Compared to Turkey, Iran has comparatively few mosques or outward signs of mass worship. If Martians landed tomorrow in both countries, there might be some confusion about which state was the post-revolutionary theocracy. There are far more signs of mosque-building in solidly secular, but Sunni, Turkey than in Iran, where Shiism makes religion a more personal affair. Following the death of the Prophet, Mohammad,

---

3. Not to be confused with the Afghan *burkha*, a cover-all garment with a lace grill over the eyes.

the Shiites backed Mohammad's cousin and son-in-law, Ali, in the battle for succession. Iran was converted to Shiism in the sixteenth century, when the rulers of the time saw it as a way of rallying the population against the all-powerful Ottoman Empire, dominated by Sunni Turks. It was also a way of unifying the widely differing ethnic groups, ranging from Baluchis in the east to Kurds in the west, which make up the Iranian nation. Culturally, there are some distinctive differences in the Shiite tradition. There is much emphasis on political opposition, and on the rituals of martyrdom and suffering, commemorating the deaths of Ali and his son, Hossein.

The great variety of ethnic origins and different lifestyles make it a hopeless task to try to describe a typical day in the life of an Iranian woman. Many highly religious women stay at home, cover themselves carefully and center their lives on their children and husbands. Yet others from the same traditional backgrounds go to work, leaving their children with relatives or putting them in the office daycare. Some told me they would die of boredom staying at home. Others lead lives a Westerner could identify with. If they have the means, they shop in supermarkets, own two cars, take holidays abroad and wear international brand-name clothes. Most people's social lives revolve around their family, yet in the big cities, youngsters go to parties and cafés to socialize. One young friend who had just finished film school in the United States told me she went to far more parties in Tehran than she ever had in California.

While the revolution changed many lives, throwing women (and men) out of their jobs and forcing whole families to flee into exile, for others it barely changed things. Village life continues much as it always has, dominated by the sheer hard work of making a living. Erika Friedl's book, *Women of Deh Koh,* documents the minutiae of everyday life in a hill village in Iran. Friedl, an anthropologist with a wonderful eye for detail, has been going back to the same community for years. Yet the revolution plays a small part in her narrative. One historian working on a social history of Iran told me that the paucity of documentation never bothered him, as in general, people's lives changed very little even over centuries.

The big change for women occurred in the nineteenth and early-twentieth centuries, when women began to take part in public life. Contact with the West became more frequent, and shahs were embarrassed by criticism that they kept their women secluded and uneducated. Girls' schools were opened, in spite of opposition from the clerical establishment. The suffragette movement was widely admired, and women began to organize themselves. The defining moment came in 1936, when Reza Shah,

wanting his country to appear more modern, decreed that all women
should take off the veil or be punished. His son, the last shah of Iran,
granted women the vote in 1963 for similar reasons, pushing forward a
series of reforms against the wishes of the clergy.[4]

The 1960s and 1970s passed in a rush toward modernization fuelled by
the oil boom and supported by Western governments, notably the United
States. Iran is a rich country—at least in natural resources. It is the second-
largest oil exporter in OPEC and has the world's second-largest known reserves
of natural gas. While living standards improved, most of the people migrating to the cities did not feel as if they were sharing in the spoils. They saw
conspicuous consumption among the ruling elite and felt increasingly alien-
ated. Nor did they have a voice, for the Shah ruthlessly suppressed dissent,
banning political parties and quelling opposition from religious quarters.

For most of this time, Ayatollah Khomeini was in exile, in Iraq and in
France. He became the focus of the opposition to the Shah, supported
by religious and nonreligious factions alike. His stern face still looks down
from posters and murals all over the country. Institutes and committees
work hard to keep his memory alive, and several are run by his relatives,
including various women. Khomeini's family and the inner wheel of senior clergy have become the new elite. They remain, however, a closed
circle, closed to Iranians, let alone foreigners. The grand dinner party for
the Islamic Conference was a unique opportunity for me to meet senior
women of the regime in unusual circumstances—without the barrier of
the chador.

Khomeini's daughter, granddaughter and daughter-in-law were guests
of honor. The daughter who was present was a philosophy professor and
head of the official Iranian Women's Society.[5] The daughter-in-law, with
striking, patrician features and hair pulled back like a dancer, was head
of a research center devoted entirely to Khomeini's life and thoughts. The
granddaughter, Zahra Eshraghi, just happened to have married President
Khatami's younger brother. This reinforced the sense of a political dynasty
arising out of a tight-knit clergy class.

I met Eshraghi later in her office in the Ministry of Interior, an imposing, modern building with the atmosphere of a large police station, and
she shared some memories of her grandfather. She remembered visiting
him in exile in Iraq. "I went to see him twice, once when I was four and

---

4. His most vocal critic was Ayatollah Khomeini.

5. The Islamic Republic of Iran Women's Society "assists the intellectual, cultural and scientific promotion of
   women in line with Islamic ideals," according to an official media guide published by the government in
   2000. The society is listed as a political party and the guide notes that it supported the election of President
   Khatami. Its Secretary-General is Zahra Mostafavi, the daughter of Ayatollah Khomeini.

once when I was ten. The second time was not a very good memory, to be honest," she said. "I was wearing an Iraqi *aba*, that's a white veil that is more open than an Iranian chador, and he took one look at me and told me to wear a proper headscarf, saying, 'They might grab you and run off.'" I looked at her strangely and said it must have been a joke. But she said not. She thought perhaps he believed she might be kidnapped for her unusual looks—lighter than average hair and green eyes. She met him again later in the Parisian suburb of Neauphle-le-Chateau where he plotted the downfall of the Shah. He would not allow her to accompany him on the plane for his triumphal return to Iran, for fear it would be shot down by the Shah's forces. Mostly, she stressed his kindness and fairness, and her memories of him in his role as grandfather.

Of all the "regime women" I met Eshraghi was the only one to deliberately take off her chador in my presence, something I found all the more surprising given the surroundings. She kept on a headscarf but revealed an expensive-looking tailored jacket underneath. She and an English-speaking friend appeared to be wearing light makeup. Their main accessories were cellular phones. Eshraghi presented an equally modern face some years later, giving interviews to visiting journalists covering elections in the late 1990s, when her husband headed a new reformist party.

The more religious women I met, the more I realized that the Iranian clergy class has changed with the times. Ayatollah Khomeini married a thirteen-year-old girl who stayed at home and kept house. He would not let his daughter go to school, although he allowed her to be educated at home. For his granddaughter, it was different, however, even though she was brought up in the conservative religious city of Qom. "My father encouraged us, although it was taboo in Qom at that time for girls to continue with secondary education. Not only did he encourage us, he wanted my sister and myself to go to a special school in Isfahan, which was like a fast track to university. But I was only fifteen at the time and it would have meant boarding school, and I didn't want to leave my family."

For an ayatollah to allow his teenage daughter to go away to school was clearly out of the ordinary. During the 1960s and 1970s, education took on increasing importance among the clergy class but also in the population at large. The revolution gave it high priority, and the long-lasting social impact of education is only now beginning to be felt. Far from keeping women at home and in ignorance, the revolution has succeeded in getting many more girls into school. The emphasis on segregated education and compulsory Islamic dress, which outside Iran symbolizes women's oppression, has enabled many girls from conservative families to go to school for the first time. And one of the most delicious ironies of recent Iranian history is that newly educated women have used their votes to redirect the course of the Islamic revolution.

Even in 1979, women played an important part in deposing the Shah. They took part in mass demonstrations forcing him to leave. When Khomeini took power, it seemed unthinkable that he would abolish their right to vote. He stopped short of that but was personally responsible for imposing religious dress regulations, with the support of religious women activists. One of these activists was Mrs. Amiri, a government official who was helping organize the same Islamic Conference, who told me proudly how she was the first woman in the foreign ministry to adopt Islamic dress, just after the revolution. "Oh my goodness—the reaction there was among my colleagues. When they heard there was a woman wearing *hejab* and even chador in the Deputy Minister's office, every day a group of people would come to my office to say hello, just to look at me." She met with a lot of resistance from other civil servants, but within a few months it became law for all women working in government offices to cover up or lose their jobs. "They had to accept it or go," she said.

I had always been rather in awe of Mrs. Amiri. She was always extremely helpful to me in my UN job, during the period of the conference and afterwards, when I told her I was planning to write a book. A sweet manner was well hidden under one of the most severe hejabs I had ever seen. Her black coat was covered with a black hood or *maqna'eh*, like a nun's wimple, so tightly wrapped around her jaw it surprised me she could talk. (Of course, her chador never slipped.) I asked if the chador was important to her. "Not in itself—my sisters don't wear it, for example," she said. "But when I'm working it's simpler. If I wore a manteau I'd have to go to the bazaar and buy different colors and different scarves." Her answer was an example of the striking pragmatism for which Iranians are famous.

At the same time it came as no surprise at all to find she still described herself as a "revolutionary woman." Prior to the revolution, Amiri studied psychology in the U.S., where her husband was also a student. She read writers, fashionable at the time, who popularized a heady cocktail of left-wing ideology and Islam. Among them were Ali Shariati and Ayatollah Motahhari, prominent intellectuals who rejected the Western view of the "modern woman" and conjured up a vision of a "new Muslim woman." This is the image Iran attempts to present to the West.

The guest I sat next to at dinner, who was married to a deputy foreign minister, put yet another slant on why some women covered their heads even at an all-female gathering. I asked her if they were ultraconservative or very religious. "It's not because they are very religious that they're wearing it," she laughed. "It's more that they don't have the proper clothes or hairdo to appear in public," she said. Maryam Imanieh had also studied abroad with her husband, in California. She asked me if I'd seen the pictures of that year's Army Day, when phalanxes of women volunteers marched past carrying automatic rifles. "It gives such a wrong image," she laughed. "I'm a practicing Muslim and I'm happy with my hejab, but I'm just like women in other countries." She worked as Director of International Affairs at the Institute for Iranian Contemporary History, and I met her again later in her own office. Her newly created post seemed to be aimed at opening up the institute to the rest of the world. In Iran, contact with the West was still often referred to with hostility as "cultural invasion." Yet the Khatami presidency was opening up the floodgates to the modern world. The institute had just set up its own Website to enable worldwide computer communication. "We went on the Internet two months ago," she said. "In the first month the response was about 180,000 'hits,' as they call it. If you don't become part of it, you're really missing out."

The conversation turned to the problem of malnutrition in Iran, which affects almost one in five children under five, and, in some areas, girls more than boys. Imanieh had visited homes in a deprived area of Denver as part of a university degree in nutrition: "It was unbelievable that in such a city you could see such poor people. The kids were chubby, but you could see signs of malnutrition in their eyes."

At this point the sound of the midday call to prayer threatened to drown us out. Imanieh got up and shut the window—Islam sat lightly on her shoulders. There was none of the dour fanaticism or sanctimonious show I had encountered routinely in other officials. I told my husband how much I had liked her. "Is she someone you could get to know socially?" he asked. As I hesitated to reply, I realized that the women of the revolutionary establishment remain a closed society. They have benefited tremendously from their connections, their closeness to the new center of power, and they have had a substantial impact on the situation of women since the revolution. But they remain a class apart—theirs is the official face of women in Iran.

2

Births, Marriages, Divorces and Deaths

My Iranian friend Pari was due to travel from Tehran to London along with her newborn baby, three-year-old daughter and mother. Her husband was to join her several days later, after attending an international conference. But late that night she called me to say they had not been able to leave. They had forgotten that they needed her husband's written permission to take the baby out of the country. "We got to passport control and the man said, 'Where's the baby?' and I said, 'Here.' But he said, 'There's no exit stamp for her. She can't leave.'" Even if Pari's husband had been with her at the airport, his word would not have been enough. It took another three days of running around government offices and lawyers to get the necessary papers.

Ironically, it had been Pari's mother they had been worried about. She had been unable to leave the country for seven years, as Pari's father had repeatedly denied her permission to travel. Their marriage had long since broken down, and while the mother had been living in London, they had divorced on grounds of separation. But when she returned to Iran, her ex-husband refused to recognize the divorce, and, reluctant to accept the breakup, he took his revenge. "When she came back, my father took up a court case against her out of spite and bitterness. He made my mother *mamnu al-khoruj*, meaning that she could not leave the country," said Pari. "She felt trapped. My grandmother died in Australia and her son died in India, but she could not go to either funeral." The family went to Qom, the seat of religious learning in Iran, to seek guidance. But even a legal ruling in their favor from a Grand Ayatollah, one of the most senior legal and religious experts in the country, failed to persuade the officials to change their minds. Pari's father only relented after the birth of his second grandchild. He agreed to a divorce by mutual consent in the Iranian courts and granted his estranged wife, at long last, her freedom.

The legal system touches almost every aspect of a woman's life, from cradle to grave, and not just since the revolution.[1] A mixture of Islamic *sharia,* revolutionary regulations and an earlier civil code, the law is often contradictory but usually inescapable. Islamic law in Iran, as in other Muslim countries, comes from the Koran, taken from the sayings of the Prophet Mohammad, and is subject to a mass of interpretations by religious scholars. While the Koran stresses the equality of men and women as human beings, it also sees them as playing different roles. Men are expected to provide for their womenfolk financially, whether as fathers, brothers or husbands. One reason women appear to have so few legal rights of their own, is that men are expected to protect them and maintain them.

The different treatment of men and women begins in childhood. In Iran, the age of criminal liability is taken to be "maturity," or puberty, which girls are said to achieve earlier. A girl of eight years and nine months, or nine lunar years, could be executed or sentenced to life imprisonment for murder. A boy would have to be fourteen years and seven months before he could be tried for the same crime. Similarly, a girl of nine can, in theory, be married, while boys have to wait until fifteen. Yet at the same time, Iranian law says that neither girls nor boys can be legally employed until they are fifteen and cannot hold a driving license until they are eighteen. The same girl who could be married off by her family, have children or enter legally binding contracts cannot vote until she is fifteen. When President Khatami swept to power in a landslide, widely credited to young people and women, there was a suggestion that the voting age should be raised. One of his supporters mischievously proposed to the press that, in fact, it should be lowered, to enable girls to vote from the age of nine.

The mass of conflicting rules and regulations makes plenty of work for lawyers. One leading expert on the legal situation of women is Mehrangiz Kar. She worked as a legal adviser to the government for nine years before the revolution, then, like many others, lost her job. "All the lawyers' offices were closed," she said. "They didn't like lawyers. A lawyer for them was like a friend of the imperialists."

The Shah had been hugely unpopular, but most people had expected Ayatollah Khomeini to retreat into a seminary and remain aloof from politics once he returned from exile. Women, in particular, still express surprise at how the revolution changed their lives. Mehrangiz Kar grasped the implications right from the start. "I understood right from the beginning," she

---

1. The rule requiring the husband's permission to travel is part of the Passport Act of 1972.

said. "I was working for the state social security organization after the departure of the Shah. The day the Shah left, I was walking down the street near my home. I was wearing a long coat because it was winter and it was cold, but I didn't have a headscarf on—some did, some didn't, then. For the first time, somebody in the street shouted at me: 'We got rid of your bad Shah and it's your turn now, you bitches without hejab!' At that moment I understood how it would be."

In her office, Mehrangiz Kar wore a bottle-green coat and scarf, excusing herself, saying that her hair was a mess. Her teenage daughter, Lily, opened the office door to me completely covered but later took her coat off to reveal trousers, a skimpy top and platform shoes.

I had the idea of trying to establish exactly which laws were the worst offenders against women's rights, but it soon became clear that this was an impossible question to answer. The law impinges on everybody's lives—men's and women's, private and public, regardless of wealth, poverty or social standing. Indeed, when I asked Mehrangiz Kar how the law touches people's lives, she told me a personal story about how a small dinner party had been ruined by unwanted guests, the Komiteh, or "Morals Police."

"We had a dinner for family and friends. There were about fifteen people, every one of them over forty. Of course, we were not wearing headscarves." Her daughter took up the story: "We heard the sound of boots and everyone rushed to put on a scarf." Mehrangiz continued: "My daughter was crying, they grabbed a camera that was lying around and took a photo of us—but under the table, of our legs—they wanted to show we were not properly dressed. That's on our files now! They didn't know who I was and I said I was a housewife. They arrested me and my seven-year-old daughter for a while, and they kept my husband for five nights," she remembers "Instead of flogging us they got money from us." The fine was 70,000 tomans, several months' wages at the time. They could have been sentenced to seventy-four lashes for having a party with mixed company outside the immediate family.

It is rare to meet anyone who has actually received lashes. Kar told me she had never seen a public flogging in her life. Lawyers say they handle very few such cases, as the sentence is generally carried out quickly and the defendant is unable to seek legal advice. Some tell stories of bribing the guard to go easy and lessen the severity of the flogging. Since the revolutionary fervor has died down, it is nowadays more common to get away with a fine. Yet two days after I wrote that last sentence, a party held by friends of friends in the street next to ours was raided and all the guests were flogged. The men received seventy lashes, the women got sixty, and the hosts were sentenced to a year's imprisonment for keeping a house of ill repute. Some guests needed hospital treatment. The arbitrary nature of the justice system instills as much fear as the laws themselves.

In 1996 the law on flogging for violating the strict dress code was amended to reduce the penalty to two months' imprisonment or a fine. Yet I found that few people were aware of this. Most had no idea what the law actually said, and one well-informed philosophy professor assured me that there was no law on the dress code, just rules and regulations. In practice, women, especially young women, were still being picked up on the street and harangued by revolutionary volunteers, or *basij,* twenty years after the revolution. They may be taken to the quaintly named Centers for the Prevention of Vice and Enjoining of Virtue and questioned about their morals. They are frequently asked to sign confessions and make written promises that they will not "offend" again.

The enforcement of the law on *hejab,* or Islamic dress, is a symbolic battleground. For the establishment, it is a touchstone that signifies nothing less than the success or failure of the Islamic Republic. For some sectors of society, in particular for the more educated, Westernized women of northern Tehran, violating the dress code is an act of resistance. Visiting journalists take the political temperature by observing how much hair women are showing, how much makeup they wear and whether they dare wear see-through stockings or even no socks at all.

During my time in Iran, the law was enforced arbitrarily and inconsistently. I lived there for two years without once being told off for my undoubtedly "bad" hejab. Then, at an international book fair, I was reprimanded six times in one day. A friend with me was told, literally, to pull up her socks. Some places are worse than others—airports and government offices are among the strictest. In ministries, I was usually careful to wear black and cover myself well to avoid attracting attention. On one occasion, however, in an elevator at the Ministry of Agriculture, a group of women told me to "adjust" my hejab. Hot under the collar, I pulled my headscarf down so it flopped over my forehead. Surely this was Islamic enough. They nudged each other. "No, you can do better than that," said one of them firmly. "Look in the mirror and make it nice." They wanted me to show more hair. This, incidentally, was in a special elevator for women, where up until the eleventh floor we had to squeeze in against two handymen and a desk.

Hejab was officially defined in 1980 by the Council of the Revolution as "covering of the head and all of the body except for the circle of the face and hands from the wrist."[2] The regime first enforced it in government offices, then gradually extended it to a nun-like school uniform. In 1983 it was made compulsory for all women, with sentences laid out in the draconian "Islamic Punishment Law (Flogging)." Yet there have been innumerable crackdowns since, and continuing attempts to define what exactly is "good hejab" or "bad hejab." Ten years after the revolution the following bylaw was still trying to clarify Islamic dress for government employees:

> The complete Islamic clothing for use of sister employees is the following:
> 1. Simple trousers and manteau, loose and long, from thick material.
> 2. Trousers and manteau must be chosen from sober colors. (Preferred colors are navy blue, brown, gray and black.)

The law goes on to categorize six different types of "mal-veiling," including "use of facial makeup, lipstick, eye shadow, in a seductive and vulgar manner; use of clothes that exhibit in a seductive manner curvatures of the body; use of clothes that have symbols or pictures or writings that are vulgar and contrary to Islam."[3] My Persian teacher was ordered to take off a baseball cap (worn over a headscarf) that was shading her eyes at a show-jumping competition. Baseball, it seems, is non-Islamic.

At times, the authorities seem to despair of making people conform. The Chief Public Prosecutor told a journalist in 1986: "I believe the question of hejab should be left to the people to deal with. We obviously have not solved the problem by patrolling the streets. How many patrols should we allocate to this?"[4]

Living here, I found it irritating that the law could dictate how I dress (and that some people feel it is their right to stop strangers in the street to tell them what they should be wearing!), but there are other aspects of the Iranian legal system that cast an even greater shadow over women's lives. "There are many laws, and we cannot say that one article is important and another is not," said Mehrangiz Kar. However, she homed in on the laws governing divorce and custody, as well as the ruthless law on retribution, or *Qesas*, which decrees, on occasion, death by stoning, and lays out the unequal compensation laws for men and women.

In cases of compensation, where a woman has been the victim of a road accident, her relatives receive only half the "blood money" from the driver

2. Paidar, *Women and the Political Process in Twentieth-Century Iran*, 338.
3. Najmabadi, "Power, Morality and the New Muslim Womanhood" in *The Politics of Social Transformation in Afghanistan, Iran and Pakistan.*
4. Paidar, 343.

Posters urge women to observe the rules on Islamic dress. Traditional women wear the black chador, a black hood or maqna'eh on top of an overcoat.

Shiite cleric Ayatollah Sadr stares down from a massive mural in northern Tehran. Note the featureless female face behind him. Scaffolding was erected for repainting, but when it was completed, the woman's face remained blank.

Newlyweds preparing to receive guests on the stage of a public hall in Tabriz. Western-style wedding dresses are popular.

of the vehicle that they would get if a man had died. Similarly, in a court of law, a man's testimony is worth twice that of a woman. This means in practice that in some cases, two women need to be called to the witness stand where one man's evidence would do. Article 91 of the law on retribution, for example, states: "Adultery is proved on the basis of testimony by four righteous men, or three righteous men and two righteous women, whether it leads to flogging or stoning." Not surprisingly, such cases are difficult to prove. Moreover, there are heavy penalties for falsely accusing someone of adultery. In this case, men and women receive the same penalties, but it is a curious fact that while the punishment for male homosexuality is death, the punishment for female homosexuality is 100 lashes.

The principle of "an eye for an eye, a tooth for a tooth," which is the basis of the law on retribution, grabs the headlines and dominates Iran's image abroad. But it is not limited to Iran and appears in similar forms in other Muslim countries. In everyday life, one is struck much more by the impact of family law. Marriage and divorce are fiercely contested areas where the clergy have repeatedly tried to exercise their power. Women have distinctly unequal rights, and while they do have certain bargaining chips, the system, on the whole, is stacked against them.

An Iranian wedding is a beautiful ritual, with no expense spared to give the couple a spectacular start to married life. In the cities, the bride is often decked out in a white, Western-style wedding dress. At one marriage ceremony I attended, Mitra, the bride, wore a purple and green silk designer outfit based on a tribal costume. Her family came from the Bakhtiari nomads, and several of the guests wore traditional dress. This wedding party was at the house of Mitra's employer in northern Tehran, and it was mixed (men and women together), with dancing and music, whereas bigger parties, at hotels, have to be segregated. When the mullah arrived to perform the ceremony, some of the guests donned nothing more than a headscarf. On the other hand, others, including several teenage girls, kept their coats and scarves on throughout the whole party. The mullah, wearing a white turban and brown robes, was jovial but business-like. He sat down with the men from each family to examine the marriage contract. The bride hovered anxiously in the background. When it was time to sign the document, there was no chair for her at the table. She confessed to me afterwards that she did not even read the dozen or so places where she had to sign her name.

Once the signing was over, the women began to whoop and ululate, and the traditional ceremony began. A kind of bower had been prepared for the couple, draped with scarlet and white satin and velvet, and decorated with flowers and special candies. The groom sat on a sofa and called for the bride to join him. At first, her sisters and cousins gave picturesque excuses, such as "She can't come, she's gone to pick flowers." When she joined him, her relatives held two cones of solid sugar above them. As they rubbed them together, the sugar fell like snow onto a lace cloth held over their heads. The sweetness symbolizes a blessing for the future. Divorcees are expected to make themselves scarce at this point, for fear of jeopardizing the couple's future happiness. The mullah read out the contract once more, they accepted, he departed and the party got under way. The couple was showered with gifts, especially gold. In some families, in particular in more traditional and tribal ones, the different parts of the ceremony last for days.

Mitra's was a modern Iranian marriage. While the vast majority of marriages are still arranged by the parents, she had been introduced to her future husband by a cousin. The approval of her father, a cook, had been vital, however. *Khastegari,* the process of formal introductions leading to marriage, has always been popular in Iran, and the post-revolutionary restrictions on socializing with members of the opposite sex have brought it back into fashion with a vengeance. The sheer cost of getting married is a major headache for young people and their parents. One sociologist reminisced that when she got married, the outlay was around three months' salary. Now, incomes have declined, yet families sometimes spend five years' wages or more on dowries, wedding parties and furnishing the young couple's home.

All marriages have to include a contract, and since 1984, the officially printed ones have included a list of thirteen conditions the couple may choose to sign. The first twelve lay down circumstances in which the woman may seek a divorce. The thirteenth states: "Other conditions." At her father's suggestion, Mitra had planned to include a stipulation that the couple reside in Tehran, where she lives and works as a housekeeper, rather than in her husband's hometown, the northwestern city of Tabriz. She later discovered that this was not in the final document, but she told me she was confident that her husband would respect her wishes.

Some brides use the "other conditions" section to specify their right to work or, perhaps, their right to continue their education. Interestingly, the list of conditions was introduced after the revolution, in response to pressure from inside and outside the government aimed at reclaiming rights women lost in the revolution. It's not uncommon, however, for clerics or family to try to dissuade the couple from signing. Among my Iranian friends, two different, well-educated couples ran up against mullahs who tried to talk the husband out of giving his wife the right to divorce. "Are you mad?" one cleric asked. Of course, social pressures are also strong, making it almost taboo to discuss divorce at the time of marriage. A friend of mine was invited to a society wedding, which was called off the day before because the groom's family objected to the wording of the contract at the last minute. They felt it was unnecessary to spell out the bride's right to divorce. Some of the four hundred guests still turned up on the day, to be met by a tearful relative explaining that the whole thing had been cancelled. This was a terrible loss of face in a society where family honor is sacrosanct, and I was left wondering how much worse the pressure could be in traditional families or village society.

A frequent source of wrangling is the size of the *mehr,* a financial pledge made by the husband, which can be cashed in at any time by the wife. Mitra's mehr consisted of fourteen gold coins and a substantial sum of money. In some, more Westernized families, this is looked down on as a rather distasteful "bride price," and it's not uncommon to hear of women who set their mehr at $1, or a car, or, more fancifully, a ton of jasmine or a kilo of flies' wings. But in reality this is one of the few sources of power a woman has within a marriage. It acts as a financial brake on a flighty husband, and if the marriage fails and it comes to divorce, it is the woman's main, sometimes only, bargaining chip.

The civil code states baldly that a man has the right to divorce his wife at will. He does not even have to give grounds for a separation. In general, a woman cannot even initiate a divorce if her husband opposes it. However, she can establish her right to divorce under certain conditions if she has them included in her marriage contract, as Mitra did. A woman who has no right to seek a divorce generally offers to give up her mehr in order to buy her freedom. The other tactic she can try is to prove that her husband is neglecting his duty to maintain her in the style she was accustomed to in her own family. This right is the husband's obligation under Islam to provide financial support, or *nafagheh,* within the marriage.

Many women who go to court are, in fact, trying to rescue a difficult marriage. Ziba Mir-Hosseini, a London-based anthropologist who co-produced a fascinating documentary, "Divorce, Iranian-Style," has written a book comparing women's experiences of divorce in Iran and Morocco. At first sight, Morocco's more Westernized legal system might be expected to favor women, yet in fact, the women she saw there appeared cowed by tradition and the formal setting of the courtroom. "In Morocco, I never saw a woman raise her eyes to look at the judge," she told me. "In Iran there are often no lawyers (they were banned at one time by the revolutionary courts) and I've seen women banging on the table, demanding their rights." I showed Ziba's film to several groups of women in Iran. It reduced many, including myself, to tears, but on the other hand we were all impressed by the confidence and determination with which the women pursued their cases.

Iranian divorce cases are long and bitter, as they are the world over. But if children are involved, the nightmare enters another dimension. For in Iran, custody of the children is the right of the father. I met Parisa—a smart, single mother, at a particularly civilized coffee morning. It did not seem unusual to me to meet a woman holding down two jobs to make ends meet. It was only when she told me her story that I realized how extraordinary an Iranian divorce can be. She met her husband-to-be, a bright medical student, through a matchmaker. Her family disapproved of the whole idea of divorce and her mehr was set at just one gold coin. "My family did not believe in *mehriyeh*," she said. "They thought it was kind of buying and selling a woman." This was something she later regretted.

The marriage was not a success from the first. "He was very bad-tempered," she said. "He humiliated me all the time mentally. He used to call me ugly and old, and I got very depressed. It got worse and worse every day, but unfortunately, the day I decided I needed a divorce, I realized I was pregnant." Parisa tried to make the marriage work and in the meantime her husband became a successful surgeon. He began to have affairs and appeared to have fallen in love with another woman. When she threatened to leave him again after seven years, he launched a charm offensive, and she got pregnant again. Finally she put it in the hands of a lawyer. The attorney expressed amazement that Parisa had not had the foresight to give herself the right to divorce. He warned that it could take two or three years to persuade her husband, and the courts, to release her. In fact, it took about a month and she considered herself lucky. "It's not like that for other women," she assured me.

Under Iranian law, custody of the children automatically goes to the father, or even to the father's family, rather than to the mother. A woman has to hand over sons above the age of two, and daughters from the age of seven. From puberty onwards, the children can choose which parent they prefer to live with. Parisa had to give up her son, who was then nine, but was able to keep her eighteen-month-old daughter. When I met her, she was living in fear that she would lose her daughter too: "She is six and a half now, and I don't know what his reaction will be when she turns seven. Then, he can take her at any time that he wants. Whenever we have a quarrel now, I'm scared he'll do it for revenge."

As she told her story, Parisa mentioned that her husband had pleaded with her to come back to him. Pretty, educated, and loyal, she must have been an asset as a doctor's wife. As she finished her story, I said I was surprised he had let her go so easily. Uncomfortably, she revealed the missing piece in the puzzle. During the Iran-Iraq War her husband had been jailed for ten days for providing draft-dodgers with false medical papers. It was a secret not even his mother knew. Parisa had threatened to reveal it and ruin his high-flying career if he did not release her from the marriage. "It was my ace," she explained but the specter of her failed marriage still hangs over her life, both because of the social pressure and because of the law. Even though she has custody of her daughter for the time being, she will forfeit that right should she remarry. "My ex-husband can marry whenever he wants, but if I remarry they can take the child away from me right away. It means that I cannot have a normal life and that he can dominate me even after divorce," she said.

Divorce carries a great stigma in Iranian society. Social pressures mean that it is extremely difficult to live the life of a single woman. Most divorcees have no option but to return to their parents. Parisa was living in her parents' house, which, in typical Tehran style, was split up into apartments for various branches of the family. Many parents of divorcees do their best to marry their daughters off again as soon as possible. At least Parisa was able to find a well-paid job, unlike many women I met. But she described how her male colleagues automatically assumed she was "available."

"At first I was very proud to tell people I was divorced, but then I noticed that people's attitudes changed. In fact I suffered what you'd call sexual harassment, and I started to wear a wedding ring again," she said. "When I said no, they didn't think I was serious. They said, 'you're young and beautiful—you have to have someone.' For a period of time I really wanted to remarry because I thought I needed a protector, but fortunately I've found a group of friends now where I can be myself. Otherwise I think I would have been forced to marry again. The pressure from society and family was very heavy—socially, emotionally and economically."

In other social classes the pressure is even greater. One researcher told me that village women who go through a divorce become "outcasts," whose only hope of becoming part of the community again is to remarry as soon as possible. "I had a case of a woman who lived in a village," the researcher said. "Her husband fell in love and wanted to take a second wife, and she would not go through with it. In the end he agreed to divorce her and give her half of their assets. But she had five or six brothers, and *they* stepped in and said she should not take anything because she had become *biaberu* [disreputable] even though she had four kids. They went on to abuse her and beat her into marrying the first guy that came around. She ended up marrying a Kurdish laborer seven years younger than herself. She was living in absolute poverty when I came across her. All her family and the villagers had just disowned her." In the cities, there is more anonymity but also less of a safety net in the form of the extended family. "You were looking at total tragedy and ruin," said the researcher. "Many of these women were just sitting around waiting to die."

One of the possible conditions listed in the marriage contract that entitle a woman to seek a divorce relates to polygamy. It states that if the husband takes another wife without the consent of the first wife, or if the court finds that he does not treat his wives fairly, she can ask for the marriage to be ended. Islam gives men the right to take up to four wives. However, polygamy is a typical example of something that is possible according to *sharia,* but tricky in practice. Religious law insists that a man can take more wives only if he can afford to treat them equally. The financial burden that this entails and the social pressure of modern society therefore make polygamy a rarity. Iranian law does not even mention it directly, although there are indirect references, for example laying down the law of inheritance "in the case of the presence of several wives." Polygamy has never actually been banned in Iran, but the far-reaching Family Protection Law of 1967 restricted it, by stipulating that a man had to have the consent of his first wife before he took a second. It is interesting that Ayatollah Khomeini suspended this law within the first few days of coming to power.

The revolutionary regime, in the early days of its zealous attempts to "Islamize" Iranian law, abolished the restrictions on polygamy. But public opinion, led by Islamic feminists close to the government and supported by many of the judges who had to actually deal with family law, paved the way for the introduction of other curbs.[5] This is one reason why in 1984 the government introduced the standard marriage contracts, which lay out the conditions of the union and effectively give women an alternative way of protecting their rights.

Iranian law differs from general Islamic law in certain respects because Iranians are part of the minority Shiite branch of Islam rather than the Sunni majority. There is one uniquely Shiite legal institution and it attracts a large amount of attention: temporary marriage, or *sigheh.* Temporary marriage enables a man to marry as many women as he likes for a fixed

---

5. Paidar, 282.

period of time, from one hour to ninety-nine years.[6] It is a marriage with few responsibilities, undertaken mainly for pleasure, unlike permanent marriage, which is principally designed for having children. Indeed the Arab word for it, *mut'a*, means enjoyment. As Shahla Haeri explains, in her extraordinary book, *Law of Desire*, the Shiite clergy purport to believe that every new temporary marriage brings a blessing from God, a *zabad*, or a kind of religious brownie point. For women, the religious reasoning is rather different. They are allowed to enter only one temporary marriage at a time and women, the theologians argue, do it mainly for money. It is hard for an outsider to see the difference between sigheh and prostitution. Or as a professor of religious philosophy told Haeri: "Yes. Mut'a is like prostitution, but because it has the name of God, it is permissible."[7]

Historically, temporary marriage may have been useful for travelers, soldiers and merchants away from their wives for months at a time. It is still associated with pilgrimages to the shrines of Qom and Mashhad, leading the famous British traveler Lord Curzon to describe Mashhad in 1892 as "probably the most immoral city in Asia."[8] Haeri, the grand-daughter of an ayatollah, describes her research methods, including hanging around notorious pickup spots and discovering the secret signs that indicate that a woman is available for sigheh. Female tourists may wish to note that one of these is wearing your chador inside out.

Before the revolution, temporary marriage had fallen into disrepute. However, there is evidence to suggest that it has since made a comeback. Ayatollah Motahhari, the architect of revolutionary policy on women's issues, described it as "one of the brilliant laws of Islam," and argued that far from being an anachronistic curiosity, it was in fact a most "progressive" phenomenon. This view was taken up by the revolutionary leadership, notably by former president Rafsanjani, who proposed it as an outlet for young people's sexual needs. He suggested that women widowed in the Iran-Iraq war could invite male friends to "marry" them so as to pursue a sexual relationship without fear or shame.[9] A state-sponsored dating agency was set up to find new partners for war widows. Some young people, scared of being picked up by the Morals Police or arrested at parties, are said to carry temporary marriage forms around with them, which they fill in with their boyfriends or girlfriends names. Older, more religious

---

6. Haeri, "Temporary Marriage: A discourse on Female Sexuality in Islam," in *In the Eye of the Storm.*
7. Haeri, *Law of Desire,* 186.
8. Ibid, 18.
9. Haeri, *In the Eye of the Storm,* 98.

people, may use the custom to make everyday contact, with, say, a servant or traveling companion respectable.

I came across the phenomenon in connection with a long matchmaking saga involving the Iranian father-in-law of an Irish friend of mine. Anne-Marie's father-in-law was a diabetic, was partially blind and had never really recovered from the death of his wife some years before. Gentle and easygoing, he was looking for a companion to take care of him in his old age. Friends and relatives wheeled in a succession of totally unsuitable women: "The very first one I met, they told us the husband had died and there were no children and that she was looking for a companion to spend the rest of her days with," said Anne-Marie. "But it turned out that it was all lies. When we got to the house she was a giant woman with long nails. She was divorced with two children whom she hadn't seen for quite a while." The next candidate was a divorced schoolteacher who seemed promising but insisted on very favorable marriage terms. Then came a woman Anne-Marie's father-in-law (whom she called Baba) had found for himself. "She's a woman to die for," he insisted.

"Baba said she had had a terrible life," said Anne-Marie. "Her husband was an opium addict who had put a knife to her throat. She hadn't seen her children for years because custody had been given to their grandfather." But Baba's son, wary of inheritance rights, was dead against the idea of marriage. He persuaded his father to take out a temporary marriage contract for five years, as a kind of trial period. Within a year the "bride" had spent her marriage settlement and was demanding that Baba should put a house in her name. They parted soon afterwards.

Next came a very religious woman from a traditional family. Their temporary marriage was blessed by a mullah. She wore her chador even inside the house and performed her regular prayers, or *namaz,* five times a day without fail. Anne-Marie's family, not quite so devout, had difficulty telling her which way was Mecca in their Tehran apartment. "My mother used to line herself up with the fridge," said the son. The new "wife" proposed that the driver who worked on their fruit farm should also perform sigheh with her, so as not to jeopardize her reputation. "She started asking Baba why he kept on shaving [beards are an Islamic fashion statement], so he asked her why she kept on praying, and it came to the point where it just wasn't working—they were like chalk and cheese." They parted after about four months and Baba apparently gave up his search for the perfect wife.

Even in death, women and men are not equal. Complicated inheritance laws are based on the assumption common to all Islamic countries that men are duty bound to provide for their womenfolk and that single women, whether spinsters, widows or divorcees, are a rarity or an aberration. So, for example, if a woman dies, leaving children, her husband inherits half of her estate. But if a man with children dies, his wife inherits only one eighth of his estate. Moreover, boys with a share in a legacy receive twice as much as their sisters.

In addition, strict laws lay down exactly what a woman can or cannot inherit. She can inherit fruit trees, but not the orchard itself, as this counts as agricultural land, which she is not entitled to. Her portion of an inheritance in general is based on a share of the building and the contents, including moveable objects such as cars and furniture, and not from the farming land on which the building is built. One leading lawyer, Shirin Ebadi, has campaigned against this, pointing out that it particularly penalizes farmers' wives because farming families tend to devote all their resources to buying more land. "You can say that farmers' wives have virtually no inheritance…which is completely against all wisdom, logic or religious law," she writes.[10] She argues that inheritance laws in different Islamic countries vary widely and that the ban on inheriting farmland is peculiar to Iranian Shiite law. On the other hand, a woman keeps whatever assets she possesses, including land, in her own name. There is no concept of pooling resources within a marriage, so if the relationship breaks down, the woman takes out whatever she put in at the beginning.

I went to the house of Mahin Sanati, a children's rights campaigner who worked alongside Ebadi, with the idea of asking her about her famous aunt, Sedigheh Dowlatabadi, a leading figure in the women's rights movement in the first half of the twentieth century. As I took off my coat I told her I was glad to find her in Tehran, as I knew she spent a lot of time in the United States with her children. "You know why I stay in Iran— it's to get my inheritance," she explained. Her father had drawn up a will that specified that his eldest son, who was well off and did not have children, should not inherit anything. However, because the son contested the will, the family had been wrangling over it for twenty-five years, and the case had never been settled. Mahin was no longer on speaking terms with her brother. She described the estate as "substantial," adding that it included land in the heart of Iran's historic second city, Isfahan.

Ironically, half a century earlier, her aunt had managed to claim a better inheritance for herself. Sedigheh's father had encouraged her to study at home, where she learned French and Arabic from a tutor. "Her father said to her, 'If you get yourself educated, you'll get the same kind of

---

10. "The Woman's Share of Inheritance of Agricultural Land," in *Negah Zan.*

inheritance as your brothers.'" Sedigheh, who later studied at the Sorbonne, kept her side of the bargain. "The interesting thing is that my aunt was strong enough to implement this promise," said Mahin. "In fact, the five brothers were intimidated by her, and the two younger sisters only got the smaller female share whereas she received the full portion."

Time and time again in Iran you hear stories about women who struggle against the laws ranged against them, and who frequently beat the odds, triumphing through sheer force of personality. It may take years, but they have a confidence and a tenacity that belies their downtrodden image. In everyday life, women confront the laws of covering up, traveling, marriage and divorce. They hope they never have to deal with the more extreme forms of Islamic law. They have become experts at beating the system, and living their own lives.

*Two male faces out of hundreds carved in stone at the ruins of Persepolis, the fifth-century-*B.C.E. *palace of King Darius. Representations of women are noticeable by their absence.*

Khorshid Khanum, or the Sun Lady, on a piece of pottery from Meybod, near Yazd. Her face and flowing locks adorn everything from paintings to pan scrubbers.

3

Twentieth-Century Woman and the Sun Lady

Sunbathing holds very little appeal if you're wearing a raincoat and head-scarf, so I saw very few beaches and a lot of ruins during my time in Iran. The country is stuffed with archaeological remains, monuments to great rulers such as Cyrus, Darius and Xerxes, who still exert a romantic pull on travelers in search of ancient Persia. But at the great ceremonial site of Persepolis and elsewhere, women are notably absent. In beautifully preserved rock carvings, kings, princes and ambassadors queue up by the hundreds to offer presents to the ruler of the day, but there is not one rep-resentation of a female. Yet the queen's quarters are clearly marked, and in later periods several women took the throne. One historian has described the history of Iranian women as a patchwork.[1] There is no shortage of colorful cameos but little sense of continuity or development. As in the making of a quilt, the individual patches have been regarded as scraps of little consequence. Other writers argue that the sources are there, but that the material has never been considered worthy of study. In modern times, the debate over the status of women has continued to rage. The image, appearance and even dress of Iranian women has repeatedly been held up to scrutiny and exploited for political ends.

I wanted to try to find the origins of the debate in history, so I visited the museums, hoping to find some clues. At the Archaeological Museum of Iran, a willing student showed me around the small but stunning col-lection. Pride of place was given to a rotund fertility goddess from the sixth millennium B.C.E. found in western Iran. "This is the oldest exhibit in the museum," my guide said proudly. "You can see that part of the lady's body was…exaggerated," she said. None of these goddesses had any head, because that was not important. Ladies who couldn't have children

1. Najmabadi, *The Story of the Daughters of Quchan*, 182.

used to use this." The books I had read said that the heads were smashed off after the death of the owner so that no one else would be able to profit from the luck-bringing charm.[2] But the guide made her point. The museum's other star attraction was a huge block of stone inscribed with the world-famous Code of Hammurabi, which laid down the law in ancient Babylon. Found in the south of Iran at Susa, the student confessed ruefully that the original was in the Louvre. Article 153 of the Code states: "If a woman has brought about the death of her husband because of another man, they shall impale that woman on stakes." There were more all-male friezes from Persepolis, and plenty of pottery and jewelry. I thanked my guide, went next door to the Islamic Art museum and found, not surprisingly, even fewer images of women.

Yet at one time the entire region was dominated by matriarchies. Goddesses, rather than gods, were worshiped. The father of Persian archaeology, Roman Ghirshman, reported finding "quantities of figurines of the Dea Mater, deity of procreation, fertility, and abundance" (dating back more than four thousand years B.C.E.) at the oldest known human settlement in Iran—Tepe Siyalk near the central city of Kashan.[3] He believes the goddess cult originated among cave dwellers who respected women's roles as the guardian of the fire, the probable inventor of pottery and the expert on cultivation. Among certain hill tribes, such as the Guti, who raided Babylon in the third millennium B.C.E., women served as army commanders. The Elamites, who founded the first great civilization on Iranian soil around the beginning of the first millennium B.C.E., practiced descent through the female line. When the Aryans, considered the forefathers of the Iranians, arrived from central Asia, they adopted many of the customs of the peoples they conquered. The main mother goddess of this time was known as Kirririsha, then later Nanaia. Ghirshman speculates that she may have been transformed into the most famous of Iranian goddesses, Anahita, equated with Artemis or Athena in the Roman and Greek pantheon.

Anahita was known as the source of life and the source of all waters on Earth. She is variously described as strong and bright, tall and beautiful, pure and nobly born.[4] She remained popular throughout the period of the Achaemenians, who built Persepolis, but was increasingly part of a trio that included two male gods, Mithra and Ahura Mazda. Nowadays, traces of goddess worship lives on in dozens of place names, such as "Girl's

---

2. Ghirshman, *Iran*.
3. Ibid.
4. Hinnells, *Persian Mythology*.

Bridge" (Pol-e Dokhtar) or "Girl's Castle (Qal'e-ye Dokhtar)." Many places of pilgrimage or small shrines now dedicated to Islamic female saints were originally dedicated to Anahita or other goddesses. In time they were transmogrified into holy places for Muslims.[5]

I was puzzled about what became of the goddesses, so I went to see historian Jaleh Amuzegar for guidance. A lecturer in pre-Islamic history and languages at Tehran University, she is an expert on Persian mythology. With the arrival of the Aryans and other roaming tribes from central Asia, the nature of society changed, she said. "Always with these civilizations which travel, it's the men who command, whereas when there's a tradition of cultivation, and of civilizations which stay in one place, it's the women."[6] She explained the absence of images of women in the pre-Islamic period. Followers of the pre-Islamic Zoroastrian religion, for example, were not very keen on any kind of images, wary of setting up false idols. The Zoroastrians were increasingly influential at the time of the Achaemenian empire, which saw the construction of Persepolis in the fifth century B.C.E.

The rows and rows of men depicted in the stupendous remains near Shiraz were meant to represent foreign powers paying their respect to Darius. Women may not have appeared in official artwork, but they did play a role in public life. The historian Josef Wiesehöfer has found references to women in twenty-five separate texts originating from Persepolis.[7] "All the women of the royal house, in so far as they are mentioned in the Persepolis texts, appear as positively active, enterprising and resolute. They participate in royal festivities and banquets or organize their own feasts, they travel across the country and issue instructions, they watch over their estates and manpower." The favorite wife of Darius (he married six times) claimed an allowance that included two hundred jugs of wine and one hundred sheep. And it was not just the royal women who ran their own lives, manageresses often distributed rations and supervised groups of workers.

The decline of the Achaemenian empire ended with the conquest of Persia by Alexander the Great. But its fall was also widely blamed on the intrigues of a series of scheming queens and princesses, such as Atossa,

---

5. Frye, *The Golden Age of Persia,* 140.
6. As my pleasant chat with Professor Amuzegar came to an end, the modern world intruded, in a way it can only do in Iran. She suddenly let drop that her husband had been assassinated three years previously, because of his opposition to the regime. I had known that he had been murdered, but it didn't seem to be the kind of thing to raise in polite conversation. They had been living in Paris at the time, but after his death she insisted on coming back to Iran. She had been interrogated many times but had been able, she hoped, to convince the authorities that she herself was purely an academic, and not involved in politics.
7. Wiesehofer, *Ancient Persia,* 68–88.

daughter of Cyrus. Heleen Sancisi-Weerdenburg has argued that this view was promoted by Greek historians, who saw Persia as decadent and effeminate. The notion is still influential today. "The majority of women in the ancient Orient have left no trace in the historical records," she writes. "They remained nameless and unnamed. Exceptions that escaped anonymity are mostly of a notorious kind."[8] She sees the favorite Iranian tales of jealous vindictive mothers and cruel, heartless lovers as literary prototypes, rather than historical figures. Yet their presence resonates through Iranian history and well into the twentieth century. Mahd-e Olya, the mother of a nineteenth century ruler, plotted ruthlessly and unceasingly to win power for her son. And in living memory, the Shah's twin sister Ashraf, was widely believed to control her brother.

One of the most intriguing questions in the history of women in Iran is whether their lot was any worse or better after the coming of Islam in the seventh century. Some scholars argue that women's rights improved. They point out that in Arabia, at least, women were subsequently allowed to inherit property, infanticide of baby girls was banned and women were respected as mothers. But the evidence is miscellaneous and contradictory. One influential writer, Leila Ahmed, points out that all over the Middle East, women were being kept in their place. In sixth-century Iran, before the coming of Islam, when Zoroastrianism was at its height, the Sasanian wife supposedly swore obedience to her husband every day. She was required to declare, "I will never cease, all my life, to obey my husband," and was subject to divorce if she failed to do so. She was also expected "every morning on rising" to "present herself before her husband and nine times make her obeisance…arms extended…in greeting to him, as men did praying to Ormazd."[9]

Others, however, have pointed out that during the long period of Sasanian rule (from 224–642), attitudes towards women in society varied tremendously during different reigns. One historian who holds that view is Katayoun Mazdapour, a linguistics professor specializing in the Pahlavi language, which was spoken before the Islamic conquest. As I tried to find her house in central Tehran a neighbor showed me the way. "You mean the Zoroastrian lady," she said.

The Zoroastrians follow a religion laid down by the prophet Zoroaster. They worship one god, Ahura Mazda (also spelled Ormazd), and believe life is a constant battle between good and evil. Only a small community of about thirty thousand remains in Iran, mainly centered on the desert

---

8. Sancisi-Weerdenburg, "Exit Atossa," in *Images of Women in Antiquity*, ed. Cameron and Kuhrt.
9. Ahmed, *Women and Gender in Islam*.

city of Yazd.[10] They are tolerated by the authorities, being considered "people of the book," like Christians, Jews and Muslims. Mazdapour, a plump, homely figure surrounded by piles and piles of papers, pulled out a file containing a legal document, "The Book of a Thousand Laws," from the Sasanian period. As a linguist, she makes the point that Persian is not gender specific. There is no "he" or "she," which can make interpretation of historical documents even more of a puzzle. It is clear, however, that women were divided into two classes—those who could own property and those who worked for a living. Either way, it suggests they enjoyed some form of financial independence. "Some scholars have said that women were like objects during the Sasanian period. But in my view this is not true," said Mazdapour. "There was polygamy, but one wife was always considered the main wife," she said. "The Padishah wife had power over the financial affairs of the husband and household, and if the husband died, she would take over all of his effects. If she married again she would keep all her own things and bring them to the new marriage." These two characteristics of polygamy, coupled with a degree of financial independence for women, are typical of the Islamic world. The expanding Muslim empire took on many of the customs of the territories it conquered, especially as political alliances were often formed through marriage.

Mazdapour believes we can learn about women's lives in the past from stories and folktales. For example, the women who figure in Iran's best-loved piece of literature, *The Book of Kings (Shahnameh)*, are few and far between, but they play particularly strong roles. The author was a tenth-century poet, Ferdowsi, and his female characters are prototypes. "Women have a very high rank in the story and they often take the initiative," she said. In one of the most famous stories, Princess Tahmineh asks for the hand of the great hero Rostam, and not vice versa, for example. This is one of several cases in the saga where a woman marries a foreigner, underlining the importance that women played in cementing political alliances.

Women from the higher classes were often educated, even in the Sasanian era. "Do not withhold your wife and child from culture, so that trouble and great sorrow does not reach you, and you may not be regretful" is the advice from one writer of the time.[11] But examples of women writing about their own lives are rare, according to Farzaneh Milani, author of *Veils and Words: The Emerging Voices of Iranian Women Writers*. She says

---

10. The 1996 census puts the number of Zoroastrians at 28,000. Mario Vitalone, of the University Institute of Oriental Studies in Naples, who has studied the Zoroastrian community, suggests the figure could be nearer to 40,000.

11. Frye, *The Golden Age of Persia*, 20.

that the first Iranian woman known to have written poetry was the tenth-century princess, Rabe'e.[12] The story goes that Rabe'e fell in love with her brother's slave. When her brother learned about the affair he had her put to death. Legend has it that she was imprisoned in a bathhouse and her veins were slashed. As she died a slow, lingering death, she is said to have written love poems in her own blood on the bathhouse wall.

Another exception, much later, is the thirteenth-century poet, Padishahkhatun, whose name is a title meaning "Queen-woman" and who ruled in the Kerman area of central Iran. Writer and historian Banafshe Hejazi who has researched Padishahkhatun's life, quoted the following lines to me:

> I'm the woman who does all good deeds
> Hidden under my maqna'eh (hood)
> Not everyone who wears the maqna'eh is a kadbanu
>   (woman of authority, lady)
> Not every man who wears a headdress is a leader.

Padishahkhatun lived to be forty, when she was killed in a battle—some say by her sister-in-law who wanted to rule herself. Other women of the time included astrologers, calligraphers, mystics and teachers, but Hejazi is particularly interested in the poets. "There were women poets in that period, and I attach a lot of importance to it because they could say a lot of things which other women could not," she said. Hejazi has written books with titles such as *Women under Suspicion of History,* and *Women under the Scarf.*

Nicely framed pieces of calligraphy on the walls of her modern apartment turn out to be her own work. Hejazi's apartment is decorated with colorful, silky patchwork fabric, which she also made. She, like all the other historians I spoke to, insisted that the practice of banishing women to their own quarters, keeping them covered up and secluded, was confined mainly to the upper classes. While the princess was in her tower or the queen was in her chamber, poor women were working away in the fields in traditional dress. This was unlikely to have been the chador, which would have been utterly impractical for manual labor, as it is held closed by one hand.

What, exactly, women did wear is very sketchy indeed. All the experts agree that in a dusty, desert country like Iran with extremes of temperature, covering up, including covering the head, was the norm for men and women

---

12.Milani, *Veils and Words*, 220-221.

alike. Anthropologist Soheila Shahshahani believes the chador, a peculiarly Iranian form of dress, can be dated back to Achaemenian times. In this period, both men and women wore skirts, and the only distinguishing feature of women's dress was a short, semi circular veil that came down to the waist. When the chador became long is shrouded in mystery, although it certainly was by the fifteenth century. The black color is a surprisingly recent development, said Shahshahani, who has written a book on the subject. Previously, black was generally only used on specific occasions (when one was in mourning for example). But with the growth of urban life in the twentieth century, black became a symbol of respectability.

During the reign of the Safavids (sixteenth to eighteenth centuries), when Iran experienced a long period of wealth and stability, Hejazi believes that women were freer to take part in public life. The empire was centered on the splendid city of Isfahan, and women are depicted against a stunning backdrop of turquoise domes and elegant palaces. "Women were present in great numbers at all public events," she said. "You see them in miniatures. The public speakers are up on a podium but there are women listening to what's being said....One overall image is that in all these miniatures the beautiful women were shown with full face, long beautiful hair piled up, with a headdress, but older women were shown in profile, with chador."

Portraits of women were often of female acrobats or musicians and used for decorative purposes, as they were in the Qajar period that followed. The women of nineteenth-century paintings, with their short skirts and bare breasts, present a curious picture, a hybrid of East and West, as Afsaneh Najmabadi, professor of women's studies at Harvard, has pointed out. "We have an abundance of representations of women from the realm of male fantasy and pleasure but very few representations of real women."[13] Such portraits probably adorned the walls of hunting lodges and palaces. However, at this time, women began to find a voice of their own, and with increased education and contacts with the West, started to demand more rights and freedoms. A woman, Tahereh Qorrat al-Ayn, played a prominent and outrageous role in a religious sect whose members followed a leader known as The Bab.[14] At the time, Babism was seen as a serious threat to national security. Forerunners of the Baha'i faith which is still persecuted in Iran today, the Babis were thought to preach free love and a heretical version of Islam. At one notable prayer meeting, Qorrat al-Ayn, apparently the only woman present, stripped off her veil and proclaimed Babism to be a faith in its own right. In the ensuing panic, one

---

13. *Royal Persian Paintings,* ed. Diba with Ekhtiar.
14. Milani,86–99.

man reportedly cut his own throat and fled. Qorrat al-Ayn, one of the leaders of the sect, was later detained by the government and died after being strangled and thrown into a well.

Women were increasingly influenced by contacts with the Western world. Naser al-Din Shah wanted to improve Iran's image abroad and encouraged Western visitors. Historian Mansoureh Ettehadiyeh tells the story of how he took a favorite wife with him on a tour of Europe and the Caucasus hoping to get medical treatment for her failing eyesight. He had to send her back home, however, because of criticism by the clergy, who thought it was inappropriate for him to be accompanied by a woman.[15] Ettehadiyeh notes a change in the life of women at the royal court in the 1880s, as observers found they were becoming "loud" and "notorious." Naser al-Din Shah's mother, Mahd-e Olya, undoubtedly deserved her reputation for scheming. Her plotting famously led to the assassination of the respected prime minister, Amir Kabir. "Naser al-Din Shah's mother, the leader of the Andarun (women's quarters), is the perfect example of the power behind the throne theory. She was very important and she was quite a powerful woman," said Ettehadiyeh. "They were not just plotting for themselves, but for the power of this prince or that prince."

In the lower classes, too, women were beginning to question their traditional role. In 1890, women joined in street demonstrations, protesting the government's decision to grant the British a monopoly on the production, sale and export of tobacco from Iran. Even in the royal household, women stopped smoking and broke their pipes.[16] The tobacco boycott had repercussions some years later when the country entered the period of reforms known as the Constitutional Revolution (1905–1911).

When a male writer preached that women should stay at home in a tract entitled "The Chastisement of Women," he was answered in satirical fashion by a woman named Bibi Khanum, whose essay, "The Vices of Men," was published in 1896. While the man argued that wives showing anger and disobedience towards their husbands would go to hell, she advised women to ignore such unwanted advice, as it was aimed at perpetuating a male-dominated society. Backwardness or corruption in the country should not be blamed on women, she argued, as they were excluded from power.[17]

---

15. Mansoureh Ettehadiyeh, personal communication. But see also Abbas Amanat, in his introduction to Taj al-Saltana's *Crowning Anguish*, who writes that two wives were returned because of the embarrassment caused to the Shah and his European hosts by them appearing in public and heavily veiled, 30-31.

16. Poya, *Women, Work and Islamism*, 32.

17. Paidar, *Women and the Political Process in Twentieth-Century Iran*, 48.

At the Qajar court at that time was a princess, Taj al-Saltana, who lived to see the passing of the nineteenth century and the birth of the modern era. She became one of the most notorious figures of the age. Her story is all the more remarkable as it only came to light in 1975, with the discovery of memoirs written in her own hand. Historians pounced on the document, because for once it gave a first-hand account of a woman's life and an insider's view of the royal court. Some have even doubted its authenticity, perhaps because Taj emerges as a daring, unconventional figure.[18]

Taj, born in 1884, describes the harem at the Golestan Palace, where she was raised. The palace still stands in the heart of Tehran, sumptuously decorated with marble, mirrors and tile-work, and reopened to the public. The Shah, her father, had eighty wives, some of whom had as many as twenty servants each. Concubines also lived there—they were often beautiful women captured in battles with the Turkomans or Kurds. Including visitors, there were sometimes as many as nine hundred women in the harem.

Taj passes harsh judgment on her mother, who handed her over as a baby to a wet nurse. At the age of eight she was married to a youth she had never met. Although her father, Naser al-Din Shah, did not expect her to live with her husband until she was twenty, the marriage was a source of great unhappiness. "Truly, what greater misfortune could one suffer than to have to take a husband in childhood, at the age of eight?" writes Taj in her memoirs. Or, elsewhere: "Ay me! Like a captive slave with all her outward accouterments I was sold off to a husband whom I had not had a chance to observe and to whose character I was not accustomed."

Pastimes in the palace were limited, but Naser al-Din Shah's parties seem to have been rather decadent affairs. With the installation of electricity, his favorite game was "Lights Out," where he controlled the light switch. "The game consisted of turning out the lights. In the darkness the women had absolute freedom and license to kiss each other, beat each other, bite each other, blind each other, or break each others' heads and limbs." Her father dropped the game when Taj was badly beaten by another woman.

The princess was increasingly able to compare her lot with women's lives abroad. "Alas! Persian women have been set aside from humankind and placed together with cattle and beasts," she wrote. "They live their entire lives of desperation in prison, crushed under the weight of bitter ordeals. At the same time, they see and hear from afar and read in the newspapers about the way in which suffragettes in Europe arise with determination to demand their rights…" She wished she could travel to Europe to meet

---

18. Taj al-Saltana, *Crowning Anguish*.

these "freedom-seeking ladies." At the same time she realized that her closeted life was not typical of the masses who worked the land. "Traveling
along the Tabriz road, I saw men and women everywhere working side by
side in the villages, the women unveiled.…[Besides] since the women do
not cover their faces, mates are able to choose one another for themselves.
After they are married, they always work together as partners in their farming and herding."

As the century progressed, the clamor for reforms took hold. Taj came
to blame the lowly situation of Persian women on two things: lack of education and the practice of veiling. She herself became less and less religious
and flouted convention more and more—taking lovers and riding a bicycle. The last sentence of her memoirs in the existing version states that
her desire to go to Europe became the cause of her separation from her
husband. She died an obese and impoverished woman in 1936.

Pictured, looking plump and faintly ludicrous, on a bicycle, Taj has
the moon face, thick hair and eyebrows almost joining that characterize
the typical image of a Qajar female. The brows were made to join by being
drawn in with silver nitrate if necessary. A similar, stylized image of beauty
is known to Iranians as *Khorshid Khanum,* "the Sun Lady." The image is
seen everywhere, even today, when the authorized face of feminine love-
liness is an unadorned triangle framed by a chador. I became fascinated
with this modern contradiction after a trip to Uzbekistan to visit the
ancient cities of Samarkand and Bukhara. I was surprised to find the Sun
Lady's face staring out at me from the ornately decorated, grandiose gates
of a seventeenth-century *madrasah,* or theological school. She was depicted
as a rising sun on the back of what looked like a tiger. Elsewhere the
woman's face, with curly hair and distinctive eyebrows is seen like a rising sun ascending behind a lion's body. But where did she come from,
and why was she sometimes, but not always, in the company of a lion?
Until then, I had thought of her as just a folksy piece of Iranian pop culture familiar from a children's nursery rhyme.

> Khorshid Khanum
> Come and make us a panful of rice
> We're the children of the Kurds
> And we're hungry

Some have said the Sun Lady has pre-Islamic Zoroastrian origins, others that she came from Turkic Central Asia. The ultimate puzzle is how
she came to be female at all, as in almost all mythologies, the sun is male.
Zoroastrian origins have been claimed for a series of embroideries of

Khorshid Khanum found in the Yazd area.[19] The small, circular pieces of needlework were made by brides-to-be before their marriages. The recognizable round faces are embroidered in colorful thread and adorned with sequins. Some were found walled up in houses, presumably to protect the household, and most are 100 to 160 years old.

Most historians believe Khorshid Khanum is not a particularly ancient creation; however, there are plenty of old stories about her. The historian Hamid Nayernouri, the father of a good friend of mine, recounts a delightful story about a thirteenth-century Seljuk king, Ghiaseddin Keykhosrow, who fell madly in love with a Georgian princess and decided to have her face stamped on the currency. His devout Muslim entourage thought this was inappropriate, not to say scandalous. They insisted that her likeness should be combined with a lion and made to look like the sun so as to imply that the image was purely an astrological reference to the sun rising in Leo, the fifth sign of the zodiac. Astrology is popular in Iran, where an astrological calendar is still used and the months coincide with the signs of the zodiac.

Afsaneh Najmabadi confessed to harboring a "scholarly obsession" with Khorshid Khanum, and by sheer chance was working on a book on the subject when I contacted her. She is positive that the image reached its zenith in the nineteenth century, when it was generally paired with a lion. The symbol of the Lion and the Sun was made the official emblem of Iran in 1836, at a time when the Qajars were busily inventing a glorious past for their recently established dynasty. Najmabadi has traced how the insignia became more and more stylized, and the facial features of the woman slowly disappeared, in what she calls a "gradual setting of the sun." Around the time women were ordered to abandon the veil, in 1936, a royal decree officially erased the lady's "eyes, eyebrows and hair," altogether an irony that is not lost on Najmabadi. "As real women became more publicly visible, the symbolic woman of the national emblem disappeared," she comments.[20]

Meanwhile Khorshid Khanum, in her solo incarnation, had become a popular icon, almost a nineteenth-century sex symbol. Her face pops up frequently in the new genre of paintings. "The female sun face of the emblem belonged to a particular set of female representations in Qajar court paintings," writes Najmabadi. "The same female face inhabited the

19. Herman Vahramian, "La Donna Sole: Ricami Khurshid Khanum," *FMR, Journal of Franco Maria Ricci*, No. 116, June 1996. Mario Vitalone, of Naples University, cast doubt on the historical accuracy of the theory.
20. Afsaneh Najmabadi, *The Eclipse of the Female Sun: Masculine State, Phantasmic Females and National Erasures*, (work in progress).

ceiling of a reception hall in a Qajar palace and was the face of dancers, musicians, wine-servers and other female entertainers…" The leading court painter, Sani al-Mulk, used her image in his depiction of *One Thousand and One Nights;* he also put the motif at the top of the *Official Gazette* as part of the emblem of the Lion and the Sun. However, when he painted a real woman named Khorshid Khanum, a cousin of his father's, she was demurely dressed, wore a scarf, showed little hair and had an oval, not a round, face.

A medal was instituted, the Sign of the Sun, to be awarded to royal women, or women who had given exceptional service to the state. It was bestowed on Queen Victoria during Naser al-Din Shah's visit to London in 1873. A painting of Victoria commissioned to commemorate the event now hangs in the British Embassy in Tehran. Najmabadi notes that apart from the Queen of Belgium, the Shah's favorite wife seems to be the only other woman to have received the order.

In the latter half of the twentieth century, Khorshid Khanum made a massive comeback. Before the 1979 revolution, her image appeared on pottery popularized by the *Sanaye'-e Dasti* handicrafts organization, a government-sponsored movement aimed at promoting Iranian culture. Along with a handful of other traditional designs, such as fishes in the desert or the rose and the nightingale, her face adorns bowls, plates, saucers and mugs. Interestingly, much of the pottery comes from Meybod, a small town not far from Yazd, the traditional stronghold of Zoroastrianism. But the Sun Lady also beams down from calendars, book covers and packets of pan scrubbers. She is one of the most popular marketing symbols in Iran today.

Khorshid Khanum adorns the cover of one of Banafshe Hejazi's books. When she asked a commercial artist to put her own photo on an anthology of poetry, she was told that this would be difficult to get past the censor. "I'd rather have had my own picture on it but I couldn't show myself properly so I asked the designer who did the cover to use a symbolic woman with full face and apparently the only woman you can use is Khorshid Khanum. He put this rope, like a strand of knitting yarn, in front of her mouth to show that she's silent," she said. It is a supreme irony that while the official image of Iranian womanhood has been restricted to a practically faceless triangle in a black frame, Khorshid Khanum—plump, curly haired and sexy—beams down benignly and silently mocks.

* * *

The feminist duo of publisher Shahla Lahiji and lawyer Mehrangiz Kar wrote a book about the whole question of the image of Iranian women. They completed it in the turbulent days after the revolution when neither of them could work in their regular jobs.[21] They called it *The Quest for Identity: The Image of Iranian Women in Prehistory and History* and set out to answer one big question: "Where do we come from?" Their first volume attempts to trace the image of women in pre-Islamic times. The introduction asks: "How can we get rid of all the dust that has collected on the history of women?...." It tries to explain: "This is how you are and this is how you lived and this is what happened and this is why you are now unseen." It urges women to understand their origins so that they can "rise and find their true position in society." The book concludes that women throughout history were not just mothers and wives but played an important role in the development of cultural, social and civic beliefs.[22] Unfortunately, this ambitious work raises many more questions than it can answer, and a later volume about women after the coming of Islam was never completed. What Lahiji and Kar do say, though, is that modern women are questioning their status as second-class citizens and looking for answers in history. "Today, in this part of the Middle East, women's whole identity has changed qualitatively and quantitatively, whether under pressure or because of their own interests, and if you look at the true face of women in this region you realize that women's lives in society have changed tremendously, whatever their class or social position."

While historians scratch around for images, artifacts and obscure references to women in history, the twentieth century should seem like an open book. Yet the idea of women's history is, of course, a new one, and methodical, unbiased accounts of women's lives in the last hundred years are few and far between. While work has been done, it has often been partisan and patchy, aimed at showing the revolution in a positive or negative light. As I tried, not very successfully, to get an overview of the upheavals of the modern age, I came across a woman who seemed to have lived through the changes and, in some cases, shaped them.

Mehrangiz Manouchehrian, an elderly lawyer in her nineties was born in 1906. She died in 2000, just a few months after my meetings with her. She lived through the whole gamut of social movements and reversals of fortune that have transformed the lives of Iranian women today. This formidable woman lived in a house in the center of town not far from the former U.S. Embassy. As luck would have it, my first appointment coincided with the

---

21. Lahiji and Kar, *The Quest for Identity.*
22. Ibid, Preface.

annual anti-American, flag-burning day, the Anniversary of the Hostage-Taking of the Den of Spies. My four-year-old son, Sasha, in the car with me on his way to school, watched with curiosity as students filed past chanting, "Death to America" and "Down with the traitors." Outside the embassy wall, women in chadors were assembling in an orderly fashion and I counted dozens of buses bringing conscripts to take part. I wondered uncomfortably if our UN license plates would attract any attention. But the days of revolutionary fervor had passed. Indeed, that year, at least one student group had announced that they would not actually burn the Stars and Stripes, but would set fire to an effigy of Uncle Sam instead. This, they said, would make it clear that their protest was against the U.S. government, not against the American people. At the school of a friend's son that year, as always, the deputy head laid out an American flag in the hall for all to trample on. But the boys walked around it and then, when he put it in the narrower school gateway, they jumped over it.

So we arrived late, and to our mortification, the wizened Dr. Manouchehrian, a tiny figure in a flowered smock and dark trousers, did not accept our excuses. "I am always very punctual," she said, reprovingly. "I was always early, even for my tennis lessons." I was accompanied by a close friend, Soudabeh, whose grandmother and great-grandmother founded the school Manouchehrian attended, one of the first girls' schools in Tehran. While Soudabeh swapped the usual Persian compliments and gave detailed news about family and friends, I rather slyly asked Manouchehrian's husband how he had met his wife. I was curious because I had heard that he was much younger than she was. My ploy failed, because he fobbed me off with "Oh, that goes back sixty years. I really don't remember." Quick as a flash, Manouchehrian chipped in: "I remember—he was *half*-human!" She explained, only half-jokingly, that the majority of Iranian suitors were not even that. After her death, her husband, Hossein Hosseini Nejad, confided that he was younger by seventeen years.

Mehrangiz Manouchehrian grew up in the northern city of Tabriz, where her father was a civil servant at the court of the heir to the Qajar throne. She remembers the closeted life of the *andarun,* or inner quarters, where the women and children lived. "A male servant worked for my grandmother, and he used to bring in messages from the outside," she said. We asked if he was a eunuch, and she hooted with laughter. "Male eunuch? No! By the way, have you read Germaine Greer's *The Female Eunuch*? What a nice woman she is. I translated it into Persian, you know."

Her mother wore not just the chador but also a white horsehair mask that covered her whole face. But she did not force it on her daughters.

Manouchehrian recalled that as a girl she was keen to wear the flowery, pastel-colored prayer chador, to appear grown up. "It was me who did this terrible thing to myself, because my sister had a chador and I said, 'Why can't I have one, too?'" Five-year-old girls on the streets of Tehran today are just as keen to wear a headscarf and chador for the same reasons.

Typically, for traditional families, her mother and father were cousins. But in this family, there was also a tradition that the men limited themselves to one wife, and that the women learned how to read and write. In the early days, going to school outside the house was frowned on, so Mehrangiz was taught the alphabet by her grandmother. Then, around the time of the Russian revolution, the family took in a lodger, a White Russian princess fleeing from the Bolsheviks. She gave the mother and daughter French, ballet and music lessons. Yet the family hesitated to send Mehrangiz to the French missionary school. At that time, girls' schools were considered breeding grounds for vice. When Mehrangiz did eventually begin at the Jeanne d'Arc School, she completed four grades in two years. She remembers fumbling with her chador while trying to write her final exams. She was not used to wearing it because girls of her class rarely left the house. "I couldn't hold it so I tied it under my chin with a ribbon." When asked to conjugate the verb *aimer*, she wrote, cheekily, that the imperative form did not exist. "You can't order someone to love someone," she explained. The examiner from the French Embassy, whom she remembered as handsome, awarded the eleven-year-old full marks.

The family moved to Tehran, and she and her sister attended the newly opened *Effatiyeh* school, run by Soudabeh's grandmother. The name, meaning "house of chastity," was typical of the attempt to bring respectability to the then scandalous field of girls' education. Other schools opened around that time, with names as pure as the driven snow: *Namus* (honor), *Esmatiyeh* (house of purity), *Ehtejabiyeh* (place of seclusion) and *Nosratiyeh-ye Pardegian* (Nosratiyeh School for Veiled Girls).[23] Although a model student in some respects, in others, Mehrangiz showed a streak of rebellion. She played truant, skipping classes to play with her jump rope. As she got older, she studied music, learning several instruments. But she realized she could never be a performer—the only female musicians playing in public were regarded as loose women.

By now, the women's rights movement was in full swing, backed by Iranian intellectuals and influenced by increasing contacts with the West. The status of women was one of the main topics for debate during the years of the Constitutional Revolution when many voices pushed for liberal

---

23. Milani, 57.

reforms. Women began to play a more prominent role in politics, on one occasion marching on parliament to urge the government to stand up to Russian pressure. Periodicals began to spring up, tackling issues such as women's education and the suffragette movement, as well as matters of housekeeping and family. By now, individual women were challenging convention on a daily basis.

In 1936 Manouchehrian was present at the famous occasion when Reza Shah abolished the veil, one of the defining moments of twentieth-century Iran. She had been attending teacher training college, where for some time, women teachers and students had been urged to appear in school without the veil.[24] "The Shah was visiting the teacher training school with his wife and daughters for a parade and he had asked that everyone should come without hejab," she said. "I and a number of teachers brought as many women students as we could to support it. We didn't realize at the time that it was going to become law, we just thought it was an event. Everyone was very excited that the Shah was coming." Other writers have described the shock, for both participants and onlookers. Badr ol-Moluk Bamdad, in her book *From Darkness into Light*, describes the looks of astonished disbelief on the faces of men in the street as they saw schoolmistresses walking by, unveiled. The Shah, during the ceremony, urged women to play a more active role in society. "Ladies, know that this is a great day, and use the opportunities which are now yours to help the country advance," he ended his speech. But, according to Bamdad, "Some of the elderly ladies among them, however, were visibly so upset by the loss of facial cover that they stood almost the whole time, looking at the wall and perspiring with embarrassment."[25]

Although Manouchehrian was delighted with the announcement, she realized the consequences were far-reaching. "There were girls who were completely rejected by their families afterwards," she said. "Girls started to just wear scarves instead of chadors, and their families didn't like it. Many of them were stopped from going to school altogether by their parents." The abolition of traditional covering became a royal decree and was brutally enforced. Police had orders to strip off the veils of women on the streets. Even today, some women can recount stories of the pain and embarrassment their mothers and grandmothers endured at suddenly being forced to appear uncovered in public. Some simply stayed at home. Men were also forced to adopt Western-style dress; tribes were ordered to give up their traditional costumes. The ban on wearing the veil was

24. Bamdad, *From Darkness into Light,* quoted by Milani.
25. Ibid., 33.

lifted in 1941, when Reza Shah abdicated in favor of his son, Mohammad Reza Shah. When compulsory Islamic dress was enforced more than forty years later, some women had a feeling of déjà vu, a sense of outrage that their clothes and their appearance were still not theirs to control.

Manouchehrian's frustration at being unable to study music led her into taking up law. "At that time there were no female law students. I wanted to break this forbidden thing about women and music, and in the end that's why I went to law school—to fight it. I had to wait for five years to be accepted." It was at Tehran University that she met and married one of her fellow students, Hossein Hosseini Nejad, who remained devoted to her. "I married because I wanted to be free," she declared. A married woman would no longer be pursued by suitors and had a certain status. As more girls received an education, women were playing an increasingly active role in public life, and Manouchehrian had many women clients.

At the beginning of the 1960s the Shah attempted to push through Western-style changes, culminating in what he called the White Revolution. A package of legislation including far-reaching land reforms and a proposal to give women the vote ran into heavy opposition from the clergy, led by Ayatollah Khomeini. In the end, after months of wrangling, the Shah simply granted women the vote by decree in 1963. The same year, he named Mehrangiz Manouchehrian as one of the two first women senators. Years later, Khomeini relied on the support of women to swell the mass demonstrations that brought down the Shah. The question of whether those women were entitled to the vote was scarcely even raised in the new Islamic Republic.

Manouchehrian helped reform the divorce laws, which were heavily weighted in men's favor, and worked on a revision of the civil code, rewriting parts which discriminated against women. She drafted the Family Protection Law of 1967, possibly the single most important piece of legislation relating to women ever passed in Iran. It established family protection courts to rule on divorce and custody (previously husbands had been able to terminate a marriage at will and automatically take custody of the children). Women were granted the right to initiate divorce proceedings, men were forced to seek permission from their spouses before taking a second wife, and the age of marriage was raised. On the wall of Manouchehrian's small sitting room was a picture of her in 1968, meeting the UN Secretary-General to receive an award for outstanding achievements in the field of human rights. Another framed certificate commemorated her being made Honorary Life President of the International Federation of Women Lawyers.

After the revolution, the Senate was abolished. The regime ordered senators to pay back all the wages they had ever received, accusing them of being the stooges of the Shah. Predictably, Manouchehrian fought the case in the revolutionary courts—and won. Nibbling pumpkin seeds, with a defiant look in her eye, she said with an air of finality: "That was my salary, and I didn't have the money to pay it back. They dropped the case." When she died, newspapers paid tribute to her as a fighter for women's rights. In Manouchehrian, all the strands of the historical debate over girls' education, marriage rights, and the right to hold public office and speak in a voice of one's own seemed to unite in one twentieth-century woman.

→fought
for women's
rights

4

Working Women

The perfume of *narenj* blossom, from bitter orange trees lining the path through the tea plantation, made me swoon. "Welcome to paradise," said the guide. A handful of men lolled against the tea factory door and watched us go by, on our way to talk to dozens of women working in the fields. The northern province of Gilan is a green garden of Eden in a desert country, the most fertile area of Iran, where you can grow tea, rice and just about anything else. It is also famous for its working women.

Down the road near Rudsar, I perched on a paddy field wall to talk to Hava Sedaghat, planting rice in pouring rain, up to her knees in muddy water. She was at the head of a long line of women workers. "Is it heavy work?" I said to get the conversation going. "Is it heavy work for a woman?" asked the male translator. "All work is difficult," said Hava. Dressed in a leopard print headscarf, an orange striped top, blue check skirt and black leggings, she had a large sheet of plastic tied around her shoulders to protect her from the rain. A nearby group of officials from the Ministry of Agriculture, all in regulation black coats and hoods, looked as if they were from another planet. Hava organized her friends and relatives into a group of twenty women to work in the paddy fields on this broad coastal strip on the shore of the Caspian Sea. They earned thirty thousand rials a day, (worth around $3.50 at the time), some of the highest farm wages in the country. At the age of forty-four, with six children to support, Hava needed to go out to work. "We spend the money on the house, and lots of us need it to save up towards a dowry for our daughters," she explained. "That's very important." She left primary school after just four years, but two of her daughters have finished high school and a son is at university.

Hava Sedaghat, planting rice near Rudsar, in the Caspian Sea province of Gilan. Her skirts are hitched up, and the scarf tied around her waist provides back support.

Women in rice fields organize themselves into informal cooperatives and earn some of the highest agricultural wages in the country.

Roghiyeh Pashali runs a rice plantation in the top rice-producing area of Astane, in Gilan. The local office of the Ministry of Agriculture named her a model farmer.

One of the puzzles about Iran is that, officially, women figure very little in the workforce, but in many areas they are very visible. Official statistics suggest they make up only fourteen percent of employees, and even less in rural areas.[1] Yet women work in fields throughout Iran, not just in the north. Sociologist Jaleh Shaditalab explains how the figures come to be so misleading. "The reason is that in Iran when they ask a woman what her job is, the first thing that comes to her mind is 'housewife' and they put her down as 'not economically active.' The reality—especially in rural areas—is that women sometimes have full responsibility," she said. "In rice production almost seventy percent of the labor is provided by women, but you don't see this in official statistics." Nonetheless, a government report on rural women concluded that, in general, women provided half the labor in country areas and that in some activities, such as raising livestock, dairy farming and rice growing, almost all the work was done by women.[2]

On a neat, prosperous farm near Astane, an area famous for producing top-quality rice, Roghiyeh Pashali sits at the head of the table. She has managed her own farm since her husband died, and she has been named as a "key farmer," who advises other growers in the region how to improve their yield. Confident, with strong features, she leaves the running of the house to her daughter-in-law. "I don't do the housework, my work is outside," she said. "I don't do the cooking; why should I? I do the shopping, and I get up at 5 A.M. every morning and go to town to look after my other business, a clothes shop."

As she talks, her adult son serves the guests with watermelon and cakes. Then he sits down and looks after his sleepy four-year-old daughter. He does the heavy work on the farm and will eventually take over from his mother. When I ask his mother why more women don't run their own farms, seeing as they do most of the hard work, she says, "They don't want to; it's tradition." He mutters *mardsalari,* "patriarchy," and laughs.

At the Rice Research Institute, outside the regional capital of Rasht, the deputy director Dr. Ali Reza Tarang is proud of Iranian rice, which he says is the best in the world. He's also proud of his female colleagues. "The head of our budget and program division is a woman, as is the head of our library, and all the laboratories are headed by women. There's no difference here between men and women." In a spanking-new lab, Farahnaz Farrokhzad is head of quality control. "Quality is very important because Iranian consumers are prepared to pay more for aromatic rice. Long-grain

---

1. From the 1999 *Human Development Report,* copublished by the Plan and Budget Organization and UNDP.
2. *Rural Women in the Islamic Republic of Iran* by Dr. Parvin Maroofi, Rural Women's Affairs Coordinator, Ministry of Agriculture, 1994.

rice with a fluffy texture is important." She introduces me to other women researching soil composition and genetic engineering.

In the north, women's roles in agriculture are openly acknowledged. At the headquarters of the Gilan Agriculture Organization, in Rasht, a senior official explained that the ministry had opened girls' clubs. "In areas where there are girls' clubs, and women are involved more in agriculture, the yield is higher than in more isolated areas where we haven't opened them," he said. At a nearby village, rows of girls dressed in strict black or navy-blue uniforms were packed into a tiny classroom for a club meeting. I asked them what kind of things they did, and they mentioned day trips to Tabriz, Mount Damavand and the seaside resort of Ramsar, as well as learning about rice growing. On field trips to other farms, they are paid for their labors (ten to twenty thousand rials a day, not bad for a teenager). "When we go to the fields with the club, we help farmers, but we get money, too," said one bright-looking girl with a beauty spot. "We learn new techniques from here. My family has an old farm, and they use old techniques. We can teach our own families." Selecting the seed can almost double the yield and the space between the seedlings is crucial. I asked her what she spent her money on. She had helped her family renovate the kitchen. Others shouted out *"Jahizeh"*—they were saving for their dowries. One club member was already married. In the classroom, macramé work and soccer trophies from the boys' club were on display. There was not much opportunity for girls' sports, they said, only ping-pong. I inquired whether there were other activities for young girls in the village. "Shooting, weapons training, Koran classes," they answered. The ubiquitous *basij,* or "volunteers' movement," keeps alive memories of the revolution and the war with Iraq while providing a social focus in villages with few facilities.

On the wall of the Rice Research Institute I had noticed a picture of President Rafsanjani, performing an opening ceremony at the organization. A row of ministry officials stood alongside him and in front of him. In a flooded paddy field, was a single man with a mechanized tiller, or rotivator. Where mechanization is introduced, women are squeezed out. Outside Astane, a row of three women were sowing peanuts, walking barefoot or with plastic sandals, behind a man with a heavy mechanical tiller. Maryam Jalali has been working this land with her husband's family since she married, at fifteen. "I left school when I was thirteen because I didn't like it. I prefer working on the farm or in the house," she said. "Also, one of the factors was marriage." Now she's twenty-two and her five-year-old son plays at the edge of the plowed field. Child care is not

*Planting peanuts outside Astane. ~~Men take over~~
as soon as mechanization is introduced.*

*Great-grandmother Roghiyeh Shabani supervises
work on a tea plantation at Kumle, Gilan.*

Women Pick tea in Gilan, northern Iran.

Tea Research Institute, Lahijan, northern Iran.

a problem; either he comes with her or stays with her sister-in-law at the farmhouse. A few fields down the road another family is planting peanuts; they are poorer and have no rotivator. They use a wooden pole to make holes for the nuts. Three good-looking teenage girls are working alongside their mother and father.

Further inland, on the vivid green slopes of the Kumle tea plantation, the elderly manager, Mr. Sabunchi, has been supervising a female workforce for more than sixty years. In the factory, the workforce is all male, but in the fields, he has four or five men and forty-five women. "I've tried with men but never had any success and even though they've suggested that I bring in three or four men and mechanize the plucking, I don't want to," he said. "I'm so satisfied with these ladies that I don't want to change. If I got a machine, what would I do with my ladies?"

The women walk among the knee-high, emerald tea bushes, deftly plucking the two newest shoots from each shrub. It's not as messy as rice planting, but it's heavy work. Many of the women wear shawls wrapped tightly around their waists as support for their lower back. When they have filled a huge rush basket with tea leaves, they carry it on their heads to the factory. Some carry children on their backs as well. As I toured the plantation, an older woman came up to me quietly and whispered into my ear that not only were the wages low, the company paid no health insurance or social security.

Mariam, thirty-two, earns seven thousand rials, or less than $1 a day, for picking seventy or eighty kilos of tea leaves. She left school at eleven and would have liked to have given up work when she got married, but her husband's job as a construction worker could not support the whole family. "Nowadays in Iran the cost of living is very high, and for most families, for the woman to stay at home and be a housewife is just not possible." She has three children and uses her wages to buy them clothes and school equipment. Her supervisor, Roghiyeh Shabani, was not even sure how old she was when she started work in the tea plantations. Her mother and father worked on the same bushes fifty years ago. A stocky, tough-looking woman, she now has children, grandchildren and great-grandchildren, some of them university graduates, one killed in the war. She can't stop working, even though she's near retirement age. "I just like to work," she said.

All the women channeled their wages into their children's education or "household expenses." No one mentioned pocket money, or financial independence from their husbands. Jaleh Shaditalab explained: "Even in Tehran, women who work don't consider their income as their own money," she said. "We have done two different pieces of research in rural and urban areas. In both cases money earned was considered as income for the family. If they consider it their own that's considered as the starting point of problems in the family."

As my visit came to an end, I sat around with officials, drinking tea just a week old. The color was quite beautiful, but I tried to hide a grimace as my tongue curled up. Iranian tea has a distinctive taste all its own. At the Tea Research Institute in Lahijan, they told me it was due to the cool climate and the variety of the bushes. In the deputy director's office, we were eleven women and three men around the boardroom table. After starting a speech "In the name of God," the deputy introduced his female staff and pointed out what responsible jobs they had. "You have chosen the right place to come, because as you know our ladies are very active in agriculture," he began. I braced myself for a barrage of propaganda. Then, to my surprise, he and the other men withdrew, and left us to it. Even more women arrived.

I was trying to get to the bottom of why the women of northern Iran are so different. A whole genre of "Rashti" jokes casts them in the role of sexy, assertive individuals married to hen-pecked, stupid husbands. In Tehran, theories had included the proximity to the former Soviet Union, and the fact that this area, and the neighboring province of Mazandaran, had been one of the last regions to embrace Islam. At the Tea Research Institute, they had a more convincing explanation. "Firstly it's a traditional thing; it's been going on for a long time and you can see references to women working here in old books," said Kobra Moghaddam. "Then, secondly, I think it's the climatic conditions which make it favorable for women to work. From April to September, there's a short period when the work is very intensive, and you have to plant rice and pluck the tea then prune the bushes, and the men alone simply could not do it. And, of course, it's delicate work which women can do well."

Shahrzad Shayegan, who had studied tea production in India, pointed out that because the land in this area is so fertile, it was possible to make a living with small family farms, whereas in other countries tea plantations and other agricultural holdings had become vast and industrialized. "Women who worked in the rice-fields were traditionally paid with a gunny sack of rice and if a woman brings in some income, then of course she feels she can have a say in the running of the farm," said another. Sociologists point out that as the north is densely populated, girls face fewer problems about going to school, as they rarely have to travel far. This is more acceptable to fathers anxious about their daughters' reputations.

Before leaving for the north, I had spoken to the Tehran representative of the UN Food and Agriculture Organization, Gamal Ahmed, who helped arrange the trip. When I had asked him what problems women farmers in the region faced, he raised the issue of the inheritance laws. Under Iranian law, a woman's share of an inheritance does not take into account the value of her dead husband's agricultural land. Instead it is calculated on various other factors such as the number of fruit trees and the value of the farmhouse and household effects. I had assumed this would be quite an issue, as women clearly played a huge role in farming here. Yet when I asked, not one of the women around the table had even heard about the law on inheriting land. They all knew about other aspects, by which, for example, a widow with children is only entitled to an eighth of her dead husband's estate. "That's a Muslim rule," said one woman. "That's how it is." I began to think I was imagining the law relating to agricultural land and let the subject drop. It wasn't until my final meeting when a female legal adviser happened to come into the room that the question was resolved. The other women looked amazed to find that I was right. Afterwards, I realized that, in a way, the law didn't matter to them. In this case, custom and practice was more important than the letter of the law.

While it is perfectly acceptable for women to contribute to the family income at home, going out to work is still a touchy issue, especially in conservative regions such as Baluchestan on the border with Afghanistan. The civil law states that a "husband can forbid his wife from taking up a profession or job which is against the interest of the family or the dignity of himself or the wife." So while, according to Jaleh Shaditalab, women make up to three-quarters of the rugs and carpets that are Iran's second most valuable export item after oil, they mostly make them at home or in small workshops, not in factories.

At a small knitwear factory on the edge of Tehran I saw a handful of women workers. They were concentrated in the quality control department, checking each completed garment. I was shown round by Jaleh Farhanpur, who designs and makes children's clothes for her own label, Zero Ten. I had hoped to chat with some women workers, but Jaleh advised me not to, saying that many of the female employees were worried their families would find out they were working in a factory. "Some of the girls face resistance from their families, but many have no choice," she said. "They have to work." When Jaleh took over, there were no women employees in the three hundred-strong workforce. Now she has a few, but it has not been easy. "There is male opposition to female workers even here," she said. The factory Komiteh keeps a close eye to ensure that there is no socializing between men and women. She's sure some of the men would

[handwritten margin note: probs women farmers had]

rather not be working for a female boss, but on the other hand, she's earned their respect, especially among employees who've worked for her for years.

Jaleh's own career has been, literally, a rags-to-riches story. She showed us into the boardroom wearing an unusually smart Islamic cover-up consisting of a tailored, gray, pinstriped long jacket, and a black headscarf. She then led us out of the front door, around the back of the building and up a fire escape to her office. Her small room is tucked away at the back so that when she is working on her own, she can take off her scarf without fear of being disturbed. Swatches of fabric, racks of samples and sketches for children's clothes littered the room. An assistant brought in the latest collection, tiny dresses knitted in gray wool and trimmed with pink rabbits. Little boys' jackets in blue and mustard were decorated with a square sailor collar in the shape of a school bus. Up to a hundred thousand garments a month leave Jaleh's factories, and she designs and checks most of them herself. The simple, sporty, well-cut Zero Ten clothes, something like an Iranian Benetton, stand out from the poorly made models decked with lace, frills and furbelows that Iranian children endure.

Her life, like that of many Iranians, changed irrevocably in 1979. At the time she was eighteen and studying architecture. Her father was fired from his job as a senior civil servant, the family house was raided, confiscated, and the money began to run out. Jaleh came up with three possible moneymaking ideas and made some samples—paintings, lampshade covers and children's clothes. "I had absolutely no money, so I sold a gold chain and bought some material," she remembers. "And with my mother's sewing machine I made three dresses for children." She hawked them around and one shopkeeper took the dresses and hung them in his window. He sold them the same day. "I stayed up all night making more," she recalls. "They were so successful that this guy was always on my back. At that time our second house was taken away by the Komiteh, so I rented a small place to work. I hired two ladies who didn't know how to sew, bought two old industrial sewing machines and had to start reading my mother's books on how to cut a sleeve, etcetera." Her mother, although from a wealthy family, had taught pattern making and physical education. "I made many mistakes, but I was really successful," she says. "Two years later I had five companies, eighty employees and I was only twenty years old." She went to Italy to finish off her studies—the universities in Iran had now closed—and remembers buying herself a Rolex watch. "I don't know why I wanted to buy a Rolex—perhaps because they stole my mother's Rolex when they broke in. So I bought one for her, one for me, and paid cash. I'll never forget the look on the shop assistant's face."

She met an Iranian diplomat and followed him to Canada, leaving the business in the hands of her family. She began to work as an architect, sinking her savings into a housing development, but the housing market collapsed. She returned to Iran in 1989 and found that her family was in debt and the business was failing. She went back to Canada but found there was very little work for architects in the wake of the slump. She drew a sketch for a large company of lady's outfitters, and they gave her a job as a designer's assistant. She started at $8 an hour, but within five weeks they tripled her salary. "They sent me to New York and Paris, they were so happy with me, and they gave me a line of my own to design." Then, she got pregnant. Her husband did not want the baby, and her marriage and life began to fall apart. She left her job and, with the help of an elderly friend, revived her Iranian business, naming it Zero Ten. She produced the garments in Iran and he marketed them in Canada. But even this plan foundered. Her partner died, and she became entangled in a legal battle with a previous business contact over the rights to the brand name. She had to sell all her jewelry again (but not the Rolex). Now she concentrates on the Iranian market, although her overseas customers include the Dutch giant C&A.

But doing business in Iran is not easy. When I arrived to visit, the factory's seven phone lines had been down for several days. The workers had recently completed an export order worth $30,000 for children's cashmere coats. The items were sent off, packed in one hundred boxes with twelve pieces in each, but when they arrived in Italy, almost every box had been opened. Iranian customs officials had cut a nick out of the sleeve of one garment in each box and muddled up the colors. The consignment was ruined.

Jaleh said she knew of no other woman boss working in the textile industry on the same scale, although many small workshops are run by women. She remembers being invited to a diplomatic business lunch where she was one of only two women guests. "When I arrived at the door, one man said: 'You know it's only for men, don't you?' Then another two said: 'I didn't know we could bring our wives, too.'" I asked how she was regarded as a single mother in business circles. "It's terrible being single, let alone a single mother," she laughed. "The problem of being a single woman here is a huge one. If anyone in the industry knows I'm single I'm going to be ruined. I keep my wedding ring on and don't say anything." Being a single mother is not so bad, however. "You have support from your family, whereas being a single mother in Canada is miserable!"

Women managers are few and far between, even though in some sectors, such as education and health, women make up almost half the employees. Jaleh Shaditalab says that the few figures available show the share of women managers in the public sector has not changed in the past thirty years and is stuck at around three percent. This is even though the number of women employees with higher education has increased by a factor of almost twenty over the same period. While the laws provide for equal pay, in reality it's a different matter, as she knows from her own experience as a civil servant and university professor. "My male colleagues get a certain allowance for their wives, but I don't get it because I'm not a 'breadwinner.' Male colleagues have more chances of taking promotions, so their salary increases much faster. They get a car and we don't. They get a driver and we don't. They get trips to conferences and summer schools. You can't find any law in the country which says the pay of Shaditalab should be lower because she's a woman, but in real life that's how it is," she told a group of professional women during a lecture called "Women in Management." Another academic, Nasrin Jazani, a management consultant at Shahid Beheshti University, added that top women managers did exist, even in the car industry, but that they were subject to the same problems encountered the world over. "There's been a glass ceiling here for working women, but it is not as bad as I thought when I came back fifteen years ago. The glass ceiling is the same one I see everywhere, even in America," she said.

I was struck by the fact that the impact of the revolution was barely raised, either in the lecture or in the question and answer session that followed. There was a general belief that the main obstacles in women's paths came from culture and tradition, rather than the Islamic regime. The percentage of women in the workplace did dip after the revolution, as women were encouraged to stay at home and concentrate on motherhood. But the numbers recovered to much the same levels for two reasons. Firstly, the war with Iraq meant that many women took over men's jobs while they were away at the front. Hundreds of thousands of young men did not return and in some cases the women stayed in the jobs. Secondly, the economy has slowly deteriorated to a point where most families need two incomes to survive.

In the early days of the revolution, women were indeed cast in the role of homemakers. Work was only appropriate if it did not affect family life. Night shifts for women were frowned upon, for example, as they could interfere with a man's conjugal rights. Women lawyers and judges were fired and many government offices stopped recruiting women altogether.

Employees who remained had a difficult time. One senior official at the Plan and Budget Organization recalls how her boss tried to have her office moved away from his on the grounds that a female voice would distract him. The same woman was refused entry to a meeting at the Ministry of Jihad because the doorman could not believe that women would be present. On another occasion she was handed a black package on her way in—a chador. "I'm laughing now, but it makes me bitter when I think how they treated us," she said. "When I think about the last twenty years, I think I have lost twenty years of my life. I was left outside of so many activities, so many fields."

However, in the decades that followed, attitudes changed.[3] The part women played during the war with Iraq reinforced their presence outside the home. Mostly this was in a supporting role as the mothers, wives or sisters of soldiers or, all too often, martyrs, as those who died in the war are known. But some women were on the front line. At a 1998 seminar entitled "The Epic Role of Women during the Sacred Defense Era," women recalled their experience. When she was seventeen, Nushin Najar was training as a basij, or volunteer, in the border town of Khorramshahr. "During the siege we were hungry. There was no food because the military did not relieve us. The weapons we had were very primitive; for example I had an M1 [WWII-era bolt-action rifle] with only three bullets." The city was taken by surprise and fell quickly. "We had to gather up our RPGs so the enemy would not be able to get them," she said. "It didn't matter whether there were women or men, we just carried out all the artillery and weapons to get them out of the enemy's hands. They were all saying, 'This is not a woman's job, it's too heavy,' but we did it anyway. I remember there was even a thirteen-year-old girl helping them."

Two women who had lost relatives recited their poetry. One, with a round, smiling face, described a conversation between a "martyr" and his mother.

> I wish you were there when I gave my blood
> And saw the light and all the stars
> When the wedding ceremony began…

Other women supported the army in logistics and supply jobs. Mehrangiz Kar points out that in traditionally conservative areas such as Khuzestan and Kordestan, the wartime experience had a lasting impact on women's lives. "Women who were not previously active in social

---

3. Paidar, *Women and the Political Process in Twentieth-Century Iran*, 322–355.

affairs, ordinary women, were hired to prepare food and became involved in food processing for the soldiers, especially in the south and west near the front. For these women it was good because they were working outside their home and it meant that they could be involved in the war and in politics and other subjects, so their minds were changed in this new situation—their horizons were broadened."

Changes in attitude towards the provision of child care give some idea of the shifting perspectives on working women. Just after the revolution, Ayatollah Khomeini described nurseries for the children of working mothers as a Western conspiracy to deprive youngsters of motherly love and an Islamic upbringing, and they were closed.[4] But in 1988 the prime minister's office instructed all ministries and government organizations to set up state-run nurseries for employees' children. In 1992, a government policy document regarding women's employment gave top priority to the role of women in the family and what it called the "job of motherhood."[5] It channeled women into "preferred" professions such as midwifery, gynecology and teaching. But it did acknowledge that working women had special problems. It insisted that they should be paid on par with men and encouraged to go into management. Moreover, the drive towards segregated facilities meant that in the traditional fields of health care and education, there were many more job opportunities for women. Plans were drawn up to train an extra twenty thousand midwives, for example. Iranian labor law is, if anything, favorable to women, and a string of amendments since the revolution have generally reflected the increasing presence of women in the workforce. It specifies maternity leave, details breaks for breast-feeding mothers and prohibits women from carrying heavy weights. However the various concessions may make employers less inclined to hire women. A controversial law making it easier for women to work part time was criticized as a double-edged sword, which may, in reality, ease women out of the workplace.

There are two jobs from which women are, to all intents and purposes, banned. One is the presidency, where the constitution specifies that candidates must be among religious and political *rejal*, Arabic for "men." The other is the position of judge. A law passed after the revolution stated: "Judges are selected from among men with the following qualifications…" thereby excluding women at a stroke.[6] More recently, women have been granted positions equivalent to the rank of judge in the judiciary and have

4. Ibid.
5. Supreme Council of the Cultural Revolution, UNICEF report, 19.
6. Ibid., 36.

been allowed back into family courts. But there they sit as "consulting judges" and do not, actually, have the power to hand down sentences. The justification for banning women judges is the traditional view in Islam that a woman's emotions cloud her judgment. But before the revolution, several high-powered women judges had been appointed. One of them was Shirin Ebadi, who is now a well-known human rights lawyer. She qualified in 1969 and within a year was appointed as a judge. She thought she had a brilliant career in front of her.

"It was the first year that women had been taken on," she said. "I got ahead for three different reasons. Firstly, I was smart and came top in the exams. Secondly, my father was a commercial lawyer. He was part of the system, and we talked about it all the time at home." In her book-lined study, she took down his spectacles, his magnifying glass and the book he had been reading when he died. She fingered them lovingly. "And thirdly, I was in love with the subject of law."

Like many Iranians, when the revolution began, she backed it wholeheartedly. At the time she was close to Abolhasan Banisadr, a non-clerical Islamic reformist and the man who would go on to become the president of the first Islamic Republic. "I really supported the revolution," she said. "During the Shah's reign, my office was a place where all the people against the Shah used to gather, and I was very close to the first group which came to power. But unfortunately those same friends—I'm not talking about the clergy—once they came to power, decided that women could not be good judges from a religious point of view."

The handful of women qualified as judges were fired. The regime tried to make Ebadi work as a clerk in the court where she once presided. She refused and took early retirement. But as one door closed, another door opened. "The first day they gave me the verdict I was very, very upset," she remembers. "But at the same time I was happy, because it meant I could be more independent." She began to write, first fiction, then legal textbooks. "When I was writing about the rights of the child I had two children of three years and three months and no one to help me," she said. "I'd go to the bathroom, turn the water on and do my writing there. I used to go the bathroom about five times a day. That's the reason why I believe that for every bad situation there's always a positive side. If the revolution had not happened I'd never have become a writer. If there'd not been a revolution, the most I could have achieved was to have become Minister of Justice, but because of the revolution I've become a fighter and I'm alive."

Ebadi is known as a high-profile campaigner for children's rights and heads one of Iran's most active NGOs, but she readily admits she would have liked to have focused on human rights in general. "Working with human rights, you're taking a bomb into your hands and walking round the streets with it. I couldn't really go and start up a human rights NGO, but through children's rights I believe that you can work for everyone's rights. Instead of me banging my head against a closed door, I'll become like water and run under the door, and I know that in time I'll be able to do what I want to do, which is to help people," she said. "I know that if I live long enough, I'd like to do something about human rights." I wondered if she meant her life was at risk, as I knew she had received many death threats from extremists. Even though we were at her office, in the same building as her home, she wore a gray manteau and had a scarf draped over her shoulders, as if in readiness for an intrusion from outside. "I don't say that I'm not afraid," she said. "Fear is an instinct like hunger. You can't really control it, but over the years I've learned how to conquer my fear. Yes, I'm afraid, but it hasn't really changed my goals. I'm a religious person. I believe that whatever Allah foresees for me will come about." Some months after we spoke, Ebadi was asked to act on behalf of the families of two politicians brutally murdered in a series of killings that the government shamefacedly acknowledged had been carried out by its own agents. Her name appeared on the same death list of dissidents regarded as opponents of the regime. Sometime later, she was arrested and kept in custody for three weeks on suspicion of disseminating a videotape that contained allegations of government involvement in the violence. She and another prominent human rights lawyer were tried in camera on grounds of national security, and in September 2000 they were given suspended prison sentences. They were also suspended from practicing law for five years for "having slandered senior government officials."

"My message is that we're like cacti in the desert," Ebadi told me. "You have to be strong to survive. I sometimes wonder if I'd been born in Sweden or Switzerland would I have been so strong..."

Girl wearing school uniform over jeans plays in a Yazd park.

5

Knowledge from Cradle to Grave

Our house in Tehran was surrounded by schools. I was awakened every morning by the sound of schoolgirls reciting the Koran at 7:30 A.M. In the tiny schoolyard next door, teenagers played volleyball wearing raincoats and headscarves. From time to time I would hear the teachers haranguing parents over the loudspeaker, demanding money for books and materials. One day, my maid's daughter, Nazanin, came into the house crying after disappointing exam results. I asked what her score was, and she sniffed, "Seventeen out of twenty." I told her mother, Soghra, that I thought they sounded pretty good, and she replied crossly that Nazanin, who was then eleven, generally got a perfect score. Soon afterwards, the class teacher rang Soghra to offer the child extra coaching, for a fee. Nazanin's grades improved. In Iran, as in many developing countries, education receives almost obsessive attention. The strict Islamic uniforms and the emphasis on religious studies give the impression that children are being brainwashed. Yet paradoxically the revolution has transformed attitudes to girls' education, and the last two decades have seen a vast improvement in women's literacy. The single-sex environment may ultimately have favored girls over boys. Many girls from highly religious families were allowed to go to school for the first time, then encouraged to continue into higher education. By 2000, more women than men were entering university.

Free primary school education for boys and girls is enshrined in the Iranian constitution. At the Vahdat Elementary School, in a prosperous suburb outside Tehran, around three hundred girls lined up, class by class, according to height. A monitor at the back kept each class in order. Every girl wore bottle green trousers, a smock, and a white hood, or *maqna'eh*. At the command of the teacher, barked out over a microphone, the children shouted enthusiastically: "Come, Mahdi," to encourage the twelfth Imam to return.[1] Then they put one hand on the shoulder of the child in front and marched into school.

In first grade, a lively math class was in progress. The teacher was explaining addition, with the full attention of the children. There was no shortage of volunteers to do sums on the blackboard. Each child received an enthusiastic round of applause. I was surprised, as clapping has been frowned on since the revolution as being Western and un-Islamic. "We don't usually clap every time," six-year-old Mina explained afterwards. "Only when someone gets twenty out of twenty. And in the Koran classes they reminded us not to clap when it was [the mourning month of] *Moharram*." The children were already receiving homework, including dictation, every night. I asked if their parents helped. One child, Fereshteh, said she and her brother sometimes went to the neighbors' house. Fereshteh, explained the teacher, was an Afghan, whose parents were illiterate. She towered head and shoulders above the rest of the class, because she had started school late. "She tells everyone that people are taller in Afghanistan because they swim, but we think she's about eleven," said Mina, wisely.

In the playground there was little sign of games—running was forbidden. "We go to the bathroom, we eat something and we prepare for the next lessons," said a tall girl clutching a history book. Elaheh, a fifth grader, was just about to take a test on the Constitutional Revolution, the period of reforms from 1905 to 1911. Inside the classroom, the girls in her class had taken off their white hoods and draped them on the back of the chairs. They hastily put them on again when a male official joined us. Elaheh read out one of the questions on the board: "Why did Mohammad Ali Shah bomb the parliament?" The answer: "Because he didn't want us to be free and have a constitution." Another girl, Faezeh, said history was her favorite subject—she wanted to be an archaeologist. She had not been to Persepolis, or any of Iran's staggering number of archaeological sites, either on a school trip or with her family. "I've read about it in books," she said. Undeterred by the dry-as-dust curriculum, the girls were beavering away. They told me girls studied harder than boys.

In the early years, math, Persian and science are stressed, but as children get older, religious studies take up an increasing slice of the school day. By high school, it comprises around a third of all studies, if Koran

---

1. Iranian Shiites revere twelve different Imams, or saintly religious leaders, and for this reason they are sometimes known as Twelvers. The twelfth Imam mysteriously disappeared in the ninth century when he was a child, and he is believed to be somehow hidden from view. He represents a Messiah-like figure who will return some day to create a perfect society.

classes and Arabic are included. Most Iranian education is rote learning, sheer memorization. Until the mid-nineteenth century, formal education in Iran was provided entirely by Islamic *maktab,* private schools supported by the contributions of wealthy donors. Instruction was based on memorization of the Koran and of classical poetry. Later on it was influenced by the French system, and the approach leaves little room for creativity. Even six-year-olds' drawings are given marks out of twenty, with the emphasis on technique rather than originality.

[handwritten margin note: peculiar bdc changing in America]

In the staff room, the head teacher, Marzieh Fatahi, admitted she followed a traditional "chalk and talk" approach. "When we compare ourselves to other countries, we feel at a disadvantage, because there they have an experimental approach and the children experience things," she said. "But we don't have the facilities. Here it's more theoretical and they just have to memorize things." She gave the example of science, where, she suggested, if every classroom had a TV, they could show science films. As this was not my idea of practical science, I asked whether the girls did any experiments. She said, without a trace of irony, that they did them at home. When I expressed disbelief that first graders were already taking three exams a year, she showed me piles of scripts with neat little drawings and the first letters of the Persian alphabet. Wasn't it difficult for a six-year-old to do dictation, and constantly face exams, I wondered, thinking of my own six-year-old? "I don't think this is a negative thing. It's positive. It enables the teacher to assess how well they have done," she said. "If it's conducted with lots of stress for the pupils, then that's negative, but because of the frequency with which we give the tests, they get used to it."

Vahdat Elementary, equipped with a photocopier, computer and central heating, was well painted and cheerful. Many of children were from the families of affluent commuters, and there was an active parents' association. This school had few staffing problems, but teachers' wages were low. Hossein Yahyaiyan, the area education director, said that a teacher with twelve years' experience would get around 450,000 rials a month (just over $50) plus a bonus for traveling from outside the area. Earlier that day, one of the parents had mentioned that this was the wage she was paying her maid. As we left the school, Yahyaiyan remarked that these days girls were doing better than boys. The insistence on a single-sex environment meant that they often had better teachers and natural role models, as few men were prepared to go into teaching because of the low wages, he said. Outside the school, a cluster of girls asked for my autograph. Meeting a foreigner was an event. Two boys were engaged in a fight outside the school gate. "See what we mean about boys?" said one girl with a look of superiority.

At the Way to Jerusalem, a crumbling lower secondary, or "Guidance," school two hours' drive south of Tehran, the walls were drab and bare. Several of the teachers commuted through hellish traffic from the north of Tehran every day. Behind the local education offices, builders were laying the foundations for dormitory accommodation, for teaching staff. Iran's booming and mobile population is a headache for planners. My translator was an experienced English teacher who had to commute sixty kilometers a day and was scraping to make ends meet. "Before the revolution I got two thousand tomans a month, which was worth about $200. Now, with twenty-six years of experience, I get a hundred thousand tomans (around $120) and I've had to sell my car," he said. He supplemented his earnings by running a private primary school in the small town where he was living, with girls' classrooms on one floor and boys' on another. "Why is it that girls do better than boys?" he asked me with a genuine expression of bafflement. "I teach English to boys and girls and the boys are so…noisy. The girls do much better because they are motivated—they are eager to learn."

The head teacher at the Way to Jerusalem, Ameneh Selsipur, was a past pupil from the days when the school was named after the national emblem, the Lion and the Sun. She remembers the village as being poor and remote; there had been no secondary school in the community then. Now, the village's nearness to Tehran and a boom in flower growing for export has raised the standard of living and attracted many migrant workers. The village itself has been renamed Golzar, or "place of flowers." "The people of this area are traditionally Muslim, and we respect Islamic rules, like wearing a chador or crying for Imam Hossein, but we have technology and facilities now like phones and piped gas, and some of the girls' aspirations have changed," said Selsipur. "For example, a lot more students go to university after finishing school." Few have high enough scores to win a place at the nearby state-run Abu Reyhan University, which specializes in agricultural sciences, but more and more girls were going to the Islamic Azad private university in nearby Varamin.

In the Arabic class, girls were declining verbs and learning basic grammar. To my surprise, they chorused that it was "easy." Their teacher pointed out that the authorities had recently amended the textbook, making it less ambitious. Samira, in the first row, told me she liked Arabic because it was the language of Islam. She said she liked theology because it helped her know her Islamic duty, and she added that she could have contacts in Arab-speaking countries. Another said proudly that she knew twenty verses of the Koran by heart. But many teachers privately dismiss the lessons as a waste of time. "It may be good enough for reading the Koran, but at the end of the day they can't speak it and in real life it's useless," said one. "If you want to do business, you need to be able to use a computer and that's all in English."

At this, the "guidance" stage, the drop-out rate is at its highest. The lower secondary schools for eleven-to thirteen-year-olds were introduced at the time of the Shah and modeled on the American junior high, but they have always been problematic. Said one educationalist: "Guidance is where we have the highest drop-out rate, the highest gender gap and the highest rate of schoolchildren talking about a sense of uselessness." She pointed out that the religious content of the curriculum is doubled at this stage, just as children are entering the impressionable period of puberty. At this stage, some textbooks for boys and girls differ, with boys encouraged to follow technical vocations and girls pictured passing the time knitting. Before I left, I asked the class of thirteen-year-olds if they wanted to put some questions to me. What religion was I and had I ever though of becoming a Muslim? What do people think of the Koran in Britain? What is the aim of religion? Their questions were far more searching than their grammar lesson. I beat a hasty retreat.

In a nearby high school, the shift was changing—upper secondary school pupils were finishing their lessons and lower secondary school girls were arriving. Many schools in Iran follow a shift system because of overcrowding. In the older girls' physics class, students in an all-black uniform were working with prisms and mirrors, looking at the reflection of a torch beam and a candle. The school seemed shabby and needed painting, but the science lab was well equipped and clearly put to good use. The teachers, however, complained that when the first shift went home, they never knew where they would find things the following day. The upper school deputy head teacher had a more serious concern. Because of the shift system, her girls had to finish early and were losing almost two hours off a normal school day. "The students are not getting the time they need, and then in the afternoon, all the students are falling asleep as they are not so fresh, especially in the spring, when it starts to get hot." Moreover, in the winter many parents, particularly from traditional backgrounds, were concerned that their daughters had to come home from school after dark.

At one point, the headmistress left the room briefly and reappeared with a one-year-old child. Her son, Sahan, was looked after during school hours by the caretaker. After bouncing him on the desk and letting him play with the phone, she discreetly moved her chador aside and began to breast-feed him. She was completely unembarrassed, and the two male education authority officials did not bat an eyelid. Afterwards I wondered how many British teachers would nurse a child in the presence of a foreign visitor and two male colleagues. As I left, she presented me with two bouquets of exotic-looking lilies. "From Mr. Sharifi," she said. I had heard a lot about Mr. Sharifi, a local farmer, who had made a small fortune growing and exporting flowers. He had built the main school buildings fifteen years previously and had since provided a sports hall and air conditioning. Before that, girls from religious families had often not been allowed to travel to secondary school as it was some distance away in a nearby town. "Mr. Sharifi was a rich man and he built these buildings and now the problem has been solved," she said. Ministry of Education officials estimate that out of 51,000 classrooms built in the 1990s, more than 17,000 were built with the help of public contributions.[2]

Since the revolution and the baby boom that followed, the government has struggled to accommodate the vast increase in numbers, but the regime is proud of its record of getting almost all children into school. With forty percent of the population under the age of fourteen, Iran has one of the youngest populations in the world.[3] These days ninety-seven percent of children between the ages of six and ten enroll in primary school. The revolution diverted resources into rural areas, and by accident or design, this was of great benefit to country girls, who otherwise would have missed out on school. Sociologist Jaleh Shaditalab has seen far-reaching changes in attitudes. "Education would have happened anyway, but for the girls especially, the revolution accelerated it," she said. "Before the revolution some families did not want their girls to go to school because their teachers would have been men. But since it came in an Islamic packaging, people were more willing to accept it as Islamic education. That's why you see the rate of enrollment in schools rise. Now we see the share of girls in universities—it's unbelievable. It's increased from thirty percent to more than fifty percent. Why? Because families now think the universities are teaching Islamic beliefs, and that there's no harm in their daughters going to university because they are sleeping in [single-sex] dormitories."

Even before the revolution, most schools were single sex and girls wore a long smock and trousers as school uniform. But the Islamic regime poured money into building new schools and employing more teachers. Now, only a few primary schools in remote rural areas are still mixed, but the curriculum for boys and girls is exactly the same. The laws on Islamic

2. *Basic Education of Afghan Refugees in Iran,* report for UNESCO by Catherine Squire, March 2000.
3. *Education for All 2000,* I.R.I. country report, published by Ministry of Education and UNICEF, Autumn 1999.

dress, no matter how restrictive they are for the Westernized city dwellers of north Tehran, have had a liberating effect on young village girls. Their fathers allowed them to go to school for the first time, in the belief that they were safely covered up on the streets. Moreover, they did not have as far to travel, now that practically every village had a school, the teachers were women and the curriculum was reassuringly Islamic.

Iran has won international accolades for boosting the literacy rate among women from thirty-six percent in 1976 to around seventy-two percent in 1996.[4] About two-thirds of the population of more than sixty million are either at school or employed in education, according to the Ministry of Education's Director of International Relations, Farhad Eftekharzadeh. He, too, notes the changes in the way traditional families educate their girls. "There has been a concentration of budgetary resources to villages, where people would have been reluctant to send their girls to school, and at the same time there has been a change of attitude among traditional families," he said.

A female researcher for UNICEF told me: "I honestly think that the revolution was the best thing that happened to Iranian women. You talk to girls from twenty to thirty and most of them are dead set on getting a good job. Previously everyone was dead set on getting themselves a rich husband. The revolution raised their level of awareness. You see it in the villages. When you go to a village in the afternoon, you see boys loitering around. The girls are all inside—studying. Many village girls say that study is their own means of escape." At the time I didn't believe her theory—I thought the girls were probably helping wash up. When I asked Eftekharzadeh where the modern Iranian obsession with studying came from, he said something similar. "You have to realize that our children have not much alternative to study," he said. "They are in schools for six hours, then they come home and study again. There are few sports facilities, few recreational activities; they have no other choice *but* to study." Statistics have begun to confirm the idea that schoolgirls are pulling ahead of boys, said Farideh Mashayekh, an educational planning consultant. Once girls are in school, they are less likely to have to repeat a year. "This is important," she told a women's group. "I think that our girls are achieving more than boys and the statistics prove that." This is one reason that in the 1990s women began to overtake men in the scramble for university places.

Nonetheless, big problems remain, especially for girls in remote and deprived regions such as Sistan and Baluchestan. Overall, the number of

---

4. *Human Development Report of the Islamic Republic of Iran,* 1999, copublished by the Plan and Budget Organization and the United Nations.

girls not enrolling in school is almost twice the number of boys and many youngsters drop out as time goes by.[5] Said Eftekharzadeh: "If they taste the fruit of learning, girls have a great tendency to stay in school. But when the subject matter is boring and the father thinks that if you can read a few signs that's enough and then you should go back to work…" His words were echoed by Azin Movahed of UNICEF. "After the age of nine, participation is massively reduced," she said. "Once girls reach the age of puberty, parents don't want to continue sending them to school because they think that's an age where they should stay inside the house and keep covered and not expose themselves to people." She told me of a Persian saying: "Lessons and schools open up girls' eyes and ears." It is not used in a positive sense.

UNICEF found that a third of families in poorer provinces cited lack of money as a consideration in keeping their girls out of school. A quarter of them said the girls were needed at home to help their mothers with housework or child care; the same number said they were needed to work in the families' fields, look after animals or weave carpets; the same proportion again were convinced that education was irrelevant to the girls' eventual roles as wives and mothers. Researchers also found that hidden costs such as the price of books and uniforms added up to around $60 a year and that school uniforms and transport costs were much higher for girls than for boys.[6]

In an Arab village outside the southwestern city of Ahwaz, I asked Hadida, an elderly woman dressed in black, how many children she had. She answered proudly, "Four sons," then with some prompting from my Arab translator, "and five daughters." She did not go to school as a child—her parents did not allow it. She spoke very little Persian and joked that she could not even manage to say good-bye, *khodahafez,* properly. "I just say *fez fez,'"* she laughed. She had sent all her children to school, but neither she nor her niece, Sabah, who was also her daughter-in-law, could read or write. There was not a book in sight in the bare room, furnished only with carpets and cushions. In one corner a sturdy wooden box with rope handles marked "explosives" was used for storage. The area was devastated during the Iran-Iraq war.

"I was scared to go school," said Sabah. "None of my brothers or sisters went to school—why should I go?" Shahla, one of the old woman's daughters, went from the age of nine once a school was opened in the village. "My parents wanted me to go to secondary school as well," she said.

---

5. *The State of Women,* Islamic Republic of Iran, UNICEF, Tehran, 1998.
6. *The State of the Young,* Islamic Republic of Iran, UNICEF, Tehran, 1998.

"But at the school they said I was too old." Teachers find it hard to cope with eleven-year-olds who are three years behind. Shahla said secondary school was out of the question for most girls in their community, as they would have had to travel to another village. "It's shameful for girls to go out of the house." When I asked the women to show me the village school, just a few hundred yards from their walled house, they hesitated. "I'd need to get permission from my husband," explained Sabah. Hadida had already mentioned to us that her husband beat them if they "made a mistake," as she put it, so I did not insist. They found an eight-year-old girl to act as my guide, instead. The school, alongside a date plantation, consisted of one brick-built classroom and a decrepit prefabricated cabin with broken windows. There was no playground, as such, just a shady area with trees where cows were tethered. Neighbors were baking bread in mud-built ovens using dried cow dung for fuel.

The head of the Education Ministry's bureau for women's affairs, Fatemeh Tondguyan, stresses Iran's huge cultural differences as an obstacle to education. Speaking loudly, to be heard above a prayer meeting in the ministry courtyard, Tondguyan listed the achievements in girls' education since the revolution. I had expected this and, indeed, later discovered that she was from a "politically correct" revolutionary background, the widow of a war hero. But then she took my breath away with a long list of the problems confronting educational planners. Not least of the challenges on the list was the fact that the majority of Iranian children starting first grade nationwide do not have Persian as their mother tongue. They may speak Arabic, Turkish, Kurdish or a variety of tribal languages or dialects. Without a year of preschool or special help from locally engaged bilingual teachers, many of these children fall behind or drop out.

Another problem, said Tondguyan, was the tendency of girls in rural areas to marry early. Once a girl is officially married, she is forced to leave school, though she may attend literacy classes. In spite of the Islamic ideology prevalent after the revolution, the average age of marriage had climbed to a respectable 22.4 nationwide according to the 1996 census. But Tondguyan estimated that there were still 617,900 girls under the age of eighteen who had married before completing their studies. She wanted to set up special schools for these young married girls.

Many children feel the content of the classes is irrelevant to their lives. In 1999 the Education Minister announced that school textbooks would be revised in an attempt to change the image of women. The revisions were proposed by the ministry's own Bureau of Women's Affairs: "To reflect the changing role of the family, we are going to make a drastic change in the content, subject and images of women in textbooks to make them appropriate for today's way of life," said Tondguyan. She criticized existing texts for emphasizing women's roles in the house and giving few examples of city life. The range of jobs women are shown doing would be expanded and men would be depicted helping with the housework. But this was not all. "Also we don't have any image of Muslim women in our textbooks, which means we have ignored the way Islam looks upon women. For example in the history of Islam you see that the wife of the Prophet was active in political affairs, but unfortunately we don't have such images of women nowadays."

Interestingly, a Western study of the revisions made to textbooks just after the revolution concluded that very little had been changed even though a fundamental review was promised.[7] The researchers found that only ten percent of the texts used in the Islamic Republic were completely new. The study found that men were more "visible" than women, but that this also applied to the Pahlavi era books. These days, families are more often shown sleeping and eating on traditional carpet-covered floors rather than on Western-style furniture. The researchers acknowledged that this was a more realistic picture of life in Iran and suggested that it might help children from poorer backgrounds to relate to the teaching material.

Textbooks are state-produced and centralized, allowing teachers very little room to introduce issues of local interest. When I asked schoolgirls at a high school outside the eastern city of Mashhad, where forty percent of the youngsters were Afghans, what they learned about Afghanistan, they clucked *"hitch,"* or nothing. "We've been here a long time and I was born here, so it's like my second home," said one girl at Moghtaderi High School in Golshahr. "Although we have problems here, I've not seen Afghanistan, so I don't know what it's like." Another, Zahra, said she liked to read books about the lives of the prophets and the "great leaders of Iran." Then she burst into tears. "Our country is at war, how can we go back?" she asked.[8] "People here say we should go back, but how can we go? My cousin, he has children, they took him back." The teacher tried to soothe her, but the whole class looked upset.

There were thought to be more than a million Afghans in Iran, which at this time was host to the biggest population of refugees in the world. Most of them came in the wake of the Soviet invasion and were taken in with open arms as fellow Muslims. Since then, the economic situation

7. "Women's Education in the I.R.I." by Patricia Higgins and Pirouz Shoar-Ghaffari, in *In the Eye of the Storm*, ed. Afkhami, Mahnaz and Friedl.
8. I conducted these interviews in April 2000, before Taliban was removed from power the following year.

has deteriorated, and later arrivals have not been made so welcome. Around 180,000 Afghans from the first wave of refugees are allowed to attend state schools in Iran, causing a considerable financial burden and over-crowding. Others attend informal schools run by the Afghans themselves.[9] At another state guidance school outside Mashhad, where half the girls were Afghans, classrooms were bare and run-down. Fifty girls were packed into one small classroom. Maryam, a fourteen-year-old Afghan, had drawn a good likeness of Ayatollah Khomeini on the bare classroom wall.

But in spite of the poor resources, the lessons these girls were receiving were far superior to what they could have expected at home, where the Taliban had banned girls' schools. Even before the Islamic militia came to power, Afghanistan was a far more traditional and restrictive place for women. Aid workers reported that many Iranian-educated girls who returned became teachers in their home country. And life in Iran has had a big impact on them, said Nastaran Musavi, Iran representative of the refugee charity, Ockenden International. The average age of marriage among refugees has increased, and women say they are consulted more. "They say they can't 'force' their girls into marriage any more because they have adopted Iranian women's marriage customs. They say things like: 'We can't do anything about it—boys and girls meet each other here. They [the Iranians] are not as Islamic as we thought.'"

To put Iran's achievements in the field of education into context, by the year 2000 the adult female literacy rate was around seventy-two percent, comparable to that in its western neighbor, Turkey, and in contrast to twenty-four percent in Pakistan and a miserable fifteen percent in Afghanistan.[10] The credit for the reduction in illiteracy goes not just to schools, however, but to the Literacy Movement Organization (LMO), which tackles the problem with revolutionary fervor. There had been literacy campaigns under the Shah, but Ayatollah Khomeini called for Iran to be turned into one big school. Said Mohammad Mehdizadeh, the LMO's director of educational affairs: "This organization is a revolutionary institution, and we have very strong religious beliefs in Islam and education." A thickset man with an intense manner, he looked a true revolutionary, wearing the usual tieless gray suit and sporting a designer Islamic stubble. He prefaced his briefing with the words "In the name of God, the most merciful," and continued: "The Koran says you should seek knowledge from birth till death, and that's our motto and we try to carry it out." The LMO holds classes in schools, houses, tents, prisons, mosques—anywhere it is asked

9. UNESCO report, and personal communication from UNESCO with author.
10. *Human Development Report, Iran 1999*; UNICEF State of the World's Children, 1999.

*Afghan refugee children wait for the bread
to cool outside a baker's shop in Kashan.*

Maryam, fourteen, an Afghan refugee at school in Mashhad, is pictured next to the portrait of Ayatollah Khomeini she sketched on the classroom wall.

Batul Youssefi (right), 40, reads out loud at a literacy class with the help of her eleven-year-old daughter, Fatemeh.

6-
70
yr old

to. He said proudly that the organization had students who were six years old and students who were seventy. "In these programs, our main focus, or seventy percent of it, is on women, because we believe that if a woman is literate, there is no way that her children will be illiterate. If a woman works and earns money and has power in the family, it means that family is more likely to succeed and for the children to grow in a more secure environment," he said.

During the ten-day celebration for the twenty-first anniversary of the revolution I visited the Ershad Elementary School in Shahr-e Rayy, south of Tehran. The school was shabby, even crumbling, with ceiling tiles missing everywhere, but the head office was being decked out with green leaves and bunting. Parallel to the regular school lessons, three LMO classes were under way. In the first, sixty-four-year-old Zoleikha Hassani was just completing the beginners' course. "I'd like to be literate, now that there's the possibility," she said. "Before the revolution we were not allowed to come and study, but now we are free and our husbands have realized that and given us the freedom to seek knowledge." A hint of hennaed hair peeked out from her chador and headscarf. She added: "It helps me in my life very much, in my marriage and with my children, communicating with my children."

B/U &
after
the
revolution

In the front row, forty-year-old Batul Yussefi painstakingly read out loud while her eleven-year-old daughter, Fatemeh, dressed in a blue and white school uniform, leaned over the desk, mouthing the words. "Every night she sits beside me and says, 'Mommy, I want to help you, come and do your lessons,'" said Batul. Some women told me they decided to come because they were ashamed at not being able to help their children with their homework. I asked what book they would like to be able to read, and they chorused, "The Koran." This was not for the benefit of the visitors. Most of these women's social lives revolve around prayer meetings, trips to the mosque and charity work for the local community. "Last week I personally sewed 219 flags and wrapped up four thousand packets of chocolates for the Sepah, the Revolutionary Guard," Batul said, proudly.

edu.
in
rural
vs.
urban

Like many of the inhabitants of Shahr-e Rayy, forty-two-year-old Fatemeh Allah'do is a migrant who moved to the city from a remote rural area. "I was in a village in [the province of] Sistan and Baluchestan," she said. "My father was a farmer, and in those days they just didn't take girls to school. My father didn't see the need and didn't have the financial means. He didn't realize the value." Then when she married and moved to the city, she met with opposition from her husband. "Some have financial difficulties, some have interfering husbands," she said. "Ten years ago

I started classes, but my husband admitted to not wanting his wife to be literate!" Later, when her three children started school, she found the headmistress at Ershad was sympathetic, encouraging her to join a literacy group. "I held up a Koran in front of me and told my husband: 'You won't stop me!'" Now, Fatemeh is in the intermediate class. Another classmate's father was a clergyman. "It's very important for me that the classes are women-only," said Ashraf Sadat-Hosseini, speaking through her chador, showing nothing of her mouth. "My father was a clergyman and that's why I was not able to attend school. I did start night classes with the help of my mother, but my father found out and put a stop to it."

In a more advanced class, Fatemeh Naghdi held a sleeping three-year-old on her knee with an older preschooler by her side. Her third child sometimes babysits to allow her mother to attend classes. Many of the LMO students are girls who married early, and no woman is turned away because she has a child in tow. These girls are keen to learn, and teachers said the drop-out rate was low. Several women had newspapers on their desks—they said they liked to read human interest stories, economics and sport.

At the other end of the educational spectrum, the women at the prestigious Sharif University of Technology represent the country's elite. The administration claims that twenty-five percent of its six thousand students are women, and that twenty-five of its three hundred faculty members are female. The percentages compare well with similar institutions in the West, said Professor Abol Hassan Vafai, chairman of the Office for International and Scientific Cooperation, who organized a seminar for the diplomatic community. He introduced Assistant Professor Azam Iraji-Zad, head of the physics department, and asked her if she had ever suffered any discrimination at work. Her answer had a familiar ring, recognizable to working women the world over. "I try not to think or emphasize gender issues; however, this matter does affect me," she said. "For example, at lunchtime, when my secretary is off for an hour, I have to answer the phone. Many times when I say, 'Hello, can I help you?' they ask me to put them through to the head of the department, or even to Mr. Head of Department." Her husband, also a lecturer, was now junior to her. "It is a joke at the university," she laughed afterwards. "'Poor Mahmud,' they would say. 'His wife is his boss at university and at home as well.'"

Sharif University, in Tehran, regularly accepts virtually all the top two hundred students in the fearsome nationwide university entrance exam, taken by around one and a half million young people. The women on the panel were consequently extremely impressive. They included a young professor of electrical engineering who described traveling twenty-five kilometers each day from her village to the nearest high school. None of her family had ever been to university. Another was a twenty-one-year-old pure math graduate, the youngest woman Ph.D. student in Iran. "People say that women are not interested in pure math, but I think differently," she said. She added that her family had wanted her to become an engineer, which the majority of Iranians consider, along with medicine, to be the most prestigious profession.

Many of the women had studied abroad, most of them accompanied by their husbands. They seemed either unaware of, or confused about, legislation enacted in 1985 banning single women from taking government scholarships to study abroad unless they were married.[11] One woman assured me that the law, in any case, did not affect privately financed study. Another believed it also applied to single men. This seemed to be another example of Iranian women carrying on regardless, blithely unaware of the legal shackles that surround them.[12]

While the university management was proud of its female stars, it seemed taken aback by the rising tide of women applicants. The president confessed that the numbers had grown so fast they were having to build new dormitories. The pattern of increased university entrants has been repeated nationwide, with the post-revolutionary population boom swelling the figures by staggering proportions. In 1979, around 180,000 students were in higher education, whereas by 1998 the number had risen to 1.3 million, said Abbas Bazargan, a lecturer in higher education at Tehran University. "During just twenty years it's a great achievement. Almost ten times what it was at the beginning of the revolution. Then almost one out of ten could get to university but now the number of students is almost half the number of applicants." He told a meeting of the Professional Women's Group that admission policies now favored relatively disadvantaged candidates from the provinces. Critics of the system point out that special quotas for the families of "martyrs" who died in the war with Iraq or for other groups favored by the regime are extremely unpopular and seen as robbing ordinary candidates of a place. And there is widespread concern about falling standards.

Professor Bazargan gave a breakdown of the thirty thousand students at Tehran University. He showed that more women than men were studying

---

11. UNICEF Women report.
12. An attempt to repeal the legislation was made in 2000 but it had a difficult ride through parliament and was opposed by a leading ayatollah and the conservative Guardian Council. In 2001, the Expediency Council approved an amended law that stipulates that a single woman may be granted a scholarship if her father has no objection.

humanities and basic science, and about the same number had chosen engineering. "One would expect women to be concentrated in the arts subjects, but they are not," he said. However, in the private, or Islamic Azad, universities, established in the 1980s, sixty percent of all students study humanities. These institutions, often in provincial towns where previously no university existed, have done much to encourage youngsters to enter into higher education.

But the big concern preoccupying parents, planners and students is quality. Surely the quality of education must have suffered with the huge population explosion? Bazargan took off his quartz watch and showed it to the audience. "This watch keeps perfect time, but I don't think any of you would call it a quality watch." He declined to elaborate. Iran's first *Human Development Report*, however, puts it more baldly. "The main challenge the education system has to meet is simultaneously to maximize access to education and improve the quality of education at all levels." Moreover, the system is weak at providing vocational training to supply skilled workers for technical jobs.

With its emphasis on rote learning, the school system does little to prepare students for high-quality academic life. Azin Movahed of UNICEF holds a doctorate in music and teaches in her spare time. "I see my students at university, and they are very lacking in social skills. They are afraid even to say a word. They are not willing to present ideas. They don't have the skills to analyze or give their own opinions, even if we're just doing a review of a concert. They have always been told what to think." But history lecturer Mansoureh Ettehadiyeh, also from Tehran University, stresses that university life transforms students. "In the universities, they wanted to separate the classes, then they said they'd put up a curtain to separate men and women, or that women would sit on one side only," she recalled. "But students are students—they work together, and they talk together and after four years of study they begin to question things." She gestured at a handful of young women at work in her office. "These girls are interesting," she said. "They are all ambitious, but they are all chadori. In class they work better than the boys because they know if they don't, they won't get a job."

Professor Ettehadiyeh remembers the days when many academics were thrown out of their jobs in the purges of the early 1980s. "I only escaped the 'purification' as it was called, because I was doing my Ph.D. outside of Iran at the time when they closed the university. When they reopened it all the leftists and other political activists had been ousted and every student was scrutinized." In recent years, the climate has been freer, easier in some ways than it was at the time of the Shah, she said. "In class, I'm not stupid, I'm careful what I say, but you can talk about Communism, Mao or Marx, which I could never have done then." However, strict Islamic vetting means that many able academics have been excluded from teaching jobs. I once met a linguistics graduate at a party who told me she had been turned down at the interview stage when a panel member objected to the fact that she had plucked her eyebrows. Ziba Mir Hosseini, a Cambridge-educated anthropologist, remembers the ordeal of the "cultural interview" when she applied for a teaching job. She was vetted for her commitment to Islam and the revolution.

"It was not like an interview it was like a trial....I failed the interview because of hejab. They asked me what was people's reaction in the West when I wore hejab. I didn't want to lie, but I didn't want to say I didn't wear it, so I tried not to answer. In the end I lost my temper and asked them why they thought it was so important....Then finally they asked me to recite some verses from the Koran. We learn them all by heart at school and I knew them, but I was so nervous I made a mistake and missed out the most important verse. I knew it didn't sound right and I got quite angry and said: 'Look what you've made me do, I can't even remember the Koran now. Why are you putting me through this?' They said, 'It's very important who is teaching our children now...'"

After the revolution, women were banned from studying a host of subjects, such as agriculture, geology and accounting. They were channeled into other subjects, so that, for example, a woman could become a doctor, but not a veterinarian. Meanwhile men were also banned from certain areas of study, such as midwifery or gynecology. It has always been difficult to establish exactly which fields are open, and which are closed—the rules appeared to change from year to year.[13] But the campaign to get the restrictions lifted was spearheaded by an influential Islamic feminist, Zahra Rahnavard, wife of former prime minister Mir-Hossein Musavi and a member of the Women's Social and Cultural Council. Now chancellor of the all-women Al-Zahra University, she assured me that all fields are now open to women. "From 1985, I started fighting not to have this discrimination between boys and girls for entrance to university, and I was successful in taking this prejudice away. In those days there was a quota basis—five percent for mathematics and ten percent for agriculture and some courses which were not permitted," she said. Lifting the ban required the intervention of the the president at the time, Ayatollah Khamenei, later the Supreme Leader.

---

13. Higgins and Ghaffari, 27–32.

Al-Zahra University was founded in 1964, when it was known as the Higher Educational Institute for Girls. Unofficially it was called the Farah Pahlavi Finishing School, a reference to the empress. It offered languages, secretarial courses and psychology. In the second year, it expanded to include "housewifery," a course that has since been discontinued. Nowadays faculties also include engineering, social sciences, theology and arts. Here, too, there was building work going on to cope with the dizzying expansion in girls' education.

On her résumé, the chancellor describes herself as "Mrs. Zahra Rahnavard, Ph.D., sculptor, author and activist in politics." One of her sculptures, commonly known as *The Mother* dominates a busy roundabout in northern Tehran. It is one of the best-known landmarks in the city. From out of her desk drawer, she produced a multi-colored silk-screen print, depicting a jumble of images of women in world mythologies. Professor Rahnavard, dressed in a candy-pink cardigan with a geometric pattern, admitted she would rather see more color amid the sea of black chadors. "I'd prefer it if all the girls in the university would wear colorful clothes, but for that it would have to come from a political authority, not from me," she said. "Hejab is a requirement under Islam, but this black color is not mentioned." The rules on Islamic dress are strictly enforced at Al-Zahra, as at all Iranian universities.

To my surprise, Rahnavard said she did not subscribe to the widely held view that many girls perform better academically in a single-sex environment. However, she said she believed single-sex establishments could increase the number of places available for girls, thus enabling them to enjoy their "natural right" to study. I asked her about girls' expectations on leaving university. "To have a good job, especially in the specialized fields which they train for, and also in management," she said. "To have a good income, a good husband and to have what I'd call a clean life, which is religious but free and happy."

Whether these expectations are met is another question, especially where jobs are concerned. Graduate unemployment is a fact of life for both women and men, as the president's adviser on women's affairs, Zahra Shojaie, told a 1998 Women's Week conference at the Institute for Political and International Affairs. "Unemployment is one of the great anxieties and concerns of our economy.... The new graduates who are the offspring of families since the revolution outnumber the other graduates, so we may face an even greater crisis in the near future," she said. The issue worries sociologists. Homa Zanjanizadeh, of Ferdowsi University, told a *Zanan* magazine roundtable that Iran had reached a point of transition. "It is natural that when we allowed women to go and achieve high levels of education, those women would demand employment....Our traditional families have been transformed. We encourage our daughters to go to higher education. Then we see that we are faced with a multiplicity and a clash of roles."

Sociology professor Jaleh Shaditalab agrees. "Now, an illiterate mother can have a daughter at university," she said. "That's made a very curious situation because the mother doesn't understand her daughter any more. They don't speak the same language. That's why youth is a serious problem. There's a huge gap in understanding, and they don't have anything in common to talk about....I'm expecting very serious problems in this country in the next ten years," she said. "It could end in social movements or political moves because young people have been to university and they want jobs, but they are unemployed." In none of the cultures she had studied had she ever seen such a gap, she said. Not only is she one of the country's leading sociologists, Shaditalab has a personal interest in the matter. As our conversation drew to a close, she made a confession. "To tell you the truth, my father only had an elementary education and my mother is illiterate. She keeps asking, 'When will your reading be finished—is there no end to it?'"

6

You Can Leave Your Scarf On…

On the low-lying plain near Dezful, between the Iraqi border and the Zagros Mountains, a group of Bakhtiari nomads were preparing for their spring migration. Leaders of the tribe had gone on ahead to pick out a route to their summer pastures in the hills. Eight families were clustered around deserted outbuildings, some living in the traditional dark-brown woolen tents of the pastoral nomads, others in drab canvas shelters.

A young woman in a purple dress was baking bread over an open fire in a tumbledown cowshed. Her dark headscarf revealed two long ringlets on either side of her face. She first prepared the dough, occasionally swatting flies off it, flattening it out with her hands until it looked like a large pizza. Then she placed it on a dome-shaped metal hot plate to cook. The whole process took only minutes; the thin bread tasted crisp and delicious. They invited us to stay for tea, rolled out factory-made carpets for us to sit on and gathered around to chat. It appeared there were only two glasses to be had, and I drank my tea from a metal water beaker, first washed scrupulously in front of me. They had a health problem, and they wanted our advice.

The men wanted our guide, a university professor, to look at a five-year-old boy with a suspected broken arm. It had been strapped up with bandages and homemade wooden splints. "Why don't you take him to the hospital?" we asked. "Too expensive," was the answer. An average hospital consultation would cost around twenty thousand rials, or less than $3, but hospitalization or an operation could prove costly. The arm seemed perfectly normal, but they kept the dressing on. The boy was barefoot and dressed in rags. "Play clothes," one woman assured us, but their poverty was evident.

Other health problems were also dealt with on a self-help basis. Maryam, a mother of seven, told me an elderly woman known as Mamani or Granny

Afshar, a Bakhtiari nomad, holds her baby in front of her tent near Dezful.

Bakhtiari nomads bake bread over an open fire in an
abandoned building, which serves as part of their winter camp.

helped with childbirth. "We go to hospital if the labor is very difficult or too hard to bear, but otherwise we have our children here in the tent and Mamani helps us." Mamani, all in black, was tending to the livestock, mainly sheep and goats, while the younger women sat around with the visitors. "But where are your husbands? And what about your children?" they asked, baffled. "And if you are from Britain, how did you meet your other friend, from Canada, in Tehran?" One quiet woman, Katun, told us she married at eleven and was now sixteen years old. Her husband. Ahmad, was twenty-five and appeared impatient to have children. When my British friend told them she did not have her children until her thirties, they raised eyebrows. "Our husbands would beat us if we did that," said one. Katun said little. Ahmad answered most of the questions for her. We asked how they had voted. "For Khatami, of course, for the true Islam," said Ahmad. Katun explained that her husband had told her who to vote for.

Early marriage, a lifetime of childbearing and sheer poverty take a toll on a woman's health. There are problems of malnutrition, anemia and death in childbirth. Yet women's health is another area where the revolution had an unexpectedly positive impact. As with education, the government channeled resources into remote, deprived areas. It set up a grassroots primary health care network that has transformed access to health care and is the envy of other developing countries. From 1985 to 1997, the maternal mortality rate dropped from 140 deaths per 100,000 live births to 37.4 per 100,000. The infant mortality rate has also been slashed. The revolution led to a massive population boom, however, which brought with it intractable problems. Family planning clinics were dismantled and large families were encouraged. By the end of the 1980s, policy-makers had realized the error of their ways. In a spectacular reversal, contraception was again officially encouraged and the country saw the population growth rate practically halve.

A large part of the success in improving health care has come from better communications, access to safe drinking water and the rise of literacy among village women, said Giti Hedayati, the government's director of maternal health. "Before the revolution, the main concern was in urban areas, and we didn't have any facilities in rural areas, just some physicians who used to go there when they were doing their military service," she said. "But we didn't have health houses, health workers and some rural areas didn't have any road or a phone. Rural areas have changed a lot."

Village health care starts with two health workers, a man and a woman, who run what's called a health house. "They are known as *behvarz*," she said. "Most of them are married, both of them are from the same village. They select them from that village and then train them for two years in mother and child care, family planning, et cetera, and send them back to that village." When a woman goes into a health house and announces that she's pregnant, she is entitled to free checkups, first monthly, then every fortnight, then every week. If she does not appear at the expected time, the behvarz will go to her house and seek her out. "People in the village will all know each other and they know this girl—she's the girl of one of their relations, and they trust her and they listen," said Mrs. Hedayati. In the two years' training, they are supposed to learn everything about their village, about population and environmental issues, how to distinguish between a child with a cold and a child with pneumonia. They do vaccinations and hand out condoms, pills, even give Norplant contraceptive injections. They visit the school and check hearing, and eyesight, and carry out vaccinations. They keep a file on every family in the village and record vital statistics such as births, diseases and deaths. The woman partner is usually busier than her husband, who is often occupied visiting nearby hamlets by motorbike. For, in conservative provinces, women are not encouraged to travel unaccompanied and have to guard jealously their respectability.

One of these health workers, Zinat Daryaii, has become a celebrity since her life became the subject of a dramatized documentary. I met her at a Women's Day meeting in Tehran. Wearing a blue and white prayer chador over a bright-orange traditional trouser suit, she appeared like an alien flower amid the sea of dark raincoats, sober headscarves and black hoods. When she spoke, she set the meeting on fire, gesticulating freely, tossing her chador around her head and revealing silver spangles and embroidered sleeves underneath. Zinat comes from Qeshm Island, the largest island in the Persian Gulf, which forms part of Hormozgan, one of the poorest, most conservative provinces in Iran. She began with a recital of her own poetry, delivered in the dramatic Iranian style, then told the story that has made her famous, about how her life changed when she abandoned the Arab-style face mask, the borqa.[1]

Zinat was interested in health care even as a girl. From the age of eleven she would help foreign doctors working on the island, but when the government ordered them to leave, the Iranian who took over told her she

---

1. The borqa is not unlike the Arab face masks seen in other parts of the Persian Gulf, but the origins are unclear. "An interesting local tradition which will be seen in Bandar Abbas and many other coastal towns of Hormozgan province are the borqa or the 'masks' worn by some women, which are fairly hideous, semi-rigid contraptions surrounding eyes and cheek-bones and covering the nose. The Iranians believe that no religious taboo explains the wearing of these masks: rather it is a fashion which originates from the period of Portuguese occupation when ladies wished to walk about unrecognized or simply to protect their face from the scorching sun." Faramarzi, *A Travel Guide to Iran.*

needed a permit to practice as a health worker. She would have liked to train as a nurse, but she had only had a few years' primary school education. She decided to go to the mainland port of Bandar Abbas to train as a behvarz. "For that I needed to unveil myself," she said, "and in our village that was like walking around naked." She would leave her village still wearing the mask then take it off on her way to the training school on the mainland, replacing it with a headscarf or maqna'eh. When she qualified and returned to the village to work, she was ostracized. "At first people didn't recognize me, but when they did, everybody isolated me. My friends disowned me, saying that if I could take off my veil I was capable of doing worse things. This went on for ten years. I was totally alone," she said.

Then one night she saved the life of a child, and the tide turned. She became a local heroine and stood in Iran's first local elections in February 1999. "The same people who would throw stones at me before, voted for me, and I won with a lot more votes than most men," she said, triumphantly. Flashing glances around the lecture theatre, making eye contact with the audience, she made a natural public speaker, who, I imagined, livened up municipal authority meetings.

In some provinces, the situation is even worse. Mrs. Hedayati, an Iranian-trained nurse who worked in Britain for some years, singled out the eastern province of Sistan-Baluchestan, near the border with Pakistan and Afghanistan. "In Baluchestan, women are not allowed to go out of the house for forty days after the delivery of a baby. This is their culture," she said. "One of the obstacles we have there is that they don't let girls go to the district center to be trained as behvarz, so we have a lot of problems. We recently started to train rural midwives in their own villages because so many of them are not allowed to go out of their homes, especially at nights." At this point, a Tehran-based ministry official interrupted in disbelief to check if this could really be true. She asked if it meant that women were restricted from going to hospital. But, it seems, with the husband's permission, there is no problem.

Hospitals were clearly only a last resort in the Arab-speaking community outside Ahwaz where I had tried to visit the village school. Our hostess Sabah said that while some women went for checkups, others didn't bother. "I just waited for my stomach to come out like this," she said. "Then, when I was ready to deliver I went to the house of the local traditional birth attendant and had the baby there." For other health problems they went to the doctor in the next village, with or without their husbands. They said there was a woman doctor there. "What would a male doctor do, prod around and feel me inside? I'd be scared of that," she said. She and her relatives said they had all heard of women having problems with pregnancy and child-birth. Shahla said that when she was ill after giving birth, her uncle, who knew about these things, made a hot compress filled with salt to put on her head. "After a few days it was a bit better. I didn't go to the doctor because the women I knew said there was no need," she said.

Most maternal deaths are due to the absence of a trained midwife or doctor, said Giti Hedayati. "We had these trained birth attendants, or TBAS, and these were old and illiterate women. It was in their family for many, many years, but because they are very old they do not know how to care for women if complications arise and most of the deaths happen because of this." A project to increase the number of rural midwives, who can at the very least identify mothers at risk, has had some success, training around seven thousand women. But in the poorest of provinces, there is no trained health worker present at the vast majority of births. Moreover, the UN Population Fund (UNFPA) has raised concerns that because of all the empha-sis put on training women doctors, male medical students receive little or no practical training in dealing with pregnancy and childbirth. The orga-nization's 2000 *Country Population Assessment* notes that in many remote and hard-to-reach provinces the doctors in the rural health centers are men, who cannot adequately deal with obstetric emergencies.[2]

The conversation moved from birth to death. It seemed natural to me to ask what was the leading cause of death among women. I soon dis-covered this was a sure-fire way of making a health professional uncomfortable. No one seemed sure what it was, although a well-known woman gynecologist told me it was "probably one of the cancer group." A female neurologist friend told me that doctors were in the habit of put-ting down "heart failure" on death certificates to cover all eventualities. Mrs. Hedayati had invited Dr. Mina Majd, director of the Health Ministry's Elderly and Female Health Programs, to join the discussion, so I thought she would be able to give me a definitive answer. After much hesitation, she singled out breast cancer as the leading cause of death. Mrs. Hedayati then pointed out that death statistics were not broken down into male and female figures, so that it was hard to know. I ventured, rather mis-chievously, that road traffic accidents must be a leading killer as so many women insisted on wearing their black chadors at night.

In urban areas, primary health care is similar to that offered by rural health houses, but there is little or no follow-up. "We have health centers, and they provide the same service to the mother and child, but if a woman

---

2. UNFPA *Country Population Assessment*, Tehran, 2000.

does not show up for an appointment or refer to the health center, nobody will bother. In a big city like Tehran it's very difficult to make home visits," said Mrs. Hedayati.

At Hakimiyeh Health Center, among the sprawling suburbs of east Tehran, community health volunteers were preparing for a visit by the wife of the UN Secretary-General. A young boy sang a verse of the Koran in front of a roomful of chador-clad women. The front row was taken up by male officials. But when it came to showing us around, the women took over. They were particularly proud of a computer-based records system, designed by the son of one of the workers. The volunteers are usually housewives with a couple of months of health care training. They were recruited, basically, to take health information leaflets from door to door, but they have proven to be far more versatile. UNICEF cites the case of Soghra Bagheri, who has worked at Hakimiyeh for four years. When her neighbors had persistent problems with their electricity, she wrote a poem to the director of the electricity board. Within three days the supply was restored.[3]

Iran's primary health care system has been praised by the international community. Each year, the government mobilizes up to half a million volunteers, including students and basij volunteers, in immunization campaigns aimed at eradicating polio and other infectious diseases. UN agencies report that on one occasion, more than eight million children under five were vaccinated in one day. Some of the highest praise is reserved for the family planning program, which UNFPA has described as "an extraordinary achievement." At the Cairo conference on population in 1994, Iran played a role in rallying other Islamic countries behind a proposed plan of action. Its delegation had the unlikely distinction of being publicly praised by the U.S. government. Enthusiasm for population policies seems unusual in an Islamic country where attitudes toward birth control are often conservative and large families are considered a blessing. But Iran, while encouraging people to have children after the revolution, saw its population spiral out of control. A gynecologist friend of mine, Dr. Shokrou Ghorbani, who has since, sadly, died, recalled attitudes at the time of the Shah. "My first encounter with [the question of] population was in the year 1964 in connection with the Mother of the Year ceremony," she said. "She had eighteen children and was from Mazandaran. But gradually it was understood that having too many children is not a good thing for the country. So they changed the conditions for receiving the prize to having many children, but all educated. First prize then went to a mother with six children, and

---

3. *The State of Women*, Islamic Republic of Iran, UNICEF, Tehran, 1998.

they were all doctors." Dr. Ghorbani, a founder of the prerevolutionary family-planning program, helped set up family planning clinics that distributed free contraceptives. Family sizes gradually fell, and population growth decreased. However, she lived to see the whole system dismantled at the time of the revolution, in an anti-Shah measure.

While contraceptives were not banned, the hard-line clergy emphasized motherhood and the growth of the nation. Parvin Paidar reports the stand of a woman member of parliament, Monir Gorji, who opposed population control at an international conference in 1981 on the grounds that it was an "imperialist conspiracy."[4] The legal minimum age for marriage was abolished and polygamy was legalized. During the long war with Iraq, Ayatollah Khomeini called for an army of twenty million. A commonly heard slogan was that "Every Muslim born is an arrow in the side of the arrogant powers." But following the 1988 ceasefire, the economy was in tatters and the population growth among the highest in the world. Health planners met senior leaders in Mashhad, and Ayatollah Khomeini authorized a debate on population issues. This paved the way for a reversal of policy within a year. Free family planning services were reintroduced, and shortly afterwards sterilization was again allowed. Families could claim state benefits for the first three children, but from the fourth child onwards the subsidy was cut. The government managed to bring down the population growth rate from 3.2 percent annually to around 1.47 percent.

Dr. Hassan Mohtashami Khojasteh, chief executive officer of the present-day Family Planning Association of Iran, a nongovernmental organization, cites three reasons for the success of the turnaround. "I think the first one was political commitment. It was not only a U-turn, they took another route altogether, and they had the full commitment of both the government and the religious leaders," he said. "Secondly, the time was ripe, socially and culturally; and thirdly, the primary health care network was already in place—they just handed out contraceptives at health houses and clinics." Changes in society contributed to the success. Early marriages are a tradition in Iran, and before the revolution the average age of marriage hovered at around nineteen for women. Since then, although the minimum age of eighteen was abolished to allow girls as young as nine to marry in accordance with Islamic beliefs, the average age has steadily climbed. By the year 2000 the average age of marriage was around twenty-three for women, with girls staying on longer at school and couples despairing of ever having enough money to get married.[5] It

4. Paidar, 287.
5. UNFPA CPA cites 1996 census figure of 22.4

is a nice example of the limited impact of revolutionary ideology in the face of far more deep-rooted social change.

Nowadays all forms of contraception are allowed except for abortion. Access to birth control looks good on paper, but in reality, it may be less effective. A survey carried out in 1996 found that around a third of Iranian women on the pill did not know how to use it correctly, including what to do if they missed a day.[6] The same survey estimated that more than one in three pregnancies were unwanted. The government insists that every couple about to marry attends premarriage classes where men and women are counseled (usually separately) on family planning and other issues. Dr. Mohtashami, however, suggests that the classes are not very effective. His NGO believes that youngsters should receive sex education much earlier, preferably around puberty. One of its surveys found that the vast majority of girls were unhappy about the idea of reaching puberty. Half of them had found their first period a terrifying experience. Some of them were lacking in knowledge of basic hygiene. "There's nobody talking about sex or reproductive health with these young people. Not the government nor the parents—there are no offices offering services to these people," he said.

The health service only provides contraception to married couples, although, as Dr. Mohtashami put it: "Sex before marriage—we're sure that it exists, but we're not sure of the extent of it. There are no figures, only rumors…" Sexual relations outside of marriage are punishable by flogging or stoning. And the taboo surrounding talking about sex certainly hampers health education. When the FPA did a study to assess what kind of help adolescents really needed, they found that although there was a great demand for information, there was very little they could offer that would be acceptable to parents and society. "We have reached a point where we have to accept there is a kind of shame in this country regarding these issues and that ultimately we should respect that and provide services accordingly. We're not going to hold meetings where they'll be ashamed to ask questions," said Mohtashami.

There is no doubting the depth of feeling surrounding the issue. Dr. Fereydoun Forouhary, director of a Tehran vasectomy clinic, was one of Iran's best-known advocates of family planning. A green arrow painted on the ground marked the way from the car park to his office to show people the way without the embarrassment of having to ask.[7] Dr. Forouhary

---

6. Family Planning Association, IRI, *Needs Assessment on the Quality of Care in Governmental Health Units*, 1998.

7. *Christian Science Monitor*, 21 November 1999.

was murdered in 2000 by a group of unknown assassins. Press reports quoted his brother as saying that before his death, the doctor had been threatened that vasectomy was against religion, and that he would be killed if he continued his work.

Abortion, similarly, is an emotionally charged area. The 1967 Family Protection Act had given women the right to abortion under certain circumstances, but this was abolished immediately after the revolution, on religious grounds.[8] For twenty years afterwards, abortion was only allowed if the mother's life was at risk, said gynecologist and politician Marzieh Vahid Dastjerdi: "Abortion is not an option for unwanted pregnancies because of people's religious beliefs. But then, Ayatollah Khamenei gave a *fatwa* saying that abortion could be carried out if an unborn child was suffering from a fatal disease, such as thalassemia major." Other conditions, such as kidney disease and severe cases of Downs' syndrome, may also qualify. Each case is referred to a medical legal committee *(pezeshk-e qanuni)*. Illegal abortions, however, do take place in substantial numbers. Dr. Mohtashami said that one leading health official had calculated that the number could be as many as 80,000 per year. He pointed out that the issue had been raised in the cinema. In one film, *Yek Bar Baraye Hamishe,* or "Once and for All," a couple seeking an abortion visit various backstreet clinics from the north to the south of Tehran, at one point witnessing a police raid. "It's a movie, but it tells you about the real picture," he said.

Dr. Mohtashami's NGO is one of the few genuinely active, non-governmental organizations on the Iranian scene. In general, groups are either very close to the government, or marginalized and struggling. The election of President Khatami gave new momentum to movements fostering the formation of civil society. A conference in the southern city of Bushehr in 1997 identified problems of stifling bureaucracy, isolation and the need for capacity building. Many groups run into legal problems the moment they try to form, as they are obliged to register with a ministry that may object to a variety of things, including the group's field of operation and its choice of name. Bagher Namazi, who heads a non-governmental NGO technical support center, described the problems of bureaucracy as a "control mentality." In a newsletter devoted to the NGO scene, he said that most new groups were still too dependent on the government. He did, however, point out that Iran has a rich tradition of volunteerism, and traditional community-based organizations such as charities and religious groups. Dr. Mohtashami, too, draws attention to traditional grassroots organizations. "We have fantastic groups of people, particularly the women's groups,

8. Iran News, Press Review, 3 April 2000.

which have done a brilliant job. You can't imagine. I always say it's a sleeping dragon. If only you could wake her up and arm her with new management skills and communication skills, and knowledge about modern civil society like democracy and human rights, women's rights. They are the real civil society of this country," he said.

Farhat Mehdizadeh took me to a poor district of southern Tehran to see the Kahrizak Center for the Aged and Disabled, staffed and supported almost entirely by the Ladies Charitable Society. Kahrizak is a huge institution, with corridors, courtyards, gardens and roads of its own. The fifteen hundred residents are mainly housed in rows of depressing hospital-style wards, with very little in the way of stimulation. But there are workshops where men and women sit behind sewing machines making uniforms for schools, hospitals and industry. And there is a crèche for the children of the staff and the inmates, for relationships among the residents are encouraged, and separate housing exists for married couples. Above all, it is spotlessly clean and run like clockwork, with a workforce made up largely of volunteers. "Most women volunteers do it out of a religious duty," said Farhat. "They believe they are going to be rewarded in heaven." Farhat, whom I met many times at a Western-style women's discussion group, is very active in volunteerism, organizing events ranging from summer bazaars to an international conference on aging. At Kahrizak there's an army of fifteen hundred volunteers, and a waiting list to become one, said Mrs. Malakuti, who showed us around. "A busload of ladies comes every day to wash patients and teach them skills like tailoring."

Iranians much prefer to look after their elderly relatives at home. But now that many of them are living an urban lifestyle, with small apartments and couples working, some are forced to look for nursing accommodations. "But people are still very resistant to this," said Farhat. She estimated that there were only around six thousand elderly people in around seventeen homes, out of a population of more than sixty million. Side by side with the success stories affecting women's health, there are, however, persistent problems. More girls than boys die before their first birthday. More girls than boys die due to cot death, drowning, and swallowing of chemicals and pesticides in the first year of life. And in some areas, malnutrition is still worse among girls than boys. Although the gender gap has narrowed over the years, 15 percent of boys and 16.3 percent of girls were found to be malnourished according to a 1998 UNICEF report. Nutrition problems continue to be a problem in adulthood. Iran's first *Human Development Report* points out that "a startling proportion" of Iranian women suffer from anemia and iron deficiency. This is not helped by the Iranian habit of drinking tea, which inhibits iron intake, after meals. Visitors to Iran are struck by the amazing variety and quality of fruit, vegetables, meat and dairy produce. Yet it is highly seasonal and the distribution system is not very developed, so that in a remote village, fresh produce, including milk, may not always be available. In children, the critical time is from six months onwards, when mothers wean their babies onto solid foods. Instead of healthy mashed fruit and vegetables, too many mothers stuff their babies with tea, sugar and bread, leading to slower than normal weight gain. Some children catch up once they are old enough to eat a balanced diet, but others never recover.

Researchers in the southern city of Shiraz in the 1980s found that mothers gave husbands and sons the first choice of food, then served themselves and their daughters. Most women believed that boys needed more food than girls because they were more active. Dr. Robabeh Sheikh-ol-Eslam, Director of the Health Ministry's nutrition department, stresses that while problems still exist in one or two regions, such as the mainly Kurdish province of Ilam, nutritional differences between men and women are slowly fading.[9] Indeed, in one of the poorest areas, Sistan-Baluchestan, girls' nutrition is now apparently better than that of boys.[10] While poverty remains the main factor in a poor diet, the wealthier classes are now beginning to suffer at the other end of the scale. "We are facing a kind of nutrition transition so that we have malnutrition in one area and obesity in other parts, with high rates of diabetes, high blood pressure and cardiovascular problems," she said. Pilot health education projects have been successful, but they have not been implemented nationally.

In one field of nutrition, Dr. Sheikh-ol-Eslam waged her own private battle—and won. It had been known for years that Iranians suffered from iodine deficiency, which leads to goiter (the enlargement of the thyroid gland, which is visible as a swelling of the neck), hearing problems, low IQ and, in the worst cases, babies born with cretinism (severe mental retardation). In mountainous, remote areas, far from the sea, where no fish was eaten and no iodine was present in salt, the situation was disastrous. More women than men were affected. Studies had been done as early as 1968, but no action had been taken. Then, in 1989, Dr. Sheikh-ol-Eslam headed a project to introduce iodine into salt. This meant she had to visit salt producers, design new equipment for factories, involve different ministries and educate the public. She traveled the country and took photos of whole families with goiter, then showed the pictures to mine owners, engineers

9. *In the Eye of the Storm*, 51–60.
10. *The Nutritional Status of Children*, Ministry of Health and Medical Education, Tehran, 1998.

and health workers. "The fact that this whole project had been abandoned for twenty years made me very sad and somehow angry," she said, "because the percentage of people affected had risen from fifteen percent to forty-eight percent of the population and a lot of mental retardation was due to that. I thought it was shameful." She personally found the right kind of technology needed to spray salt with iodine, and within a matter of seven years, practically all families were using iodized salt.

Dr. Sheikh-ol-Eslam's Ph.D. thesis is dedicated "To the girls and boys of the Marivan mountains, into whose eyes it was excruciating to look, to the children of Semirom, who didn't know why they couldn't learn their lessons well, to the women of Zagros and Alborz who hide their goiter in shame, to the innocent girls of Kordestan who thought the bump on their neck was beautiful and wore a necklace on it, and to the women of Semnan, who could no longer talk because they lost their vocal chords after surgery for goiter." The nutritionist is one of many senior women health professionals who function successfully in a male-dominated field. "There are problems, but I've never let them get in my way. I always find a way to maneuver around them," she said. "My mothering instincts were very helpful in transferring my message to the right people, whereas if I had been a man I would not have had that emotional impact, which ultimately moved people to do something."

Another senior woman health professional, Dr. Mina Mohraz, is Iran's leading AIDS specialist. She, too, has had a lonely crusade, since she took in the country's first identified AIDS patient at the Imam Khomeini Hospital in 1984. "I remember the first AIDS patient, a seven-year-old boy. He was clinging to his father and nobody would admit him, so I took him in. As soon as I admitted him there was a scandal among the nurses but after half an hour we talked to them and they started to care for him. They are not paid any more, but they do it." Because of a lack of health education and Iran's isolation from the West, AIDS is a taboo subject, and patients are shunned and thrown out of work. "I was alone in my work for five or six years and, you know, it's very difficult to see them as patients and examine them and sit down and listen to their economic problems, social problems. One of my patients' mothers had two hemophiliac sons both infected, and her husband left her because he said she was responsible [because hemophilia follows the female line]. I used to go to the ceremonies and even pay for the funeral." Modern antiretroviral drugs are far too expensive for most people.

When I spoke to Dr. Mohraz in 1999, official figures put the number of cases of full-blown AIDS at around a couple of hundred and HIV at some two thousand cases . She estimated that the real number could be twenty thousand or thirty thousand. The following year, the government revised its figures upwards, but they were still only a third of her own estimate.[11] In a talk to a women's group, she showed a graph of the number of cases in Iran, and there was a gasp from the audience at the steep upward, turn. "There's been an epidemic of AIDS among intravenous drug users, especially in prison....One of my patients came from prison, and he was saying that thirty people used one syringe."

This outbreak in jails shocked the authorities and persuaded them to include information about AIDS in antidrug literature. Until then, it had been taboo, and the existence of a problem had been denied. "I know in conferences many times I have asked doctors, 'Do you think that if you talk about sex you encourage them to have sex?' But this is the logic of the policy-makers—don't talk about it and it won't happen." The deeply conservative TV and radio heads were also reluctant to become involved. While the Supreme Leader ordered all branches of government to cooperate in the fight, there was still a resistance among senior officials, as Dr. Mohraz found when she tried to start up her own nongovernmental organization. "I wanted to start up an AIDS society about five years ago. In developing countries, most of the efforts have been done by NGOs because governments can't afford it, but they said 'No' in extremely rude terms."

For many years, the Iranian government denied there was a drug abuse problem. It argued that opium and heroin from neighboring Afghanistan just passed through the country on the way to the European market. But more recently it has admitted the number of addicts exceeded one million.[12] Opium smoking is a Persian tradition, but in recent years drug use has escalated and heroin addiction is an increasing problem. Zeinab is a mother of four from the provincial town of Sabzevar in the border province of Khorasan: "My husband was a civil servant, and he used alcohol and opium, but I didn't think his addiction was too bad. I was very afraid that my sons might follow in their father's footsteps, so I was very strict. It worked and they got into university. I thought my eldest son was safe when he got into college and trained to be a pilot. But I'd been very strict and because they didn't know much about drugs, unfortunately he got addicted and used all sorts of drugs—smoking opium, heroin, and then injecting intravenously. He messed up his whole life because he's sold everything to inject drugs."

I met Zeinab at the Mashhad headquarters of Aftab, or Sun, a newly formed NGO that provides support for addicts and their families. Afsaneh

---

11. IRNA, 2 December 2000.
12. *Human Development Report of IRI, 1999.*

Ghavipanjeh, chair of the Family Assistance Committee, told me their work was concentrated in poor districts. Eighteen women were gathered around a big table in an upstairs room. Almost all had relatives who were addicts. Downstairs, a meeting of a separate group, Narcotics Anonymous, was in session. NGOs are a fairly new phenomenon, as governments before and since the revolution have been wary of allowing independent organizations to flourish. But Mrs. Ghavipanjeh said there was no shortage of helpers. "They have three motivations; first of all those who have suffered closely from addiction, for example sons, husbands or fathers addicted. A second reason is their religion, because religion says you should help people. And finally, some of them are just happy to help out of the goodness of their own hearts."

men
women
&
drugs
Khadijeh sat with her twenty-year-old daughter Fatemeh, who hardly said a word. She let her chador down to reveal a colored scarf as she told how her husband, a laborer, turned to opium after two years of marriage. "I worked myself, carpet weaving, to feed the children. I thought he would get better, otherwise I wouldn't have had five children. At first we didn't let them know, but they realized their father was taking things from the house to sell." Fatemeh hid her face behind her chador. "Fatemeh hates men. She doesn't want to get married. She thinks all men are like her father." Fatemeh spends her time going to the mosque, the revolutionary basij volunteer group and to religious meetings.

Aftab was founded by a prominent right-wing member of parliament, Marzieh Sadighi. When she entered parliament she was shocked to discover the seriousness of the situation. "For the first year, when I used to talk to people, especially to the women, they said they were suffering from this drug problem in their area. I couldn't believe it." She realized that only the NGO sector could tackle the problem and, with her connections, obtained President Khatami's support and premises from the government.

Sadighi had risen to prominence with her outspoken support of a highly controversial bill aimed at segregating health services for men and women. I first encountered her at a government-organized seminar on the situation of women, where her public speaking ability and extreme views set her apart. "I have twice had babies delivered in the U.S. and requested that all my physicians should be ladies and this was rendered to me as a human right as a Muslim woman," she declared. "We want to have this principle established in a country which says it is an Islamic country....We want to have a parallel system. It should conform to the framework of sharia. We want to say why, after twenty years of revolution, has this not been done?"

The bill began in 1998, as part of a rearguard action by hard-liners who sensed their power slipping away with the arrival of President Khatami. It started out demanding that no woman should be treated by a male doctor under any circumstance. But the medical profession argued that it was completely unworkable; there were simply not enough women physicians. Thousands of doctors and medical students signed a petition against it. One senior woman health professional described it as "an insult to women and the medical community."[13] The bill was watered down to give women the right to demand treatment by female doctors wherever possible and to insist on paramedics of the same sex. Even Mrs. Sadighi toned down her support, claiming it had been blown up into political propaganda. "If you read the bill it says clearly that when you go to hospital, you can't really cover your body when you are lying down with a broken leg, you really can't take care of your hejab at that moment and it's women's wish that they should not be disturbed by different health service workers cleaning or fixing things at four in the morning." But even in its milder form the draft law ran into difficulties. It was passed by parliament, then sent back by the Guardian Council, a highly conservative body that vets new laws, on the grounds that it would be too expensive to implement. Eventually, the Ministry of Health allocated new funds, and the bill was passed in an amended form. Ironically, the general policy had existed within the ministry for years but with typical Iranian pragmatism had either been applied selectively or quietly ignored.

When, for example, I tore a ligament in my knee while skiing, I was examined by a series of health professionals, and I was struck by how little attention was paid to the fact that I was a woman. Where a British doctor would probably have called in a nurse to act as a chaperone, the orthopedic consultant who examined me asked the driver to hold my clothes as I got undressed behind a screen. He prescribed a customized fiberglass splint, which was fitted in my own house by a man who took inside leg measurements with calipers. My husband was present at the time, so perhaps this made it acceptable. Yet at a smart, state-of-the-art MRI (magnetic resonance imaging) clinic with a mixed staff, I was instructed very carefully to take off all my clothes, put on a surgical gown, but leave my headscarf on. It struck me as most bizarre to climb inside a machine where male technicians would scrutinize every nook and cranny of my body while at the same time worrying in case my headscarf slipped.

The whole issue of medical segregation strikes at the foundation of the Islamic Republic, because in spite of the existence of a political will among religious circles, there has never been the consensus or, more importantly, the resources to implement it. While the regime tried to train more female doctors, it simultaneously channeled them into specialties such as obstetrics and gynecology, and plans to increase the number of qualified female physicians foundered. At the same time, men were banned from training in "women's" areas, although they could still practice if they had trained abroad.

Outside the headquarters of the Supreme Council of the Cultural Revolution in a narrow city center street, hundreds of students from Iran's only all-women medical school camped on the pavement. They had brought with them piles of blankets, kettles and thermos flasks, and erected a canopy of plastic sheeting. Sleet was falling gently. This was their fifth protest in two months—at a time when spontaneous demonstrations were still extremely rare. They had demonstrated outside the private Fatemiyeh Medical School in Qom, occupied the university for three days and, when they felt they were getting nowhere, brought their demands to the seat of government. "Iran's female students protest at segregation" the headlines read.[14]

But the students' line was that rather than challenging the Islamic system, they felt that the Islamic pilot project for training women doctors was failing to live up to its ideals. "We're trying to prove that being religious and being fully covered with the hejab that we are still capable of moving forward with technology and science," said a student representative. Another insisted that segregated health services were viable. "In our hearts we believe in segregation, but not on an emergency or clinical level," she said. "If there was a case of treating a man in an emergency of course, we would do it." A question mark hangs over whether they would be capable, however, as they had had so few men to practice on.

The school was opened in the early 1990s in an attempt to boost the number of women doctors. It took over the administration of a local hospital, but some time afterwards, the dean of the medical school, backed by some powerful, well-connected board members, decided to stop accepting male patients and employ only female staff. The whole system started to unravel. The thousand-bed hospital complex contracted to around three hundred beds, and now on average, only seventy beds were reportedly occupied.[15] Men were only treated in emergencies, then told to go elsewhere. Marzieh Vahid Dastjerdi backed the controversial bill to increase segregation in hospitals but did her best to stop the Fatemiyeh experiment. "Until

---

14. *The Guardian*, 28 January 2000.
15. *Bad Jens*, Iranian Feminist Online Newsletter, 13 May 2000.

four or five years ago I was on the board of directors but when they stopped receiving male patients for the students to examine, I went and raised my objections," she told me. "I strongly opposed this and I still do now. It was the personal opinion of the dean of the medical school, and we can see by the results that it was obviously a mistake," she said. When the school did manage to find teaching staff, they could not keep them. A neurologist friend told me the medical school had begged her to go and work for them, even for one day a week. She added that girls only applied to go to Fatemiyeh if they knew they could not make the grade to enter a more prestigious, state-run, coeducational medical school.

The case of the Fatemiyeh medical school, privately run by a board of trustees, brought to the fore questions of health service management at a national level. As well as the dismissal of the chancellor and the board of trustees, the students wanted the private medical school incorporated into the national health system to protect standards and safeguard their own future. In the end most of the six hundred students transferred to other hospitals and the school was expected to close.

Iran's primary health care system has been held up as a model for other developing countries. It has been cited as the main reason behind the dramatic drop in the death rate among women and young children. Improvements at grassroots level in water, sanitation, hygiene and nutrition have combined with far-reaching social changes, such as the growth of literacy, to transform women's lives. Achievements in health over the last twenty years are all the more remarkable given the impact of the disastrous 1980s population boom. Yet questions such as how to deal with the challenges of drugs, AIDS, and how far Islamic ideals should dictate health care are still unresolved and hotly debated not just in the health service, but on the political scene as well.

Voters at a Tehran mobile polling booth fill in ballot forms on a car hood.

7

Families in the Form of Political Parties

Voting in the February 2000 elections wasn't easy, but it was fun. The polling stations were full of people, and nearby streets were crowded with men and women clutching newspaper cuttings with lists of whom to vote for. There was almost a party atmosphere. I drove around with my American friend, Judy, looking at the long lines of people, until we found a mobile polling booth in the shape of a minibus. The bus had already run out of ballots, and a disgruntled crowd was milling about. Turnout that day was a record eighty percent of eligible voters. To the astonishment of the crowd, Judy produced an Iranian ID card and asked if they could find one extra ballot paper. Married to an Iranian she, too, was entitled to vote, and, on the grounds of hospitality to foreigners, one more ballot was found. Judy took out her "list," an advertisement placed by supporters of the reformist, President Khatami. "I should really look at the other adverts to find some more women candidates to vote for," she said. Then she began the laborious task of writing down thirty names and code numbers for the candidates of the Tehran area. We leaned on a car hood, along with a husband, wife and young girl. They were dressed conservatively but asked to borrow Judy's list. They, too, were voting for the reformers. The owner of the car stuck his head out of the window. "You can use my car to lean on, but you should know that it pulls to the left," he said dryly. In this smart district of Shahrak-e Gharb, there was no doubt that President Khatami's left-leaning reformists would win a landslide. Three different people came up to ask us if we needed help, several of them offering alternative lists. In the end, Judy let a bystander complete her form, as her written Persian was slow, and the minibus driver was keen to hurry off to fetch more ballots. She checked carefully that her wishes had been followed.

At the voting station in my local mosque, my elderly neighbor was asked if she needed help filling in her form. "No thank you," she told the young person firmly. But they saw how she had voted—for Khatami—and they were delighted. "We couldn't have done better ourselves," they said. In the same station, another woman told my husband Laurens: "I didn't vote for Khatami last time because I thought there was no point, that all mullahs were the same. But this time I really feel we can make a difference." In some lines there were more women than men. They were dressed in all kinds of outfits, from traditional black chadors to Benazir Bhutto-style open scarves. Many wore jeans, sneakers and jackets so short they would have been unthinkable only months before. Personal freedom had become an election issue. "I don't have a problem with hejab, but I don't understand why we can't have boyfriends," one student told a Western news agency. Judy and I then drove to Qom, one of the most conservative cities in Iran and the power base of the clergy. There again, women in chadors, carrying children, with or without their husbands, were to be seen at every polling station. When we returned at night, there was still a trickle of people lining up as voting was extended to cope with the massive turnout.

The parliamentary elections of February 2000 were widely heralded as the most significant since the revolution. Reformers broke the conservatives' hold on the Majles, or parliament, riding the wave of enthusiasm for the person and policies of President Khatami. But the hard-liners did not give up without a fight, and the conservative-dominated Guardian Council did not confirm the Tehran results for a full three months. Endless recounts were apparently aimed at ensuring that the conservatives would receive enough seats to maintain a power base in the parliament. One popular theory was that the votes were being shuffled to enable former president Rafsanjani to secure a constituency (he was trailing in thirtieth place out of thirty-seven candidates in Tehran). In the end, Rafsanjani declined to take his seat, but the bitter dispute was a significant stage in the escalating battle between hard-liners and reformers.

The election campaign itself broke new ground. Even though it officially lasted only one week, it conveyed a sense of excitement that Islam and democracy could coexist. It took place during a period of unprecedented openness and freedom of the press with the political agenda being set by a new breed of journalist-politicians. Iran was moving towards the creation of true political parties, rather than vague groupings of mullahs or alliances built out of expediency. And women played a vital role in the campaign, shaping election issues and throwing their support behind the reformers. Mohammad Reza Khatami, the president's brother, married to Khomeini's granddaughter, Zahra, had by now left medicine and founded the Islamic Iran Participation Front (IIPF). A series of campaign meetings culminated in a riotous rally of more than six thousand students in Tehran's Shirudi Stadium, which attracted the attention of the international media. Scenes of heavily made-up girls with hair spilling out all over, holding pictures of President Khatami, singing, cheering, laughing and even whistling, were beamed over the world on satellite TV. The BBC's experienced Iran-watcher, John Simpson, contrasted this with a subdued news conference of bearded men in shiny gray suits, the main photo opportunity provided by the conservatives. My translator told me that friends of hers living in Dubai saw the TV pictures and went straight to the travel agency to buy tickets to come home to vote. The rally also attracted attention because of the use of music, frowned on by the fundamentalists. Moreover, the crowd sang the prerevolutionary national anthem, which makes no reference to religion.[1]

Outside the capital the atmosphere was just as electric. In the northern town of Rasht, the leader of Friday prayers complained about music and singing. The right-wing *Jomhuri-ye Eslami* newspaper reported what it called "questionable methods" during the campaign. Candidates' posters were raising eyebrows in spite of a strict election law limiting them to a tiny six by eight inches. "In Rasht, one of the candidates is holding competitions and handing out prizes to people," the newspaper said. "Some women who are candidates have put up pictures of themselves taken when they were much younger and they have used slogans which are against social traditions and morals."[2] Nationwide, a record 513 women had been approved to run out of a total of 6,083 candidates. In Tehran alone, 160 women were fighting for a place in parliament.

Many women who were not standing for election were still active in the campaign. A reformist newspaper interviewed twenty-two-year-old Negar Birjandi: "It was at 8.15 P.M. when I left the district election headquarters. I started distributing pamphlets to young people. Suddenly two people riding motorbikes, one of whom had his face covered and was wearing black, blocked our way. The one who'd covered his face was swearing violently as he got off his motorbike. I was numb with astonishment. He attacked me and started kicking and beating my face." The attackers stabbed her brother in the neck, but then two policemen appeared on the scene. The officers did not pursue the assailants, and Ms. Birjandi was not impressed. "It makes me very sad to see that the people who are supposed to protect us should

---

1. Susan Sachs, *New York Times*, 13 February 2000.
2. Reprinted in *Azad*, 14 February 2000.

be so indifferent. Whereas if you make even the slightest slip in the way you dress they tend to take a hard line with a young person."[3]

The Islamic Iran Participation Front inaugural party conference seemed like a good place to meet some female candidates. The idea that a party would present itself officially with a written manifesto was, in itself, a novel event. "I wanted to come just to see for myself. This is something new for us," said veteran cameraman Kaveh Golestan. The congress began with a series of speeches introducing various aspects of policy. The first speaker, Mohammad Reza Khatami, concentrated on the need for increased political participation and clearer policies. The speakers were concise and the event was well organized. Passing reference was made to women and young people, and there was little talk of the problems of the economy. Afterwards, my Italian journalist friend, Nadia Pizzuti, asked Mr. Khatami what was in the IIPF program for women. He looked momentarily unsure but eagerly consulted the newly printed manifesto. "There must be something written here," he said, but he did not appear to find anything..

The forces for reform were all there, including prominent liberal newspaper editors and more than a hundred members and candidates, and a handful of mullahs. But where were the women? There were about a dozen women reporters, not counting foreign correspondents, but it was hard to identify any female candidates at all. "They haven't come," shrugged a woman reporter. I later tracked two down and asked them why. "As you know, the IIPF has a lot of women candidates—more than twenty—but everyone was invited late and not many people knew about the meeting. I was only invited last night. For the men it's not too difficult to drop everything and come in from the provinces, but for the women it is more difficult," said Fatemeh Rakeie, a linguistics professor at the all-women Al-Zahra University. She described herself as a founding member of the party and said she was inspired to go into politics by Ayatollah Khomeini's example. Nadia asked how it could be that both the reformers under President Khatami and the more hard-line conservative forces claimed to be the true heirs to Khomeini's policies. "As I have been acquainted with the family of Imam Khomeini over the years, I know they are close to Mr. Khatami's way of thinking. I am myself a close friend of his wife, his daughter and his grandchildren," she replied. Rakeie had been a member of the Women's Society of the Islamic Republic, headed by Khomeini's daughter, Zahra Mostafavi, for twenty years. The official media guide lists the society as a political party, but now it was throwing its weight behind the IIPF. Rakeie told me she wanted to concentrate on reforming

---

3. "Mosharekat," 13 February 2000.

the laws on divorce, custody and inheritance. "For example, divorce," she said. "There are some laws where men can divorce their wives in their absence, and this is unIslamic."

With her close links to the ruling establishment, Rakeie was typical of the kind of women who have figured in politics since the revolution. But standing next to her was a thirty-year-old schoolteacher from a small town west of Tehran called Bu'in Zahra, who had come to politics much more recently. Also dressed in black, Jamileh Jahanbakhsh carried a black and yellow mobile phone and a leatherbound organizer. I asked whether women's concerns in the provinces were very different from those in Tehran. "Oh, yes," she answered. "From a political point of view, from the point of view of participating in political affairs and jobs, there are all these traditional ideas that women should not be working outside the house. That's why I want to initiate this policy—which started with the twenty-third of May movement, the date of President Khatami's first election victory—for greater participation of women in political and social affairs. I want to implement this in Bu'in Zahra. Even with regards to marriage there is this traditional way of thinking—in some villages there are still forced marriages, for example." She added that she had campaigned in the presidential elections. "I was in charge of the women's campaign for President Khatami at Tehran University," she said. "In the district I come from, people have been very affected by him."

The change wrought by President Khatami can hardly be overstated. In the period between his unexpected landslide election in 1997 and the parliamentary polls of February 2000, the political landscape was transformed. As his name is constantly linked with the issues of women and young people, it is worth examining how the change came about. As the writer on Iranian affairs Shaul Bakhash has pointed out, Khatami was an accidental president.[4] Khatami was originally seen as an outsider put up to run against the favorite, Ali Akbar Nategh Nuri, the conservative Speaker of Parliament, perhaps to make the contest more credible. But his seemingly innocent message of rule of law, tolerance, civil rights and attention to the problems of women and young people was, in some ways, subversive. The electorate seized on it as a message that certain elements of the clergy were ready for change. When Khatami followed this up after his election by encouraging political activity and giving the press greater freedoms, the mass of ordinary Iranians felt emboldened to challenge the stagnant ideology of previous decades.

---

4. "How the Good Guys Won in Iran," *Washington Post*, 27 February 2000.

Shahla Sherkat, editor of the influential women's magazine *Zanan,* knows Khatami well, having worked with him years before at the Kayhan Publishing Group. His success was no surprise to her. Indeed, she played a part in his victory, having been part of a close-knit campaign team, working behind the scenes in 1997. She recalls how a group of former colleagues, some of them journalists, persuaded him to run for election. Khatami was reluctant, having bitter memories of his departure from the Ministry of Culture and Islamic Guidance, where he had been seen as too liberal, a liability. He left the ministry in 1992, after taking the side of the prominent filmmaker Mohsen Makhmalbaf in a fierce controversy over freedom of speech. "Remember this, Khatami never wanted to become a president. There was a group of people around him who more or less persuaded him to take it on," she said. "He didn't want to stand because he was very hurt when he was forced to resign as minister of Islamic Guidance."

Once he did agree to run, however, he ran what was, by Iranian standards, an extraordinarily professional campaign. Sherkat recalls a group of around thirty advisers, and at least one planning meeting where she was the only woman. She believes he made a conscious pitch for the votes of women and young people. "I know that he had advisers who were telling him that this was the way to win," she said. Sherkat singles out four points at the heart of his program that attracted the women's vote. Firstly, he talked of the need to establish a dialogue. This meant not just at home in Iran, where competing factions rarely talk to each other, but also in the realm of foreign policy. It led to overtures to neighboring countries and the West, as well as to his proposal for a "Dialogue Among Civilizations," taken up by the United Nations and promoted internationally. Secondly, he insisted on respect for other people's opinions, something he had demonstrated personally in his ten-year term as Guidance minister and in his position as head of the National Library. Thirdly, he stressed that the rule of law should be upheld and violence should be kept at bay. And finally, he favored what Sherkat calls the "Progressive Way." This suggests the influence of the Iranian philosopher Abdol Karim Sorush, who insists there can be more than one true path to religion and that religious interpretations change with time. Sorush, a popular figure who has wide support among young people, has been called the Martin Luther of Islam. "Both women and young people wanted these four points," said Sherkat. "They thought, 'If he's against violence, he opposes violence against women.'"

Perhaps just as importantly, Khatami's physical presence appealed to women. He was smartly dressed, unaffected and, above all, smiling, something considered most unusual for a cleric. When *Zanan* splashed his face all over their front cover, the photograph was taken against a black backdrop. Khatami's black turban marks him out as a Seyyed, or descendant of the prophet, but on the cover it virtually disappears into the background, leaving only the smiling face of a well-groomed professional, with modern glasses and a neatly trimmed beard.[5] Traditional women may have voted for him because of his illustrious ancestor; those disenchanted with the clergy found him a breath of fresh air.

The wide-ranging magazine interview laid out Khatami's political platform yet also provided readers with a host of personal details. He sometimes helped with the housework, he went to the cinema, he watched television. He said he did not expect his wife to seek his permission before leaving the house and that his daughters would be free to choose whom they wanted to marry. These details were seized upon by those women who wanted more personal freedom in their lives. On the other hand, Khatami insisted that Islamic law should be followed, hejab should be worn and that the problems of young people should be addressed through religion; thus, his manifesto was carefully calculated to appeal to conservative voters, too.

The fact that he gave *Zanan* such a scoop was, in itself, proof that he was offering voters something new. The other candidates relied on dry-as-dust political tracts and the usual slogans to get their message across. Here was a man who understood the modern world and how to use the media, although on certain issues, the presidential candidate took some persuading. "Are you kidding?" he is reported to have said when told that one of the questions inquired about his dress sense. Sherkat persuaded his daughter to intercede, and eventually he replied that he did indeed pay attention to personal hygiene and his appearance, as recommended in the Koran. The interview made it clear that Khatami favored legal reforms to improve women's rights. He talked of the need for boosting women's self-esteem in what he termed a "male-dominated culture."

In political terms, the *Zanan* election special, which sold a record forty thousand copies, paid off handsomely, and Khatami's main rival, Ali Akbar Nategh Nuri, may have rued the day he turned down their interview request. Sherkat pulled off a cheeky journalistic coup by publishing a list of questions she would have *liked* to have asked him. They included queries such as: "Is it true you call your wife by your eldest son's name?" (as is the tradition in some conservative households) and other queries that did not cast the Speaker in a very flattering light. "Nategh's people kept finding excuses

5. *Zanan,* May 1997.

and finally they said: 'You have such big pictures of women in your magazine, and we think that's taboo, so we won't be giving the interview. Mr. Nategh Nuri himself did want to give you the interview, but we won't let him.' I told them I was going to print the questions without the answers, and they said 'Go ahead!' They were very angry, afterwards, of course." The losing candidate's camp tried to sue for libel, but soon dropped the case.

Khatami began by appointing two women to cabinet-level posts, the first time women had held such senior positions since the revolution. Massoumeh Ebtekar, an immunologist, was made vice president responsible for the environment, and Zahra Shoja'i was appointed to head the government's Center for Women's Participation, a position that was upgraded to allow her to attend cabinet meetings. Critics, however, felt that he did not go far enough, and had settled for a token presence. Ebtekar, interestingly, is a woman with a past, having appeared nightly on American television as spokeswoman for the hostage-takers during the occupation of the American Embassy in Tehran.[6] Afterwards, Khatami, then head of Kayhan Publishing Group, made her editor-in-chief of the English-language *Kayhan International*. Before her appointment as vice president, she took an interest in women's issues and was editorial director of a quarterly journal on women's affairs, *Farzaneh*.

On another level, the newly elected president promoted the cause of women by making them more visible. The only female ambassador posted to Iran, Ms. Alari Cole of Sierra Leone, was delighted to find herself given a place next to her male colleagues at official dinners instead of being sidelined with the spouses at separate functions. Moreover, the president encouraged his wife to accompany him at official functions and to work on creating the role of first lady. In fact, as the all-women dinner at the Islamic conference had shown, family connections have always been paramount in Iranian politics, and sisters, wives and daughters have increasingly claimed a public role. When her husband was deputy health minister, Ayatollah Khomeini's granddaughter, Zahra Eshraghi, stayed very much in the background, even though her brother-in-law was the president. But when Mohammad Reza Khatami's newly founded political party surged forward in the 2000 parliamentary elections, Eshraghi made herself available for interviews. She commented confidently on various issues, including what her grandfather would have thought about her stylish hejab.

A BBC feature broadcast just after the 2000 elections estimated that one-third of the top-thirty contenders in Tehran had family ties among

---

6. Ebtekar reportedly nowadays plays down her role in the hostage-taking drama. Elaine Sciolino, *New York Times*, 26 December 1998.

the highest political echelons.[7] They included the brothers of the president and the Leader, and the siblings of two jailed high-profile, dissident clerics, Mohsen Kadivar and Abdollah Nuri. Indeed, these four well-connected candidates won the top four places in the politically important capital. At the hustings, Jamileh Kadivar defended herself rather impatiently against charges of profiting from her famous relatives. For not only is her brother a famous name, her husband, Ataollah Mohajerani, is a key figure in the reform movement. As Khatami's minister of Culture and Islamic Guidance, he set the tone for greater freedom of expression, not least by granting permits for dozens of new newspapers and allowing the publication of thousands of new books. At a preelection question and answer session at a Tehran teacher's center, Kadivar pointed out that she had a doctorate in political science and had served as a city councilor: "I'd like to be voted for because of myself, not because I am affiliated to some political figures, because it will be me who's sitting in parliament," she said. She addressed the virtually all-male audience speaking quickly and confidently, in contrast to Abdollah Nuri's brother, with whom she shared the platform. Ali Reza Nuri, a former surgeon, only entered politics the day his brother was jailed, and his answers were hesitant and slow.

Kadivar picked out my question from among a pile of slips of paper submitted by the audience. I had asked if women would vote any differently from men. "I believe that as women make up half of our population, their vote for anyone is very important, and the party that gets most support for women will get the most votes," she said. "President Khatami's victory was because of women and young people's participation. If women sense that they can trust a candidate and they see their own aims represented, they will vote for them and they will win. But it's a good question—we can't see women as a single group—they are from different upbringings and cultures, but it's obvious that they will pay more attention to women candidates or to candidates—male or female—who share their views on issues."

Jamileh Kadivar is not from a political dynasty, but politics is a family interest, she told me later in an interview in her office. Her parents were both teachers, but her father named her after a heroine of the Algerian war of independence. She told me how she met her famous husband. "Mr. Mohajerani was my high school teacher," she confessed with a twinkle. "I got married one year before finishing high school." She kept the marriage secret by having two identity cards, otherwise she would have been forced to leave school. At the age of thirty-six, when I met her, she already had four children. Yet she was combining her family life with a high-powered

---

7. Jim Muir, "Iranian Politics: A Family Affair," *BBC Online*, 22 February 2000.

A Khatami supporter at an election rally at Tehran's Shirudi Stadium.
The president's success was ascribed to the vote of women and young people.

PHOTO BY ALI KHALIGH

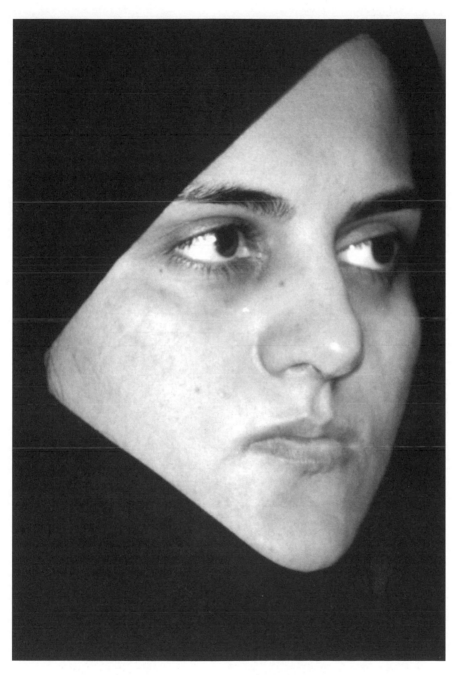

Jamileh Kadivar, prominent establishment politician.
PHOTO BY ALI KHALIGH

political career and journalism. She had written several books, including one entitled *Zan,* or "Woman," about her experiences as running unsuccessfully in an earlier parliamentary election as candidate for Shiraz.

Family links are important for male politicians in Iran. However it may be that they are one of the few areas of influence where women can also benefit, for political debate in Iran is still, by and large, conducted in people's houses, rather than in the male-dominated smoke-filled bars or town meetings of other countries. This point was made to me by anthropologist Soheila Shahshahani. "Where do political connections get strengthened, if not within the setting where women are? Therefore it's in the household, over which women have a say," she said. "If women have power, it's because they are present and they oversee all the political and economic discussions which take place. And if a woman is intelligent, she's always present." Shahshahani, a professor at Shahid Beheshti University, also drew my attention to the fact that if women have any power within the family structure in Iran, it is in the field of *khastegari,* or "matchmaking". Women generally have a say in who should marry whom, and in this way, family alliances and, significantly, political alliances, are cemented.

Perhaps the most powerful political dynasty since the revolution was that headed by Ali Akbar Hashemi Rafsanjani. One reformist newspaper, *Asr-e Azadegan,* headlined a feature on the former president's party as "The Hashemis: A Family in the Form of a Party." Government decisions and policies were being made in the backrooms of powerful families, not through national elections, it alleged.[8] Even after completing two terms as president, Rafsanjani remained a force to be reckoned with. He became chairman of the influential Expediency Council, ruling on disputes within different branches of the government. His daughter, Faezeh, is probably the most prominent female figure in postrevolutionary Iran. Another daughter, Fatemeh, lobbied for Iran abroad in an official capacity and is active in charity work. His three sons are influential businessmen, and his brother was head of the state-run broadcasting organization.

Faezeh has never been far from the headlines, whether as a sports promoter, member of parliament or newspaper publisher. She told me it never bothered her that people assumed her success was because of her family connections. "I don't get cross. I think it's realistic that some of my achievement has been because of my father," she said. "But that's not all. The boys in our family are involved in society in different fields, but maybe they are not as noisy as me. Sitting in front of a roaring fake gas fire, Faezeh let her chador fall open at the front to reveal a gray tweedy

post-revolution

8. *Asr-e Azadegan* quoted in *Iran News,* 4 January 2000.

sweater, clinging black leggings and soft black boots. "There are political families in this country, where politics are explained and talked about, so the level of understanding is quite high in these families....Sometimes politics are decided and discussed behind closed doors, but it's not so hard for women to hear what's going on; it's more open, accessible."

She explained how she and her sister came to marry two brothers of a well-known ayatollah who had been in jail together with her father during the time of the Shah. "They were very close friends, and out of this friendship they wanted to make a family relationship," she said. "After they proposed, we had several meetings. We married on the same day, the same evening. There was no love at that time. I don't believe in love before marriage. I think love that comes from marriage is much more substantial, and stays much longer." Faezeh was sixteen at the time, but in accordance with one Iranian tradition, she did not move in with her husband until she was twenty-one.

Faezeh told me she went into politics to fight for women's rights and to support her father's political program of economic reconstruction. She defended the fifth parliament's record on women but conceded that she launched her own newspaper, *Zan,* partly out of frustration that not enough progress was being made.[9] She has received widespread praise for her campaigning ability. The leading political commentator Sadegh Zibakalam defended her record in a newspaper interview with *Azad*: "I believe that Faezeh has shown more manhood than a lot of men in defending freedom and resisting powerful moves from the right wing," he said.[10] Others criticized her inconsistency, accusing her of swinging from left to right. "She has incredible energy but acts impulsively, without thinking," said the magazine *Zanan*. "Not organized or stable in her political discourse," it added.[11]

Faezeh's star has risen and fallen according to the fortunes of her powerful father. I asked if there had been times when it would have been easier for her father if she had kept quiet and vice versa. She answered, tersely, "Yes." In the parliamentary elections of 1996, when she was first elected, she received the second-biggest vote of any candidate, behind the Speaker, Nategh Nuri. Most commentators believe she came first but that it was considered unseemly for the Speaker of Parliament to be trounced by a young woman. Faezeh herself shrugged off the incident with a joke. "At the time they used to say he introduced himself by saying 'My name is

9. The fifth parliament ran from 1996 to 2000. Legislative assemblies in Iran are numbered; this series started with the revolution.
10. *Azad,* 14 February 2000.
11. *Zanan,* February 2000.

Nategh, my second name's Nuri, but at home they call me Faezeh.'" It was no joke for her in February 2000, however, when she plummeted out of office, finishing in fifty-seventh position in Tehran and losing her seat. Her father was being accused of involvement in state terrorism and corruption, and she had stuck her neck out in defending him. Moreover, the voting system worked against her, as she did not appear on the popular Participation Front slate.

In the late 1980s and 1990s there were fourteen women representatives in a 270-member house, and in spite of high hopes, in the reformist-dominated house that followed, there were even fewer. The numbers are very small, but so is the number of female representatives in most Western parliaments. Feminist analysts, putting a brave face on it, said the quality of the representatives was more important than the quantity. "There is reason to believe that, in view of the political orientation of the newly elected members, despite being smaller in number, they may make for a more promising team than their predecessors," said the *Bad Jens* newsletter.

While the female representatives of successive assemblies since the revolution have tried to chip away at various pieces of legislation restricting women's rights, they have never been able, or willing, to confront the basic laws at the root of their problems. Soheila Jeloudarzadeh was one of the two women reelected in 2000, and she was the first woman since the revolution to be voted onto the influential Presiding Board of Parliament. While her husband is active in politics, she did not boast a famous name. "I might be the only one….who got to where I am now on my own," she said. "Not only was I not supported, but I also had to overcome many obstacles." Jeloudarzadeh's credentials are the kind that would be instantly recognizable by politicians the world over. A member of the Islamic Labor Party, she studied textiles at university then worked in industry, where she got involved in trade union rights. She was also a child of the revolution, whose turning point was the bloodbath at Jaleh Square, where the Shah's forces opened fire on a crowd of peaceful protesters in 1978. "That was the last day I worked at the factory. There was a massacre and this became a defining moment for revolutionaries. We dropped everything." In spite of her claim to be independent, Jeloudarzadeh also received the support of the Islamic Republic of Iran Women's Society, led by Ayatollah Khomeini's daughter. This places her firmly within the religious establishment. She and other traditional women felt liberated by the revolution but were uncomfortable with the mass of postrevolutionary legislation that impinged on basic rights.

Jeloudarzadeh estimated that half of the members of the fifth parliament had what she called a "negative" attitude toward women's issues. She talked about a closed atmosphere, dominated by hard-liners. Parliament became a battleground where a power struggle was fought out between supporters of President Khatami's increasingly liberal government and darker forces backed by the Leader's office and the Intelligence Ministry. No one dared rock the boat. "Because we wanted to get the government policies through, we had to be a bit conservative about what we said; we had to behave within certain limits," she said. Jeloudarzadeh gave the example of the successful attempt to change the law on mehriyeh, the financial pledge made to women on marriage, usually redeemed in the event of a divorce. The proposers of the bill managed to argue that a paltry sum named at the time of the wedding should be updated to adjust for inflation and the decline in the value of the rial. Opposing the reform was the member for Bandar Abbas, known for his colorful turn of phrase. He argued that women depreciated with age, "like used cars." The bill was passed, but by a margin of just one vote. "This shows that we were working in a difficult atmosphere, but that always makes the victories more sweet," said Jeloudarzadeh. As a point of law it may seem minor, but it is an example of how the women within the establishment were left with the task of defending women's rights when the legal framework and political climate was weighted against them.

The women in the Majles traditionally sit in the third row, in seats reserved specially for them, unlike male representatives, who have to draw lots for their seats and move around from time to time. And they do make their presence felt. I watched right-winger Marzieh Vahid Dastjerdi in action as she pushed through an amendment to the law on state pensions. With a loud voice and assertive manner, she could be seen buttonholing mullahs and other members, wagging her finger at them to make her point. "This discrimination has existed for the past fifty years," she told members. "If a female civil servant happens to have a husband who passes away, she is not allowed to draw his pension if she is herself in service at the time. She is only allowed to have her salary or his pension, not both. This is very discriminatory." Afterwards she was jubilant. "There are still a few existing examples of discrimination against women and this was one of them. Basically we have fought against that and today we have won." The amendment, however, was tabled in the dying days of the parliament and Dastjerdi, like most right-wingers, knew she had lost her seat. At that time she had also proposed an amendment to the divorce law. It laid down certain cases when a woman would automatically have the right to seek a divorce, but did nothing to challenge the basic Islamic principle spelled out in civil law, which says that a man can divorce his wife at will.[12] I remarked that these were all steps in the right direction, but why didn't they just give women the same rights as men? She said that effectively, the amendment did so, and she left it at that.

Iran's first *Human Development Deport*, published jointly by the government and the United Nations in 1999, lists twenty-three laws and regulations enacted after 1979 to protect women's rights.[13] They include laws paving the way for the reintroduction of birth control and amendments to the laws on divorce, custody, widows' pensions, and employment. But critics say successive parliaments have rarely given women's rights priority or tackled issues head on. Changes to the law or the allocation of budgetary resources to promoting women's affairs were merely palliatives, according to lawyer Shirin Ebadi, a fierce critic of the regime. "We have to say that these were more sedatives, not cures," she told the reformist newspaper *Azad*. "Because the final cure for women's rights in Iran is that members of parliament should regard women as individuals."[14]

However, the continuous presence of women in parliament since the revolution may have served to provide much-needed female role models. Several of the deputies maintained high profiles in other fields of public life. Marzieh Dastjerdi, for example, kept her job as a gynecologist throughout her term of office, fitting in surgery from 6 to 8 A.M. before going to the parliament building. A fellow right-winger, Marzieh Sadighi, ran her own trucking business and was a founding member of the Aftab drug abuse NGO. They epitomize the paradox of Iranian women who find no contradiction between traditional, Islamic values and Western-style ambitions. While I met Dastjerdi in parliament, Sadighi proposed we talk at the headquarters of her international transport company in downtown Tehran. Pictures of trucks adorned the drab walls.

Marzieh Sadighi was married at the age of thirteen to a nineteen-year-old of her own choice. She did not move in with him until she was sixteen. With the help of her family, she, like Jamileh Kadivar, concealed the marriage from classmates and teachers in order to be able to finish school. When her husband decided he wanted to study in the United States, she went with him. Like him, she completed a degree in transport engineering. They returned and worked in various jobs in the field of planning. She was at one time in charge of government housing projects in the

---

12. The amendment was passed by parliament, but quashed by the conservative-dominated Guardian Council on the grounds that it was un-Islamic. (UNICEF, personal communication, 23 November 2000.)

13. *Human Development Report of the IRI, 1999.*

14. *Azad,* 21 February 2000.

conservative eastern province of Khorasan and later manager of Iran's National Transportation Planning Project. Husband and wife became parliamentarians at the same time, as members for Mashhad. She has no regrets about her early marriage and recommended it to her two daughters who married at fourteen and fifteen. "My daughters see my life and they get our whole support," she said. I like it very much because I think they are secure in society. They have someone to talk to. It's natural for a youngster to want to be part of a young couple, and it's difficult...We believe there's a limit to your conversation with the opposite sex, and if you don't consider that, you're committing a sin."

Yet when discussing the trials of parliamentary life she sounds every inch the modern, feminist realist. "It takes time for women to show themselves. There are limitations, especially financial limitations for getting into parliament. You have to spend a lot of money and have lots of connections. You have to have the support of your husband. To be a representative is very difficult. A lot of traveling, and you get calls from people in your constituency after midnight or they come to your house. Your time does not belong to you anymore." Both Sadighi and Dastjerdi were known as conservative hawks, supporting, among other things, the controversial health bill that aimed at introducing sex segregation into the country's health services. As such, they stood little chance of reelection amid the surge of support for President Khatami. Sadighi declared that she had had enough of politics and had decided not to run again. It was a joint decision with her husband. "Politics in Iran is different from other countries. You have your parties, they have worked for many years, their ideas are clear. You know that this party is going to do this or that, that party is going to do that. But in Iran the parties are new and it takes at least ten to fifteen years to establish their policies....As far as establishing Islamic government is concerned, their objectives are the same, but their ways to get to that goal are very different and they got into many quarrels. It made me tired."

When only eleven women were elected in the reformist victory of February 2000, there was little hope that women's issues would figure very greatly in the parliament that followed. Mehrangiz Kar told a post-election meeting organized by the Canadian Women's Club that the reformers had too many other problems to deal with. "They didn't have a special message on women's rights," she said. "They were only concentrating on developing the political base." She took more comfort in the far-reaching improvements in girls' education and the decisive role women were playing in voting. She singled out the local government elections of

1999 as a turning point. In Iran's first-ever municipal elections, 298 women were elected to city councils and 484 to rural councils. In fifty-six cities, women topped the election results in terms of votes received and in about the same number of cities they came second.

The local council elections were remarkable from several points of view. The respected monthly *Iran Focus* went so far as to say they "might prove to be the most revolutionary in Iran's history."[15] It was modern-day Iran's first experiment in grassroots democracy. There had been considerable doubt that they would take place at all, as there was huge opposition from conservative forces, who did their best to disqualify key candidates. And it was a test of public support for President Khatami's more moderate, tolerant approach. The reformists did even better than expected. "Apart from the clear victory of the Second of Khordad [pro-Khatami] coalition and the defeat of conservatives," *Iran Focus* concluded, "the most significant outcome is the number of women that have been elected."

"It should be considered as one of the most amazing events in the history of the revolution," said Shahla Sherkat of *Zanan*. "There were independent girls, and I mean girls, who'd just graduated from university, twenty years old, running as candidates. They were so confident that they could campaign and become council members like anyone else." If the candidates were young, so, too, were the voters, with the right to vote from the age of sixteen onwards and more than seventy percent of the population under the age of thirty. Many women, too, can be seen as new voters, and with the literacy rate having doubled since the revolution, this was one reason why President Khatami and his supporters targeted them so assiduously.

The government had encouraged women to come forward as candidates for the municipal elections through the newly established bureaus for women's affairs in the various ministries, and the Center for Women's Participation, which was allied to the president's office.[16] The center, headed by Zahra Shoja'i, organized seminars for students and leaders of women's groups. As the elections approached, an adviser to the governor of Tehran province said she hoped that women's participation in city and village councils would pave the way for a demonstration of their capabilities in senior managerial posts.[17]

The results were impressive. Two women (one of them Jamileh Kadivar) were placed among the top-five vote-getters in the crucial Tehran City

---

15. *Iran Focus*, March 1999.
16. *Zanan*, December 1998.
17. *Iran Focus*, December 1998.

Council election. They received more than a third of a million votes each. President Khatami's eldest sister, a sixty-one-year-old mother of six, came first in the central desert town of Ardakan. In one town in the northern province of Mazandaran, women won six out of eleven seats on the council. And in Saveh, an industrial town south of Tehran, four out of seven members elected were women. Once Kadivar was elected, she chose to concentrate on the problems of the south of the capital, its poorest area. She was in no doubt as to the significance. "Obviously being the first city council, the base that we created now will be built on by other successive city councils. It's important as the first of its kind because of the present efforts to create a civil society."

In the local elections, successful candidates did not necessarily have famous names or famous husbands. In Saveh, the female majority was made up of well-known figures and pillars of community life. "Their success was due to good advertising, a good campaign and their presence in public life," said one local newspaper editor. "There were meetings in mosques and schools, which were attended by all sorts of people. All the women who got onto the council are active, especially in education and in civil servant jobs." One was a respected charity worker, another was the head teacher of one of the best schools in town. I tried to interview several of them, but they proved to be elusive. One declined to meet me on the grounds that it was the mourning month of Moharram and she was too busy attending prayer meetings. She added that she would, in any case, need to get the approval from all of her fellow councilors. "We have meetings in the mornings and then there are other sessions in the afternoon and religious ceremonies in the evening, so I'm terribly sorry. And we'd all have to agree on it with the brothers." After apologizing once more, she told my assistant: "I hope that this book is going to reflect the true nature of Islam."

For all the talk of Islam and democracy, politics in Iran is far from being open to all. Candidates are screened for their loyalty to the revolution and links with "illegal organizations." Hundreds, sometimes thousands, of applicants are disqualified by conservative-controlled committees. A famous name does not necessarily help and may indeed hinder chances of selection. One of the most influential women in Iranian politics, Azam Taleqani, daughter of Ayatollah Taleqani, has been disqualified from running for public office on at least four occasions. She has tried to run for the local council elections, parliamentary elections and even the presidency. I met her when the former Irish president, Mary Robinson, visited Iran in her role as UN High Commissioner for Human Rights. Dressed all in black,

Taleqani made an impassioned speech along the lines of: "They let *you* run for president, so why won't they let *me!*" She said she had posed her candidature deliberately to challenge the article of the constitution that is taken to ban women from the position of president. She argues that the word *rajul,* meaning "man" in Arabic, is not gender-specific in Persian.

At the office of Azam Taleqani's Islamic Women's Association, I counted five portraits of her father in the little courtyard full of flowers and in her dark, book-lined office. Ayatollah Taleqani was one of the leading figures of the revolution, some would say second in stature only to Ayatollah Khomeini. He was a founder of the nationalist Freedom Movement, a party that has been banned for most of the postrevolutionary era. Azam, as she is often referred to, is associated with a group known as religious nationalists. It is partly the fact that she bears her father's name that gives her the status of a political heavyweight. Apples and cucumbers were piled high on the table, and there was a constant flow of tea as I waited. Azam was very late for the appointment, having spent the day in hospital. Almost crippled with rheumatoid arthritis, she still bustles around, a dumpy, plain figure with kind eyes and an intense gaze. Like most Iranian women in politics, she lives with a double burden of family responsibilities and work. One of her four children is handicapped, but she has always had the energy for public life. "I did all of that and looked after my family as well," she said. "I used to be up until 2 A.M. washing clothes or peeling eggplants. I'd fall asleep and end up cutting my finger." She recalls the days when her father was exiled for anti-Shah activities and sent to the poorest, most remote towns in Iran. Like so many girls from religious families, she married early, at fourteen, and had two children by the time she was seventeen, but her father encouraged her to carry on studying with private tutors at night school. She went into teaching and established a religious school where her former pupils include the Rafsanjani daughters.

Taleqani describes picnics outside of Tehran where the clergy plotted the revolution. Then in 1975, she was thrown in jail. Her father was at times in the same prison. "It was miserable torture," she said. "They used to beat you on the feet and then they used to rub salt into the wounds. We were only allowed to take a bath once a week, and one time when I peeped out from under my blindfold, I saw that people had plastic bags on their feet to prevent the wounds becoming infected." She was released two years later, as the Shah came under increasing international pressure to clean up his human rights record.

Azam Taleqani was a witness at the Jaleh Square massacre. "The women were sitting in front and the men behind, so that the soldiers would not shoot. I was there, but a relative of mine saw me and pulled me back into an alley. Then we saw the troops open fire, and I saw sixteen women being killed. The men were hit in the legs, but the women were killed instantly because they were in the front." She rushed to a phone to call Paris, where Ayatollah Khomeini had his headquarters.

After the revolution Azam was known as an outspoken member of the first parliament, and one of the only women members prepared to speak on all issues, not just women's affairs.[18] So now it makes her angry that she is banned from office for her dissident views and association with the religious nationalists. "I've been disqualified according to Article 28 [of the constitution], although I've many times shown my loyalty to Islam and to the government of the Islamic Republic," she told *Zanan* magazine before the 2000 parliamentary elections. "I've proved it time after time, and I've not only proved it, I've fought for it." She accused the hardliners of trampling over people's civil rights. But there is little place for an outspoken and fearless critic in the close-knit circles that govern postrevolutionary Iran. "They don't consider me one of them," she concluded.

Two decades after the revolution, Iranian politicians, men and women alike, were still defining themselves in relation to Ayatollah Khomeini and his legacy. His view on women in politics is one of the paradoxes that haunt modern-day Iran. In 1962 Khomeini led the clergy in opposing the Shah's plans to give women the vote. "The *ulema* [clergy] have publicly stated that the franchise for women and the abrogation of the condition that one must be a Muslim in order to be allowed to vote or to run in an election is contrary to Islam and the Constitution," he declared.[19] While many clergymen opposed giving women the vote on the grounds that they were not fit to meddle in affairs outside the home, Khomeini appears to have concentrated his case on the argument that the way the Shah was proceeding was irregular and unconstitutional.[20] Overruling the opposition, the following year, the Shah made a decree granting women the right to vote. Barely twenty years later, Ayatollah Khomeini had nothing but praise for women's role in the revolution and support for their right to involve themselves in politics. Women swelled the ranks of demonstrators, they put themselves in the firing line, and the postrevolutionary constitution recognized their contribution in its preface: "The common sight of mothers with infants in their arms running toward the scene of

---

18. Esfandiari, "The Majles and Women's Issues in the I.R.I.," in *In the Eye of the Storm.*
19. Letter to the prime minister cited in Paidar.
20. Tabari, "The Role of the Clergy in Modern Iranian Politics," in *Religion and Politics in Iran,* ed. Nikki Keddie. Also Morad Saghafi, "Votes for Women," *Goft-o-goo,* Autumn 1996.

battle and the barrels of machine guns demonstrated the essential and decisive role played by this major segment of society in the struggle."[21] In the jockeying for power that followed, Khomeini needed women's votes to consolidate his vision of an Islamic republic. Their right to vote was never seriously questioned. Twenty years on, a whole new generation of women, newly educated and newly confident, brought President Khatami to power. While they are well aware of the role they have played, women are increasingly frustrated by their failure to win corresponding power in parliament or at senior levels in government. It was a political coming of age with irreversible consequences.

---

21. Paidar, 260.

8

Making the News

After living in Iran for a year or so, my children no longer needed round-the-clock attention, and I decided to apply for a press card. The *Guardian* newspaper was keen for me to be their correspondent and gave me an official letter of introduction. I took it along to the Ministry of Culture and Islamic Guidance, which supervises the work of all foreign and local journalists. I spent several hours drinking tea with officials, discussing the possibility of getting accreditation. At that time there were only a handful of foreign correspondents working in Tehran, most of them were on three-month visas, and there were no British or Americans. Every few weeks they had to leave the country to reapply for permission to stay. Their stories were scrutinized for anything critical of the Islamic Republic. In truth, Iran's image abroad ranged from the sinister to the downright barbaric, so in my meetings I tried to argue that they might as well give me a press card because whatever I wrote couldn't make things any worse. The hospitable, tea-drinking Guidance officials were noncommittal.

On a visit to London, I tried my best to lobby at the Iranian mission, turning up in my longest dress and most sober headscarf. The press attaché seemed positive and kept saying I could be the right person at the right time. He liked the idea of the *Guardian*, which was known for its left-of-center views and, in his eyes, as less of a lackey of the British government than some other papers. Then, one day, some months after the election of President Khatami, I got a call, suggesting that I drop in at the ministry for a chat. The same secretaries were there, the same hushed atmosphere, but my main contact had been replaced. A more friendly official produced my application from his drawer. It had been lying there for about nine months, along with letters from Reuters and the BBC, who were also trying to open up offices. "I think we can do something for you, now," he said. "Come back next week and we'll ask you some questions and you can fill in some more forms."

Upon my return, I was given a detailed form: Name any country you have visited and give reasons for your trip; name any Iranian friends; name any foreign friends; have you ever visited a foreign embassy? Did you ever attend a national day celebration? And, memorably: Do you have any martyrs in your family? It was clearly designed for local journalists working for the foreign press. One official pored over my form, saying, "What's this, you visited China for 'terroristic' reasons?" The translator explained that it said "touristic." Then, a different official altogether grilled me for three hours on my motivations for wanting to write about Iran and what I thought of the "clash of cultures." I blathered my way through and realized he was becoming increasingly friendly. At the end, I asked, timidly, "When will I hear?" He misunderstood and said pleasantly, "Oh, I'm eighty percent sure that you'll get your press card, although it's not just up to us."

I went home optimistic, but then heard nothing for months. I would call, every now and then, to be told that a decision was imminent. Finally, a secretary told me, "I'm sorry, Miss Howard, the answer is no, you can't work for the *Guardian*." In Iran it is unusual to get "no" for an answer, there is usually no answer at all. So I tried to find out what the reason was. I assumed the Intelligence Ministry had blocked it, perhaps worried that I was a British spy. Later, I visited a more senior official at the ministry to find out the real reason. It turned out that it was the Foreign Ministry who had blocked the application, because of my status as a diplomat's wife. As such, it would be more difficult to get me thrown out of the country if I wrote something that upset the government. "These diplomats get up to some funny things, you know, like getting themselves arrested outside missile bases in the middle of the desert," said the official. "And you would just be able to flash your diplomatic card and we wouldn't be able to do a thing about it." It was at this point that I decided to write a book instead.

Shortly afterwards, the Guidance Ministry gave a press card to an American, Geneive Abdo, enabling her to work for the *Guardian*.[1] They allowed the BBC, Reuters and the *Financial Times,* among others, to open bureaus for the first time since the revolution. On the domestic scene there was an explosion of new newspapers, all supporting the reform program of President Khatami. The press became a battleground for the

---

1. She was forced to leave in February 2001 amid a press campaign against her and warnings from officials. "In Iran You Don't Wait to Be Invited to Leave," *Washington Post,* 4 March 2001.

power struggle between the reformers and hard-liners. Around two dozen papers were closed down within a year. But the genie was out of the bottle, and there was unprecedented freedom of expression. One magazine led the way on social issues and the debate over the role of women. The journal, *Zanan*, was edited by a woman whose life story and career has charted the course of postrevolutionary Iran.

Shahla Sherkat is a child of the revolution. She was brought up in Isfahan, a conservative city, in spite of its claim to be Iran's premier tourist destination. Her father was a civil servant who later turned to trade. He was a religious man, as she recalled in one of several meetings at her magazine offices. "He was very particular about hejab, and we even wore our headscarf to school and sometimes the chador, too," she said. "At the time I went to school, there would be some girls sitting next to me wearing miniskirts, but I was never made to feel uncomfortable." During our meetings, Sherkat did not take off her headscarf. Although her father was strict, her mother prevailed on him to move to Tehran. And it was her mother who insisted on her girls playing sports and getting a university education.

As the revolution approached, anti-Shah literature started to appear in the house, such as the work of Ayatollah Khomeini. "This is a dangerous book," her father would say. "Don't tell anyone that we have it in the house." Sherkat read authors, popular at the time, who identified the source of Iran's problems as stemming from its relationship with Western powers. They included Jalal Al-e Ahmad, who coined the influential phrase "*gharbzadegi,*" variously translated as "Westomania," "Westoxification," or "struck by the West." Like many students, she also read the work of the left-wing ideologist, Ali Shariati. She began a psychology degree, but when the revolution broke out, the universities were closed.

Sherkat went into journalism as the press was being Islamicized. One leading figure in the movement was Zahra Rahnavard, wife of the former prime minister, Mir-Hossein Musavi. "Zahra Rahnavard was asked to revitalize *Zan-e Ruz,* or "Woman of Today," and she took young people with her, including my sister. My sister called up one day and said, 'Do you want to become a journalist?' and it seemed as if the gates of heaven had opened, because I wanted to be an activist and I wanted to be a journalist." Politics dominated editorial meetings: "There were some women who were like guerrillas, who came to the meetings with guns, yet some of the men in the newspaper group were even against having a weekly for women at all." She began work on *Ettela'at-e Banovan,* or "Women's Information." Then, she took over *Zan-e Ruz,* a women's magazine popular at the time of the Shah. While covering traditional home-based interests, it had also been a major forum for the debate during the 1960s, when legal reforms were boosting women's rights. At the time of the 1967 Family Protection Law, which introduced reforms on divorce and polygamy, it published a series of articles by an influential cleric, Ayatollah Motahhari, outlining the Islamic view on women as equal to, but different from, men.[2] These later became the basis for a book that paved the way for the curious revolutionary ideology on women. When Sherkat arrived, the magazine had already changed beyond recognition: "When I got there the content of the articles were completely irrelevant to the subject of women. There were pages and pages of Hadiths, or sayings attributed to the Prophet, not even relating to women."

She tried to make it more readable and more relevant, and concentrated on legal issues. As this was a time when pre-revolutionary laws were being dismantled and the concept of an eye for an eye and a tooth for a tooth was being reintroduced, I asked what her position had been on the ruthless law of retribution. I may have imagined it, but I felt she looked uncomfortable. "The whole newspaper group was a semigovernmental institution, and the line that was followed in general was the line of the government. Of course, I tried as much as I could to take an independent position." It wasn't easy. On one occasion, a cookery feature included a picture of an imported brand of pickles. The following morning, one of the editors, also a member of parliament, made an unpleasant scene about why the picture had not shown an Iranian, noncapitalist, brand. On another occasion, the magazine interviewed the head of the UN Population Fund and printed a picture of her in traditional Pakistani dress. The management was furious, describing her as *lokht,* or "naked."

The arguments were not always to do with women's issues. Sherkat became involved in a dispute over the freedom of the press that had far-reaching consequences. She printed an essay by the filmmaker Mohsen Makhmalbaf in which he responded to criticism of one of his movies. At the time, the future president Khatami was Minister of Culture and Islamic Guidance, and he supported the director's right to reply. In the argument that followed, Khatami resigned. Sherkat's support for him then stood her in good stead when he came to power.

She left *Zan-e Ruz* in 1991, frustrated at the picture she was being asked to paint of women as homebodies in the shadow of their husbands. "My main difficulty with them was that they wanted to portray an image of women being in the house, putting on their makeup when their husband comes home. The beds are made, the table is set and every now and then

---

2. Paidar, *Women and the Political Process in Twentieth-Century Iran,* 175.

they go out to do a little bit of shopping and that's it," she said. "It got to the point when I said, 'No more.'" Seven months later, she founded *Zanan,* or "Women."

Sherkat points out that there is no word for "feminist" in Persian; the whole concept has negative connotations because of its association with Western culture. Yet she has waged a steady campaign to broaden women's rights and win recognition for women's active role in society. Many women, both Islamists and secularists, were disappointed that the post-revolutionary state failed to deliver the Utopian vision of women it promised. "The things I expected from the revolution never materialized," she said. "I had expected that the revolution would cause a change in the culture vis-à-vis women, but what happened, from the ultraleft to the ultraright just went to show that all of them feel the same regarding women."

The anthropologist Ziba Mir-Hosseini has identified Shahla Sherkat as a key figure in the growth of a homegrown feminist movement in Iran. "*Zanan* advocated a brand of feminism which took its legitimacy from Islam, yet made no apologies for drawing on western feminist sources and collaborating with Iranian secular feminists to argue for women's rights. It argued that there is no logical link between patriarchy and Islamic idealism, and no contradiction between fighting for women's rights and remaining a good Muslim," she writes.[3] At *Zanan,* Sherkat was freer to pursue her own interests. She tackled issues that had a direct impact on women's lives. The legal system, the lack of sports facilities, domestic violence, the question of the dress restrictions and the dominance of the color black, are just a few of the kind of investigations she encouraged. The magazine is stuffed full of interviews with women active in public life, whether as politicians, physicians, TV personalities or artists. Leading secular feminists, such as Mehrangiz Kar and Shahla Lahiji, are featured side by side with religious thinkers such as Azam Taleqani and, interestingly, with clerics such as Seyyed Mohsen Saidzadeh, who believe in a more progressive interpretation of women in Islam. This unlikely group of people had, in one sense, become collaborators, with Saidzadeh defending a critique of the legal system written by Kar, and Lahiji trying to get permission from the Ministry of Guidance to publish the clergyman's manuscript, *The Freedom of Women in Mohammad's Time.*[4] The three later all spent time in jail as the power struggle with the hard-liners intensified.

3. "Feminist Movements in the Islamic Republic," draft for *Encyclopaedia Iranica*, Vol IX, pp 498-503, published in Hamt@.com.

4. Mir-Hosseini, *Islam and Gender*, xvi.

The impact of this eclectic inclusiveness cannot be overstated. Living in Iran I was constantly struck by the way families and friends cling together in circles that rarely overlap. The experience of the revolution, the climate of suspicion and the legal restrictions on who can socialize with whom have reinforced that tendency. At a restaurant with a group of women friends, I overheard one guest remark to another, "I didn't know you were part of this *mahfel,* this group." I found it frustrating to see that academics worked in near isolation. "Academics hate each other's guts in the West, too," I would say. "But they do at least read others' work and get together to argue." Long-running feuds and jealousy exacerbate the situation, so that professor x will not be seen in the company of publisher y, and neither would dream of being in the same room as lawyer z. Dinner parties can, consequently, be tricky to organize.

Newspapers, once they started to multiply in the late 1990s, generally followed one particular political line; indeed, they appeared to function like embryonic political parties. Shahla Sherkat was practically the only journalist I met in Iran who knew what was going on in every camp and was on good terms with all of them. Yet she places herself firmly on what she calls the "religious side of the modern left." She has followed the evolution of Iranian politics over the years and is a firm believer in moving with the times. "The turning point for me was when Iran accepted Resolution 598 [which ended the Iran-Iraq war]. There had been statements saying that we'd go to Karbala, we can go on for another twenty years. Until then the war was on and you had to send your children—nobody even dared to question it or take a position against the war. When the announcement was made, a taboo was broken. The Imam [Khomeini] made a statement [announcing the cease-fire], saying: 'I drank poison' and everyone was dumbfounded. It was not so black and white. He made a statement to the families of martyrs, saying, 'Don't think you have given up everything because Islam values what you have done.' But everybody thought, 'Oh, so things can change.'"

At the same time that Sherkat founded *Zanan,* other publications for women were springing up, all taking advantage of an increasingly free debate on the role of women. A women's studies magazine *Farzaneh,* (a girl's name meaning wise), was launched, attempting to give the issue serious academic treatment with contributors from Iran and abroad. The editorial director was Massoumeh Ebtekar, who went on to become a vice president in the Khatami government. Within the religious establishment, there was a recognition that Iran should prepare its case before the Beijing conference on women in 1995. A Bureau of Women's Affairs, attached to the presidency, was formed and Ebtekar was a delegate to the conference.

Meanwhile the Propagation Office of Qom Seminaries launched its own women's magazine, *Payam-e Zan,* or "Women's Message." In an entertaining book, Mir-Hosseini describes a series of meetings with the journal's male editors.[5] She begins by asking them why men were publishing a magazine for women. "Ideally, women should produce such a journal," was their answer, "but men must do it for the simple reason that there are no women in the Hozeh [seminary] who can assume the task." Female theological experts at the powerful theological college were boycotting the publication, on the grounds that women were working side by side with men and breaking the principle of sex segregation. Mir-Hosseini, incidentally, never once managed to meet a female theology lecturer at the main women's college during the preparation of her book.

In 1998, Ashraf Geramizadegan launched a monthly named *Hoquq-e Zanan,* or "Women's Rights" which aimed to concentrate on legal issues. Geramizadegan had worked for years at *Zan-e Ruz* as a legal expert, and had succeeded Sherkat as editor. She told *Iran News* that indifference to women's problems was "a tragic catastrophe" and that the trouble was that newspapers were mostly owned by men.[6] At the same time, a right-wing backlash was gathering pace. The second edition of *Hoquq-e Zanan* carried a feature attacking a controversial law proposed by the conservative-dominated parliament aimed at banning women's pictures. The legislation was to outlaw "Using women as objects in pictures, belittling and disrespecting them, turning them into luxury items, deviating from Islamic Law and causing differences to arise between men and women." Geramizadegan's magazine pointed out that publishing pictures against public decency was already punishable by flogging. "Just because pictures of one or two actresses were printed in a newspaper this bill is in collision with the freedom of the press," she wrote.

The law was a taste of the bitter struggle to come between supporters of increased freedom of expression and hard-liners bent on sabotaging the reform movement. The reformist minister of Culture and Islamic Guidance, Ataollah Mohajerani, spoke out against the bill, and in an interview with the *Los Angeles Times* put the blame, tongue in cheek, on Bill Clinton. "In fact, our problem started with Mr. Clinton's girlfriends," he said. "There were color pictures of Monika and the other two. Mr. Clinton, in addition to creating problems for his society, is creating problems for our society

5. Ibid., 1999.
6. *Iran News,* 21 April 1998.

too."[7] Ultimately, the draft law was watered down in a peculiarly Iranian way, by making it to apply to men, too.

The image of women in the media was subject to strict censorship even before the new law. However, the censors operate according to a logic all of their own. While, for example, all Iranian women have to be pictured or photographed with their hair well covered, foreigners have increasingly been shown bareheaded. Nakedness is completely taboo, and no Iranian newspaper would attempt to violate the regulations. But even colorful Iranian tribal dress, which often allows a certain amount of hair to show, causes publishers problems.

women here censored

Foreign publications are allowed to enter the country, but they are closely scrutinized. They are doctored, if necessary, with a black felt pen or blue sticky tape to obliterate the offending parts. The censors have little regard for art. The French news agency AFP reported that censors on duty at Tehran airport had cut out photographs of paintings by Henri Matisse and Paul Gauguin from *L'Express* and *Le Monde*.[8] The Iranian authorities even reportedly removed a photograph of former British prime minister Margaret Thatcher in *Le Figaro,* on the grounds that her dress was too revealing.

In July 1998, Faezeh Hashemi launched Iran's first women's daily, *Zan,* or "Woman." In the few months it was published, before being closed down by the conservative judiciary, it made waves by tackling controversial political and social issues as well as stories of special interest to women. "Faezeh," as she is generally known, was still a member of parliament at that time, but the Majles had become bogged down in factional fighting. "The thought came to me when I was in parliament that Iranian women do have cultural problems and to be able to overcome those I thought a newspaper would be the best tool to reach them….Parliament was not enough for what I was trying to do," she told me. "I think I was very effective in society at raising women's consciousness. I triggered off other magazines and publications so that they showed more sensitivity toward women's affairs." However, the experiment was short-lived, as the hard-liners were drawing up the battle lines for all-out war on the press to be fought mainly through the conservative-controlled courts. Following a controversial report that two leading reformist ministers, Abdollah Nuri and Ataollah Mohajerani, had been jostled by hard-liners in a mosque, *Zan* faced seven charges in the Press Court, but got off on six of them. "I won all those arguments, but I just lost on one little charge because they couldn't say that a woman was a winner com-

---

7. "Interview with Robin Wright," *Los Angeles Times,* 3 May 1998.
8. *Agence France Presse,* 16 June 2000.

pletely," she laughed. The newspaper was closed for two weeks, then was fined. However, in March 1999, *Zan* reported that the former shah's wife, Farah Diba, had sent New Year's greetings to all Iranians, and the authorities immediately closed the paper.

The journalist responsible for making contact with the former empress was Camelia Entekhabi Fard. She represents a new generation of young reporters who barely remember the revolution. Her lively, unconventional personality has caused her difficulties with colleagues, and her fearlessness ultimately landed her in jail. Underneath a black scarf and coat Camelia was wearing a long black stretch skirt with a clingy pink floral top when I met her. She looked like she'd stepped out of a New York café, and, indeed, she was on her way to study journalism abroad. She began her journalistic career writing for the Iranian children's paper, *Kanun.* "At thirteen I was a famous poet and I was invited to gatherings of writers and I even had international recognition," she boasted. When she left school she joined the Kayhan group to work on *Zan-e Ruz.* She edited a youth page, then moved on to a new newspaper, *Hamshahri,* backed by the reformist mayor of Tehran, Gholam Hossein Karbaschi. The highly successful venture was the first newspaper to use color. "The editor wanted me because he said I had a lot of energy and initiative. I had a page of my own every week where I'd write about women and young people. But, you know, Iranians are a little bit jealous and people started to make problems for me in the office. They said: 'She's very free,' or, 'She has contacts with men and looks them in the eye.'" She left at the age of twenty-two and freelanced for various magazines. She did a postgraduate course in political science and studied alongside Faezeh.

When *Zan* started up, Camelia was offered a job. Her first story was a front-page report from Kosovo and she followed this up with a high-profile trip to Afghanistan. It was a time of great crisis when Iran and the Taliban were on the brink of war. In November 1998, she decided to try for an interview with the British writer Salman Rushdie, who lived in hiding due to an Iranian fatwa sanctioning his murder for his novel, *The Satanic Verses.*[9] Far from keeping the project secret, she rang the Iranian Embassy in London and asked if they had the number of the writers' club PEN, through which she hoped to contact him. Iranian security was alerted and put pressure on Faezeh, and within hours the project was called off.

---

9. *The Satanic Verses,* a work of fiction, contains descriptions of dream sequences of the Prophet, Mohammad. It caused a series of protests throughout the Islamic world where in some circles it was seen as blasphemous, and in 1989, Ayatollah Khomeini issued a fatwa, or religious decree, ordering the death of the writer. Salman Rushdie subsequently went into hiding. In 1998, President Khatami told reporters he believed the issue was "completely finished," which was taken as a sign that it was safe for Rushdie to emerge.

On her return to Iran, the Intelligence Ministry took a very close interest, calling Camelia daily and questioning her. This was at the time of a
spate of deaths of writers and politicians in mysterious circumstances,
which the government later admitted had been carried out by intelligence
ministry agents. In late 1998 the press got to hear of a list of 179 opposition figures, writers and journalists said to be targets for assassination.
Camelia's name was number 164 on the list. Undeterred, she covered the
story for *Zan*. "At the beginning, I thought it was a joke. We thought we
could challenge the Intelligence Ministry," she said. "It was like cat and
mouse with the ministry. They would phone me at home, in the office,
in my car."

The game reached its climax with the closure of *Zan*. Camelia was in
New York at the time. There were demonstrations by hard-liners outside
the newspaper offices in protest at its publication of the former empress's
New Year's Message, and the daily never reopened. The young journalist
returned to Iran, hoping that the furor had passed. But a few days later,
intelligence agents arrived at her house at 7 A.M. with a search warrant from
the Revolutionary Court. They turned the house upside down and took
away papers, photo albums and tapes. "They put me in a car with a blindfold on. They told me to crouch down in the back but I could tell where
we were going." This was the beginning of seventy-six days of detention.

A woman jailer showed her into a small cell, told her to take off her
clothes, and handed her a chador and plastic slippers. When the time came
for the first of many interrogations, she was told to blindfold herself again.
"You know where this place is, it's the Intelligence Ministry," said her inter-
rogator. He accused Camelia of being a spy and presented her with snapshots
of herself at a party with foreign friends, wearing a low-cut dress. "They
were keeping me in prison for political reasons, but they mainly asked me
questions about my private life, such as 'Are you a virgin, how many
boyfriends have you had?' and questions about my family. Really, it was a
very hard time," she said. "I said to myself that I had to be very controlled,
so I just tried to say, well, it's normal to have had boyfriends—I'm twenty-
seven." Her reaction was to write, and to pray, often for hours on end,
which seemed to impress her jailers.

The charges were never made clear, although her interrogators accused
her of threatening national security and failing to believe in Velayat-e
Faqih [the rule of the supreme jurisprudence], a cornerstone of the Islamic
Republic. She was taken to court three times. On one occasion, her mother
was called and allowed to see her. Faezeh was also in court, offering what
support she could. Finally Camelia was released on bail, and ultimately

fined 10 million rials (roughly $1,000). There was not much in the way of journalistic solidarity. One satirical columnist suggested that she had got herself jailed to become famous. Others were suspicious when she was freed, accusing her of spying for the Intelligence Ministry.

* * *

In the year 2000, the Ministry of Culture and Islamic Guidance reported that 89 out of 964 publications were run by female managing directors and that 71 journals had license holders who were women. Obviously, the press was still male-dominated. Writing in a feminist quarterly, *Jens-e Dovvom,* or "The Second Sex," Parvin Ardalan describes the everyday reality of life for women in the media. At the time of the revolution, she writes, men and women stood side by side, but aspirations for more equality had not been fulfilled.[10] "After the revolution, becoming a woman reporter was not an easy job. There is a lot opposition from other people and it is still a man's world." In an article entitled "Women Reporters Are Still Considered the Second Sex," she lists problems that are particularly acute for women: long hours, poor wages, no insurance and conflicts with family life. In male-dominated newsrooms, women still get diverted from the big political and economic issues of the day and directed into "human interest" stories, partly due to the decisions of their editors, and partly due to their own understanding of news. "Women reporters like to follow stories on issues like sex abuse, domestic violence, hejab, analysis of the family, relationships between girls and boys, prostitution, whether out in the open or underground, and when they cover these issues they are not completely free or safe to write openly—they are subject to censorship."

Jens-e Dovvom publisher, Nooshin Ahmady Khorasani, has waited for years to get a license for the quarterly from the ministry. In the meantime, each successive edition has had to be presented as a book. This means it has to pass the censors before publication. "They read it from cover to cover," she said. Indeed, the cover is often a sticking point, as she generally likes to use a photograph of a woman. Ahmadi has collaborated with other leading writers on women's affairs in the past, but on the whole, she prefers to work on her own. "It's easier to get work done as an individual. If you work on your own you can slip through the cracks," she said. Whereas in the West, being part of a group affords some protection, in Iran it is seen as a risky enterprise that could attract the attention of

10. *Jens-e Dovvom,* 2 Spring/Summer 1999.

the authorities. "For the person who's in charge it's a very sensitive situation: the person in charge is in the front line," she said. Moreover, Iranians are notoriously bad at teamwork, and reaching a consensus decision is difficult. "With *Jens-e Dovvom,* the good thing is that I make the decisions alone, but even then I spend fifty percent of my time agonizing about what to print, whether the climate is going to accept this or that. To be a publisher in Iran you have to know a lot more than writing. I have to think long term."

The shifting currents of Iranian politics mean that even with the increased freedom of expression of the late 1990s, what was acceptable one month could land you in jail a week later. Different trends exist side by side, and the uncertainty contributes to the feeling of insecurity in the media. Ahmadi recalls attending a book fair and being filmed by two different camera crews, both from state-run television, IRIB. The first cameraman, from the domestic broadcasting channel, advised her to tighten up her headscarf. The second, working for the international satellite channel told her to ease up, that there was no need for such strict hejab.

I heard a similar story from a black American who works as a presenter for IRIB, a stronghold of hard-liners and a powerful weapon for controlling public opinion. Marzieh, a convert to Islam who is married to an Iranian, kept her hood and coat on even as we chatted in my garden in the heat of early summer. "Of course they still make suggestions about what you can wear, but it's a lot more lenient if you're involved in the broadcasts for outside the country," she said. Ironically, Marzieh *wanted* to wear her black chador on screen, but her bosses discouraged it. She wears hejab through choice, to make a point, and she especially likes to trigger a response from young Iranians on the street.

Night after night, strictly veiled female newsreaders deliver a heavily censored version of the news as seen from an Islamic perspective. When Marzieh, a trained journalist, came to Iran in 1998, she initially worked for state-run radio. In spite of her devotion to the Islamic Republic, she found the restrictions hard to bear. "There was such a fear in Iran about saying anything negative that would reflect on the revolution itself." She remembers the cataclysmic earthquake of 1990, when around forty thousand people died in the north of the country. "We had no information, we had reporters calling from all over the world and we didn't know what to tell them."

Marzieh later joined an English-language satellite TV channel, Sahar, where she hosts a political roundtable discussion and a weekly one-on-one talk show. "There's more freedom regarding discussing certain issues now," she said. "I had a show recently discussing social problems, and we got into a lot of the questions of restrictions in society and why people have rebelled against society....However we do have a long way to go. Because it is not privately owned, creativity is lacking. We need creativity and spontaneity. They have been cut off from exposure to the rest of the world for twenty years and that has an effect." Shows are recorded well in advance, and guests are rarely critical of the regime. "How do you do a political show if everyone agrees—it's boring. You have to have pros and cons...Something I noted years ago is that it's hard for them to deal with people having different perspectives. This is one of the main problems here if you've been brought up in a Western society. *We* agree to disagree and still respect each other, but that's not the case here." Marzieh clearly believes in her job as a way to spread the word of Islam. "It has to be for something I believe in, not just as a mouthpiece for propaganda." However, the pressure to toe the party line sometimes becomes too much. "I have been given things to read on the set, and I've refused and said 'Stop!'"

From the start of the revolution, the government understood the power of public broadcasting and used it to its own ends. This continued during the war years and beyond, when the Iranian media were seen as vital in the battle to maintain unity and support for the Islamic Republic in the face of the perceived onslaught from the West. The veiled, soberly dressed women newsreaders were supposed to set an example for all women. In a book published in 1993 entitled *Woman's Image in the Islamic Order,* an influential cleric, Ayatollah Ahmad Azari Qomi, identified the role of the media as a crucial measure for the consolidation of the Islamic Republic, along with expanding what he called the culture of hejab and fostering the institution of marriage.[11] "The Islamic regime must exercise control over the press, public media, radio, and television in order to ensure that they all encourage young girls, even children, to observe Islamic dress and chador....If a woman realizes her true status and does not lose her spiritual values then she will not be overwhelmed by West-struck culture." On the other hand, another ayatollah suggested that there could be an all-female television channel where presenters would not have to wear hejab. Men could avoid being tempted by not tuning in.[12]

Before the revolution many traditional families were wary of listening to television or radio, and some even believed it was prohibited by Islamic law. Sociologist Jaleh Shaditalab points out that after the revolution, these families thought they were getting an Islamic television service, which was, therefore, acceptable. "In the first five years after the revolution, the

11. Mir-Hosseini, *Islam and Gender.*
12. Ayatollah Haeri of Shiraz, at Friday prayers in 1996. He later reportedly retracted his proposal.

number of TVs sold was unbelievable," she said. "Now almost every family has one. As soon as they get electricity, they buy a TV." And if the unrelenting diet of prayers and readings from the Koran got too repetitive, people turned to videos, often rented clandestinely. Said another sociologist, Shahla Ezazi of Allameh Tabataba'i University: "Having a video in [the southern Tehran suburb of] Nowruzabad is more important than having a washing machine." Ezazi has done a series of studies on the portrayal of women in Iranian television. She followed a popular soap opera, *Ayneh,* or "Mirror," which charts the fortune of a handful of middle-class families. Issues such as working or traveling rarely came up in relation to women, but what figured prominently were two major preoccupations of present-day Iran. "The main concern of families as portrayed on the TV was finding a husband for their daughters, or khastegari, as it's known," she said. "The other issue is that she should have a child."

Over the years, the broadcasting authorities have allowed state-run television to show an increasing number of foreign productions, censored to avoid offending religious sensibilities. One notable success was a Japanese serial, *Oshin,* about a young woman who moves from the country to the city. Anthropologist Fariba Adelkhah describes the first broadcast of the series in 1987 as an event.[13] Adelkhah points out that while the heroine is not veiled, she is modestly behaved and the program had the advantage of being from a desirable, but non-Western, trading partner. The whole country was talking about Oshin and her difficult relationship with her mother-in-law. A long-time foreign resident of Iran, the American Gertrude Nye Dorry, recalls that Iranians were addicted to the weekly hour-long broadcast. "The overbearing mother-in-law must have seemed angelic to the television audience here, used to the traditional domineering Iranian mother-in-laws," she remarks in her memoirs.[14] The success of the show brought down the wrath of Ayatollah Khomeini when a woman interviewed by Iranian radio suggested that, for her, Oshin was a more appropriate role model than the Blessed Fatemeh, the Prophet's only child.[15] He wrote to the director of the state broadcasting organization and demanded the producer be fired and punished under Islamic law. "If it is proven that there has been any intent to insult, the person guilty of insult undoubtedly is condemned to death." Ultimately, the broadcast director at Tehran Radio was sentenced to five years in jail, three directors of the organization's ideology group were

13. Adelkhah, *Etre Moderne en Iran,* 219.
14. Dorry, *Forty-five Years in Iran.*
15. Najmabadi, *The Politics of Social Transformation in Afghanistan, Iran, and Pakistan,* 366.

sentenced to four years each, and all four were lashed. The woman inter-
viewee, it seems, could not be found.

Soap operas reflect the slowly changing trends in society. When I arrived
in Iran, in 1996, Iranians were glued to the concluding episodes of a family drama called *Pedar Salar,* or "The Patriarch." The father figure tries
to insist that his three married sons should live with him. One daughter-
in-law rebels, and a huge family fight ensues, in which the mother is seen
desperately trying to reconcile the different factions. In the end, the father
falls ill and comes to his senses. He invites the family to live together in
the same building, but in their own, individual apartments, thus retain-
ing some independence. This solution, which retains the advantages of
the extended family while allowing couples a measure of privacy and independence, has, indeed, become very popular in Iranian cities.

One comedy series which enjoyed considerable success starred a young
actress, Laleh Saburi, as a lively, talkative wife with a long-suffering husband. Catchphrases from *Variety 77* entered the language of young people.
Walking in a Tehran park one evening, I realized that groups of youngsters were imitating the main characters, Ramin and Maryam, chirping
every now and then: "This is it" and "Your mother said so." Maryam is
very bossy but often messes things up, whereas her husband is mild-man-
nered and useless. Saburi, who created the character of Maryam herself,
told *Zanan* her creation was very different from most of the women portrayed on television.[16] "Women are generally quiet and don't laugh," she
said. "On our television, women play the role of mother or they're seen
doing housework. I'm a mother, too, and I'm proud of being a mother,
but women's roles on our TV are not realistic....In the end they are just
sitting in the corner of a room and cleaning their herbs or lentils or they
are gossiping about other people or nagging about their husbands." Saburi,
a former art student and aerobics instructor, told the magazine that most
of the viewers were women. "I'm not sure [why], but I've heard a lot of
women say that it's really good that for once a female really stands up
against a man, because up to now we haven't had this kind of woman on
television," she said.

While the hard-liners in the state-controlled media cautiously allowed
a few chinks in their armor to open up, they were at the same time well
aware that they were about to be swamped by satellite TV and the Internet.
Satellite dishes were banned for all but foreign officials during the time
I lived in Iran. However, better-off city dwellers installed them surreptitiously, then hid them away from time to time during periodic

16. *Zanan,* 25 December–January 1998.

clampdowns. Even members of parliament acknowledged that soon the dishes would be too small to be discovered and accepted that eventually they would be legalized.

With regard to the Internet, the clergy was one step ahead of the game. Throughout the 1990s, the Center for the Encyclopedia of Islamic Jurisprudence, based in the holy city of Qom, was beavering away, putting hundreds of thousands of pages of the texts of Shiite Islam onto CD-ROM. The clergy understood early on the potential of the high-tech revolution and the Internet. On a political level the authorities were fearful of Iranian opposition groups abroad making increasingly sophisticated use of the new media. President Khatami had his own Website up and running well before Internet cafés became a familiar sight in Tehran, although they, too, were subject to periodic crackdowns.

Websites focusing on women appeared, mainly based abroad. One, however, the ironically named *Bad Jens,* or "Bad Gender," was run by a young, U.S.-educated feminist, Mahsa Shekarloo, who returned to Iran to live. Her offerings of interviews, news stories and links with other groups attracted an immediate response when the site was launched in early 2000. "It makes me realize how little information there is," she said. "It's targeted at Iranians abroad so that they can know what's going on here." *Bad Jens,* like *Zanan,* tries to cover a wider spectrum of opinion than journals have traditionally in the past. It uses the hinterland of the Internet to develop a new space where ideas can be exchanged more freely. "One of the things that's made it easier for us is that we are putting it out on the Internet. Because it's like the Internet everywhere in the world, it's really new, it's uncontrollable. You don't need permission, but you never know, one day they might drag you to court."

Even in the twenty-first century, life for Iranian women in the media means living with uncertainty and, at the end of the day, fear. But at the same time, the image of women is changing and the change is being brought about, principally, by women themselves.

9

The Nightingale and the Rose

Concerts by women singers are rare in the Islamic Republic, where traditionalists consider women's voices to be dangerously arousing. In public, at least, they are permitted to sing only in front of all-women audiences. So I was intrigued to receive an invitation from the Ministry of Foreign Affairs to a concert by "female musicians" at Al-Zahra University. A UN driver took me to the gymnasium, where crowds of women were gathering. But when I introduced myself to the organizers, they looked surprised, then uncomfortable. "It's been cancelled," said one. I heard the words "crowded" and "security" being muttered. The concert was still going ahead, but not for foreign guests. Then the driver explained that *"Khanum,* [madam] has come a long way…" and the official assured me that I could, of course, stay if I wanted to. The strict rules of Iranian *"ta'arof,"* or "politeness," meant that she had no choice.

I asked whether it was anyone famous. "Oh, yes, very," said my escort. "Her name is Pari Zanganeh." My eyes widened. I only knew a handful of Iranian singers' names, but this was one of them. The blind Iranian diva was legendary, although her fame had been acquired before the revolution. Then, women soloists were banned from performing in public. Women do sing at private parties, but the hosts often look rather fearful of the consequences. When my Italian mother-in-law, who trained as an opera singer, launched into a resounding aria in the garden, our neighbor came scuttling out to tell her to keep her voice down. She was worried we would attract the attention of the Komiteh.

The restrictions are sometimes taken to extremes. A British friend of mine who is married to an Iranian got a note from the authorities informing her that a package from her sister had been confiscated. The problem item was a cassette of nursery rhymes. The censors had allowed the accompanying book to pass but seized the tape on the grounds that they were performed by a woman. When her husband went to the appropriate office, he found a man in a dusty room surrounded by shelves full of audiocassettes. After a brief argument, the official let him have the tape, moaning about what a boring job he had.

So a woman singing in public is something of an event. I was ushered into the front row, where I sat next to the wife of an Iranian diplomat, who introduced herself as Zahra. She could not contain herself. "People are very excited about this concert," she said. "I'm a singer myself." We watched as Pari Zanganeh, carrying a white stick, did a sound check with an all-woman crew. She was wearing a full-length fur coat (the only one I ever saw in Iran) over a long ball gown. When the doors opened to the general public, dozens of students ran to get the best places. In the end, almost a thousand people were packed into the gymnasium. They stood on the stage and sat on the floor. Two women standing in front of us were holding big paper programs, not to read, but to sit on.

The organizers made an announcement banning the use of flash photography, video cameras and cellphones, and the singer entered. Tall and imposing in bright-blue chiffon, she no longer wore her scarf and had taken off her fur coat. "That's why they made the announcement," someone remarked. "They don't want pictures of her singing without hejab." Strangely, although there was not a man in the hall, the vast majority of the audience kept on their scarves, coats and chadors. A few took them off as the concert progressed, but the mass unveiling I had expected did not materialize. As the only foreigner, sitting in the VIP section, I, rather pathetically, untied the knot of my headscarf.

Zanganeh sang various classical pieces, including Scarlatti, Schumann and Schubert. "This is German," my neighbor commented helpfully. Her voice, now aging, was still beautiful but somehow sad. Turning to traditional Iranian music, she sang a famous song based on a poem by the thirteenth-century poet Saadi, describing a traveler bidding farewell to his lover as he leaves with a *caravan*, or "camel train". Then she sang a simple lullaby about a nightingale, and many in the audience, including my neighbor, burst into tears. As she finished with an Azeri folksong, "Ayrilik," Zahra began to cry quietly again. "But her voice is not what it was," she said, shaking her head.

For older women, the concert harked back to their childhood, when singing in public was no crime and singing for your friends was a simple pleasure. "I saw her at a performance when the Shah and his wife were present," said one middle-aged woman. She was one of the few to have taken her headscarf off: "Because I am hot and I don't care. Take yours off, never mind!" Many youngsters present had not even been born at the time of the revolution. They were keen to hear the famous voice for themselves and to attend a rare, quality concert. A young translator, Mehri, suggested that the only reason the audience remained veiled was the official setting. "This is a university and everyone's being very polite, but I've been to concerts where the women were shaking their arms and legs and dancing in the aisles." She was not surprised when I told her there had been no name on the invitation. "That's because she was so popular at the time of the Shah; she's very much associated with that era," she said.

At Pari Zanganeh's big house in the smart residential suburb of Elahieh, pictures, album covers and books recall the old days. She does not hide a certain bitterness that her career was derailed at a time when she could fill the biggest theater in the country.

"It makes me sad, losing permission to work, so furious," she said. "Rudaki Hall was so alive in those days. Life was more colorful, more meaningful. Now, if they invite me to [the same hall, renamed] Validat, I never go. I feel there's a different atmosphere, a different mood. That was the house where I shone on the stage with a symphony orchestra. Now, it doesn't make me satisfied any more." To fill the emptiness, she turned to writing. Children's books, books in Braille and teaching others to sing, gave her life a new direction. But even this she found disappointing, because her young women students could not hope to fulfill their ultimate ambitions. "In all fields of your life you need your goal, you need something higher to aspire to—this is what makes the blood warm in your veins."

Zanganeh had what she called "a voice" even as a child. A lyric soprano with a wide register, she studied at Tehran Conservatory, then in Italy and Austria. Married with two young children, she had a car accident at the age of twenty-seven and lost her sight. Undeterred, she turned professional and sang abroad. On her first European tour, her husband announced he wanted a divorce. After 1979, everything was chaotic. "The first years of the revolution, we were so upset by all the changes in the country that singing was left behind." She traveled abroad and sang, but feared that she'd be arrested on her return. At home, she was no longer allowed to sing in public, although she occasionally performed for friends and at private functions. More than twenty of her cassettes circulate on the black market. "We are not allowed to sell them in the shops, because it's a woman's voice," she sighed. "There's a blind man who sits at home and records them for me." With the election of President Khatami, things became easier, and the government began to invite her to sing at selected all-women events, such as the birthday of Ayatollah Khomeini. She remembers her comeback at the Fajr Film Festival in 1998 with pleasure: "Oh, it was a fantastic reaction. Thousands of people were standing, even outside the doors of the halls." In 1999, for the first time in years, she was able to record an album, of sorts. "I had to do it with a chorus so that my voice could not be heard," she said, wryly.

A comeback on an even grander scale was made by Iran's most famous pop singer, Googoosh. For more than twenty years after the revolution she declined to sing or to record a song but remained in mute protest in Tehran. At times of national celebration, such as when the success of the Iranian soccer team in the 1998 World Cup brought thousands out onto the streets, crowds gathered outside her apartment, begging her to sing. Her absence boosted her cult status, according to Ali Sabaii in her adoring Website, Googoosh.com: "The self-imposed professional silence has only added to her fame across Tajikistan, Central Asia, Turkey, Iraq, Afghanistan and especially among Iranians." In July 2000, she gave a concert in Toronto, attended by her most ardent fans. But even to sing abroad, she reportedly needed to get permission from the Ministry of Culture and Islamic Guidance.[1]

Having to do without Googoosh and Madonna does not mean that Iranians live without music. At weddings, parties and dinners I attended, guests or hosts often started singing or produced an instrument. In wealthier homes there may be a piano, but poorer households often have a selection of traditional instruments such as reed pipes, lutes and drums. Music almost always leads to traditional dancing. A visiting musicologist told me he had no doubt that the ban on Western imports had led to a rise in interest in traditional Iranian music. One of the most famous Iranian folk groups, the Kurdish Kamkar family, consists of seven brothers and one sister. Qashang Kamkar plays a *setar,* a small, long-necked lute, which is associated with the mystic tradition of Sufism and meditation. U.S.-based musicologist Kamran Hushmand has noted that it has become the instrument of choice for Iranian women since the revolution, as it is ideally suited to a small audience.[2]

On another occasion, I saw one woman performing alongside eight male musicians all playing the *daf,* an outsized tambourine that produces a fascinating mixture of rhythm and tone. At the end, members of the audience carried flowers onto the stage. A young man presented a bouquet to the well-veiled woman player, then deliberately kissed her. He

---

1. *The Iranian,* 6 March 2000; Sadeq Saba, *BBC Online,* 19 June 2000.
2. *The Iranian,* 1 September 1999.

was probably a member of her family, and the kiss was therefore permissible, but the audience roared and applauded. At a women-only concert given by a well-rehearsed female ensemble, Ney Riz, what struck me was not so much the musicians as the audience. They seemed excited at the rarity of an all-woman performance, but not particularly well-informed on Iranian traditional music. They clapped along but seemed unable to keep the beat. By the end of the concert, one woman was dancing deliriously in her seat, while others did not even take off their coats and scarves. They seemed to have got out of the habit of concertgoing (if they ever had it before) and seemed unsure of how to behave.

In the universities, music has not been given much prominence since the days when hard-liners tried to ban it. They failed, incidentally, because it was sanctioned by Ayatollah Khomeini himself. Music students are encouraged to concentrate on theory, rather than practice. Azin Movahed, who told me she was Iran's only doctor of music, divides her time between working at UNICEF and teaching at Tehran University. A young and Western-trained flautist, she meets with some resistance from the older teaching staff. Students are still not encouraged to study performance, and a ban on college concerts was only lifted twenty years after the revolution. Azin performs the flute in public but until recently could not perform in university concerts. When I asked if it was because she was a woman, she answered cheerfully: "No, but that makes it even worse."

Music in the theater is also problematic. Yet one director, who happens to be a woman, plays to full houses night after night with plays that are, to all intents and purposes, musicals. Pari Saberi was a well-known director at the time of the Shah who has made the transition to working under an Islamic regime. She specializes in spectacular productions with a large cast. In the summer of 2000, her production of the Greek tragedy, *Antigone* was staged at the Coliseum in Rome, complete with real horses. After the revolution, the theaters were closed down and she lived abroad. Eventually, however, she was invited back. On her return, her first production made a big impact. "It was a big success because it was a mixture of poetry and music—and girls." In those days, even traditional dancing was frowned on, and a politically correct replacement, *harekat-e ma'sum* or "innocent movement," was encouraged instead. With each successive production, Saberi pushes forward the limits of what is acceptable.

The first production of hers that I saw, the tale of Rostam and Sohrab, is one of the most famous stories in Persian literature, from Ferdowsi's epic *Shahnameh,* or "Book of Kings." In the massive Vahdat concert hall, the audience was enthralled by impressive dance routines, not only of soldiers marching out to battle, but also of a seduction scene danced by Rostam's lover, Tahmineh, an assertive figure who selects her future husband for herself. What to me seemed carefully restrained love scenes were seen as quite daring in an Iranian context. My Persian teacher gasped when Rostam stroked his bride-to-be's head in passing. One of the most dramatic moments of the play involves a female warrior disguised as a man. When all the other soldiers are exhausted, Gordafarid takes up the fight, wearing a black chain mail hood, leopard skin top and big fur hat to conceal her long hair. When her true identity is revealed, she cannot let down her hair in classical theatrical tradition.

"Staging plays with women, and complying with the rules of hejab, is not an issue for me," said Pari Saberi. "I've tried to resolve the problem in an aesthetic way. For example, in my production of Rostam and Sohrab, a female character has to reveal her hair. So I used a theatrical device—she let down her hair to reveal long, beautiful ribbons. I always find a way….A man and a woman cannot touch each other, but you can create a scene by looks or words or certain action. You can show the act of love in an even stronger way. Art has no boundaries." She is philosophical about the limitations imposed by the regime. "Certain subjects cannot be staged now. In those days, certain things could not be staged either. In this country I have always worked in a framework of laws and regulations," she said.

Saberi, a short, plump figure with intense dark eyes and a striking face, sits night after night in the front row, assessing the performances and measuring the audience reaction. "Every time I go on stage I see the audience as hungry lions. If you don't tame them, they're going to tear you apart. Since I have been working on Iranian themes, I have felt happier. I'm less afraid of the lions." Rostam and Sohrab are legendary figures from pre-Islamic times, and the marriage scene draws on the ancient Zoroastrian religion. Yet Saberi draws on Islamic traditions as well. The play opens with drummers and a single trumpeter like a Shiite passion play, or *Tazieh*. A long-haired narrator tells the story, a figure familiar from the nineteenth-century coffee-house tradition, where men would get together to meet, drink and listen to poetry. In the final act, Sohrab's mother drags an Islamic shrine covered in fragments of mirrors and lit by candles on stage. These gaudy memorials, illuminated with fairy lights, are commonly seen on the roadside at the scene of a fatal accident or outside the house or shop of a recently deceased person. The dead Sohrab, slain on the battlefield by his father, ascends into the midst of the mourners dressed in white with a red headband—the typical garb of a Shiite martyr.

Just as theater needs an audience, painters need their work to be seen. In the field of visual arts, restrictions are everywhere, but they do not stop artists from working. The official artists of the revolution depict images of the ideal woman that dominate towns and cities, often painted on the sides of buildings in huge wall murals. Well-veiled, abstract and often faceless, they are generally mourning the loss of a male martyr in the war or exhorting the virtues of women wearing hejab. "A woman modestly dressed is as a pearl in its shell," is a favorite slogan. Many well-known artists stick to landscapes, still life or calligraphy. Others concentrate on faces without bodies, androgynous and fragmented. When a friend of mine took life drawing classes, I was intrigued to hear that the models kept their coats and scarves on. Their teacher was Sousan, a talented young artist who was one of a handful of postrevolutionary painters to specialize in the female nude. "In class, the model would have to have clothes on, so I explain different parts of the skeleton and if they are talented enough, they pick it up, like I did," she told me. For her own work, she meets regularly with a handful of friends who pose, without clothes, for each other. "The other side of it is that by having these friends modeling for you, there's a lot of talk about people's personal lives and you are much more relaxed, so it puts another perspective on it. I'm really after portraying that inner life of people."

In the basement of her family home, Sousan shows dozens of charcoal drawings of nudes, some delicate, some bold, many of them grim. Her first model was her grandmother, who was suffering from Parkinson's disease and Alzheimer's. "My grandmother was alive, but she had lost her memory....I was seeing a child, seeing an animal, seeing a ghost. I'd get frightened just by her appearance, but it was very educational for me. I started wondering, where did she go to. This was the beginning of my path." Sousan sees her work as a progression. Her subjects become more colorful, wear clothes, though not veils, and appear in groups rather than as solitary figures. Huge, bright oil paintings, of families and friends gathered together hang on the walls next to the fridge freezers and storage shelves of the cellar. Her later work is in vivid pastels, abstracts with bulls' heads reminiscent of Persepolis and allusions to Eastern mythology. More recently she has concentrated on animal forms and skeletons. Not a single piece of her work has been shown in a gallery.

"First of all, I'd like to have all my work shown as a progression and that would mean a lot of paintings and there isn't a big enough private gallery here, or if there is, it's a government controlled one and the nudes would be a problem. I also don't like the 'politics' of the gallery owners either, who want to charge you a lot of money to have your work framed, and set the prices, etcetera." Yet she would like her work to reach a wider audience. "I've never been outside, Iran and I don't trust other people to take my work outside so I'm just leaving it to fate and I'll wait and see if there is an opportunity to show my work." She has had a private showing of slides of her canvases, which she narrated with music as a kind of performance art. She does not believe, however, that the Islamic government has put her under pressure to choose her subject matter. "In a perverse way, all these restrictions have helped me to go about my work in a very precise, slow and careful way," she said. "The government doesn't affect my work, but having a government like this, I'm thinking about what freedom really is."

Other artists make a living from selling their work, but Sousan lives at home with her parents and makes a pittance from teaching. "Many people do work for the market and they offer people what they want, like fashion designers, something beautiful they can hang on the wall for decoration in their house, but that's not my idea of art. Here it's like a desert—you look around and there's not much activity or life going on on the surface and you think there's nothing. But there's a lot of energy. I know I've not been able to put on exhibitions, but I've been active in my own way, like a mole, working away."

For painter Farideh Lashaie, literature was her first love, and she began by writing. However, in an interview with *Zanan* magazine, she describes how she found she could not write openly about herself and her feelings.[3] "Women in Iran in writing express themselves always so very conservatively and don't say everything. We as women have a long way to go to get to this freedom and comfort where we can say what we want like other women in the world." With her painting, mostly abstract, she feels liberated. "I find cultural freedom in painting. I love the freedom that I find in painting. You can say whatever you want," she said. But she points out that artists are appreciated only by a small group of aficionados. Art is barely taught in schools, and visits to museums or galleries are rare.

Scholar Farzaneh Milani has argued that Iranian women have been encouraged to keep "solemn and silent," as well as veiled and out of sight.[4] Houses are surrounded by high walls and are divided into inner and outer areas, beliefs can be kept secret in difficult times according to the religious doctrine known as *taqiyeh,* and true feelings are masked by ta'arof, the elaborate ritual of polite conversation. Women writers have never had

3. *Zanan,* 63 May–June 2000.
4. Milani, *Veils and Words.*

a prominent voice and have rarely written about their lives. Milani's book ends with a ringing couplet from the poet, Simin Behbahani.

> O Gypsy, to stay alive you must slay silence!
> I mean, to pay homage to being, you must sing.

At her tower block home in Western Tehran, Behbahani explains the figure of the gypsy, which haunts around twenty of her poems. "The gypsy is a symbol which represents the Iranian woman who has been left wandering, stranded, not knowing where she belongs, and oppressed," she said. "It's a general universal idea of the gypsies: they are like nomads, they are constantly being assaulted by people and they are not welcome." *poems- gypsies* The poems were part of her earlier work, however, and now she feels that women have changed. Stubborn and persistent, in a sense still like gypsies, they have refused to give up their rights. Behbahani has never turned inwards or withdrawn from the world around her. At the time of the Shah she wrote a poem about a prostitute that led to a debate on conditions in brothels. After the revolution, when political violence was at its height, she wrote a critical poem that led to her being banned from publication for nine years. "It was at the worst of the times for political prisoners and I was a teacher and one of my students, just a teenager, was executed," she recalls. Referring to a poem by Nima Yushij, "The House is Cloudy," she described how "The House" had become bloody.

There have been other pressures, too. Behbahani is an active member of the influential Writers' Association, some of whose members have been threatened, jailed and the targets of assassination attempts. Her own name appeared on the death list prepared by Intelligence Ministry agents. She was arrested and detained one night along with other writers attending a cultural evening at the house of a German diplomat. And she was invited to go on a notorious bus trip to Armenia where the driver tried to drive the vehicle over a cliff, apparently on the orders of rogue elements in the Intelligence Ministry. She had declined the invitation, but many leading intellectuals on board lived to tell the tale. Receiving a human rights award in Germany in 1999, Behbahani spoke positively about the change in atmosphere since the arrival of Khatami, but at the award ceremony she also spoke out about the series of killings of intellectuals: "The dictatorship killed some of the nicest sons of the nation, but it does not know what to do with the corpses."

While many Iranian writers focus on personal experience, autobiography is rare. Author Pouran Farrokhzad, who has compiled a two-volume Encyclopedia of Women Culture Makers in Iran and in the World, told me she experienced considerable difficulty persuading women to contribute biographical data. They were reluctant to reveal their date of birth or even the ages of their children, let alone details of their private lives. She agrees with Farzaneh Milani on the symbolic power of the woman's voice. "My grandmother used to put a little pebble under her tongue to distort her voice," she recalled. When a strange man came to the door, this would conceal her identity. Farrokhzad recalled the two different door knockers for men and women that can still occasionally be seen on old wooden doors. They were shaped differently, suggestively ring-like for women and long and thin for men, so as to make a different sound recognizable to those inside.

One woman who did find a voice of her own was Pouran Farrokhzad's sister, Forough, a poet who towers above Iranian twentieth-century literature. Although she died in a car crash in 1967 at the age of thirty-two, her powerful, sensual poems overshadow present-day Iranian writing. Her unconventional, individualistic lifestyle shocked readers in the 1960s, but the legacy of her poems and her personal courage are a role model for writers and artists today. Where other writers kept a distance, Forough made her work an intimate confession.

> I have sinned, a delectable sin
> Beside a body, trembling and dazed
> O God, how can I know what I did
> In that dark and silent private place?[5]

One of her best-known works, "The Captive," describes her agony at being unable to escape from an unhappy marriage. To do so would mean losing her only son, as custody was then, as now, automatically granted to the father. The bars of the child's cot evoke her own captivity.

> If, O Sky, I want one day to fly
> From out this silent prison, cold and stern,
> What shall I say to the child's weeping eyes?
> Forget about me, for I'm a captive bird.[6]

Pouran remembers her sister as being unusually frank and honest, not just in her poetry. "Rarely in Iran people are who they say they are—everybody is wearing a mask, they pretend to be someone they are not, but my family was not this way," she said. "Nobody really looked at

5. Farrokhzad, *Another Birth: Selected Poems of Forugh Farrokhzad*, 11.
6. Ibid., 9

women from that point of view before; it was always seen through men's eyes. Since her, other women poets have had the courage to speak as women, but nobody still has had her audacity."

The Farrokhzad family has had more than its fair share of tragedy. One brother, Fereydoun, was a well-known popular entertainer. After the revolution, he moved to Germany and continued to give shows, often with a political content, critical of the Islamic regime. He was stabbed to death as part of a wave of savage killings allegedly carried out by government agents. Pouran herself has received death threats. Another brother suffered a nervous breakdown and died of an asthma attack. Pouran remembers the revolutionary authorities carrying her sick father out of the house in his own bed to take him to the police station for questioning. Their land and property were confiscated. "We lost everything. They took our house and belongings," she said. She started to cry, silently. "The family has really been destroyed. Now I'm the only one still standing, taking care of my mother. I'm no exception. A lot of families have been destroyed. What's kept me going is my work. I want to focus on life and work," she said.

Pouran has published seventeen books and had five more on the go when I visited her at home. In her day-to-day work, censorship is a problem. It took her a full year to get the Encyclopedia past the Guidance Ministry. But self-censorship is even worse, she believes. "The main thing is self-censorship," she said, "in the sense that every time a word comes up, I think, 'They're not going to let me use that,' and, in a way, it kills the imagination."

Paintings of Forough and the rest of the family hang on the wall. But Pouran does not dwell on the past. She is an irrepressible, jolly character, surrounded by her own family and her cats. She is one of many women who insist that the revolution has proved to have a positive side. "From anything bad comes something good," she said. "In the case of Iranian women, what's happened in the last twenty years has awakened us and made us realize that we have a value and an identity. At the time of Reza Shah, when they took off the veil, it was forced. By the time of his son, the Shah, things were falling into place but women didn't fight for change and the changes didn't really come from women themselves." Pouran Farrokhzad goes so far as to talk about a kind of renaissance in the arts. "In terms of art and literature there's been an explosion in terms of the numbers of writers and poets....I'm quite happy to have been part of a time in history when things were not quite so predictable," she concluded.

Her words are echoed by bookseller Goli Emami, whose Zamineh bookshop in north Tehran is a popular meeting place for writers and intellectuals.

"Despite the fact that we were deprived of every single thing we had in the revolution, it was a great blessing for us, because it was as if we were woken up from a deep sleep with a bucket of cold water poured over us….Before the Islamic Republic, we worked, we partied, and they gave us the right to vote. Everything was granted to us on a silver platter. It was once it was taken away from us that we realized we had to do something."

revolution was a awakening for women

In this bookshop, readers come not just to browse but also to chat. And one of the topics of conversation is the emergence of new women writers. "It's a very interesting point that there are more women writers writing now than ever before," says Emami. "The fact of the matter is that they have been encouraged to come out and write." She gives the example of a writer from Isfahan, Fattaneh Haj Seyyed Javadi, credited with writing the first Iranian bestseller, *Bamdad-e Khomar,* or "The Morning After," which tells the story of a love affair between a rich girl and a carpenter. Their marriage is a failure, with the husband battering the wife and the mother-in-law adding to her suffering. "I couldn't put it down," said Emami. "It's not the story, it's the way it's written, the style of writing. It's gone into its twentieth printing, that's up to two hundred thousand copies, which makes it the biggest seller since the revolution." Until the arrival of *Bamdad-e Khomar,* the record was held by another woman writer, Simin Daneshvar, for a much more literary work, *Savushun.* This work, published in 1969, paints a fascinating picture of family life and politics in Shiraz in the 1940s. Not such an easy read, but full of powerful writing, it is much loved by Iranian intellectuals.

Since the phenomenal success of *Bamdad-e Khomar*, up to a dozen other women writers have tried their luck with novels. It may be that the massive increase in women's literacy has led to a surge in novel-reading and novel-writing, much as it did in Jane Austen's time in eighteenth and nineteenth-century England. Other titles that are popular are translated self-help manuals and popular psychology such as *Men Are from Mars, Women Are from Venus.* However, while many more titles are being published, with four times as many new books available, sales of books have slumped with increasing economic hardship. But women are still buying books. "Having said all this, we know that women are reading more now than before the revolution," said Emami. "I did a very unofficial and personal survey in my own shop. For three weeks I marked down whether books were bought by men or women. The proportion of women buying books has increased."

women read more after the revolution

At the first Women Publishers' Book Fair in 1998, Iran's first woman publisher, Shahla Lahiji, was in fine form. One of Iran's leading feminists, her delightful, lively, but loud-mouthed defense of women's rights has frequently got her into trouble. Most notably she was detained in jail for several weeks in 2000, along with Mehrangiz Kar and other prominent reformers, after attending a conference in Berlin run by the prestigious Heinrich Böll Foundation. The proceedings were disrupted by Iranian opposition groups based abroad. One man stripped naked and a woman danced in the aisles. On the reformers' return to Iran the state-run television aired and re-aired a heavily edited footage of the conference, and some eighteen participants were arrested and charged with acting against the interests of national security and collaborating with counter-revolutionary groups. Lahiji's own publishing house, Rowshangaran and the Women's Studies Publication Institute, was founded in 1984. "We are the only truly independent women's studies publishing house—the others are all government-supported," she said. "The government calls me a feminist and I always have to deny it," she laughed. "It's a bad word, here. Sometimes I have to explain the meaning of the word because they think a feminist is someone who wants to go out without wearing anything and be the ruler of the world."

Lahiji said the idea of the fair was to draw attention to the presence of women in the cultural world and to promote book reading. She introduced me to various prominent publishers attending the event, including the politician Azam Taleqani. Many women in publishing concentrate on children's books, but even that is not enough to escape the attention of the censors. Roya Farsa'i, of Pamchal Publishing, showed me some of her books for toddlers. "I have one book that shows children how to dress themselves and, of course, there's a baby wearing nothing. I haven't been able to publish that book yet," she said. The fair was being held just months after the election of President Khatami, however, and already the publishers were feeling a breath of fresh air. Farsa'i told me they felt they now could print pictures of children showing hair, although long sleeves would still be necessary. She pointed out that the state-run television broadcast pictures of bare-headed foreign women but said that books were thought to have a more lasting impact.

The shifting nature of what is acceptable is something of a nightmare for artists and publishers. What is certain, however, is that since the revolution women have never let up the pressure to push the limits further and further. Nooshin Ahmady gave me some insight into the dialogue with the censors. Her Nashr-e Towse'e Publications publishes an annual women's diary that has been a resounding success. Nicely produced, the diary is full of images of women taken from photographs old and new,

some with and some without hejab. But she has to get permission for
nearly every single entry. "They gave me a really hard time about the
photographs," she said. "If a woman's neck was showing, I'd have to cover
it; if her hair was showing, I'd have to cut it out. For three or four months
I did nothing but go backwards and forwards to the ministry." On the
whole, the authorities were less strict about dead women. But they insisted
that more "revolutionary" figures, such as politician Jamileh Kadivar be
included. Even when a book has passed the censors, the publisher may
still come under pressure. For example, Ahmadi included a photograph
of Mrs. Farrokhru Parsa, the first Iranian woman to serve in the cabinet.
She was education minister in the 1970s but then executed after the revolution on charges of spreading prostitution, corruption on earth and
waging war on God. Ahmadi had to defend her decision to include her
photo after receiving a top-level complaint. "Actually my being young
helped me. I was only nine at the time of the revolution. If I had been
an older woman, I would have had a prerevolutionary past that they
could have used against me."

Like many women activists, Ahmadi is consciously trying to promote
interest and research into women in Iranian history. She told me if she had
published a book on women's history it would only reach a small group
of women. The diary has a wider impact: "Even schoolgirls can look at it
and see what women did a hundred years ago. It gives them a sense that
this can be done, and I believe it can have a positive impact on women's
self-esteem, their psyche."

Filmmaker Tahmineh Milani went back and forth to the Guidance
Ministry for seven years before she finally managed to get permission to
shoot her controversial film *Do Zan,* or "Two Women," in the Khatami
"spring." The movie tells the story of two bright university students, one
from the city, one from the provinces. The universities are closed down
after the revolution, and the girl from the traditional, provincial background loses her chance of an education. She is forced into marriage with
an insanely jealous husband who will not let her leave the house and locks
away the telephone. When he dies, she gets back in touch with her friend
from university, now, by contrast, a happily married architect. At their
first reunion she is pictured in the black chador with two children, the
image of the ideal Islamic mother, but she is miserable. In contrast, her
friend has no children and leads a comfortable, city life. When I first saw
the film I thought it was melodramatic and exaggerated, but afterwards
I heard many similar stories and realized it had struck a chord. The film
is part of what's been called the New Iranian Cinema. In the 1990s alone,

Iranian movies, including *Two Women* scooped some three hundred awards.[7] Tahmineh Milani, herself an architect, based the story partly on her own experience. "I'm not interested in winning prizes outside of Iran," she said. "I just want to make films for people right now, films like *Two Women,* which are controversial, so that when they go to see them there will be lots of arguments and maybe something will come out of it." Government figures based on interviews conducted after the showing showed that ninety-six percent of those interviewed described it as superb, she said, while only four percent said it was bad and insulting. Milani, dark-eyed and with dark hair, is extremely vivacious. I suspect the censors are bowled over when she breezes into their offices. She recalled visiting a deputy minister, who, in religious fashion, would not meet her eye and stared at the carpet. She demonstrated how she bent down in front of him and looked up, to intercept his gaze. But in her light, airy apartment, hung with bright paintings by her husband, she told me that after one particularly acrimonious row with officials, she suffered a miscarriage and lost a baby.

There was more trauma in store for her. When I met Milani, she had just finished shooting a new film called *The Hidden Half.* She knew it was controversial, but she did not know then that it would land her in jail. A husband goes to Shiraz to see a woman. He tells his wife: "She's been a political activist for ten years, not like you." On his arrival he finds his wife's diary in his briefcase and discovers in fact that she does have a political past that he never knew about. "I'm trying to show in this film that values are not just based on religious values but on other beliefs, too," said Milani at the time. "I've made the film, now I don't know how I'm going to get the approval." Perhaps to her own surprise, she did get permission from the Ministry of Culture and Islamic Guidance, but then in September 2001, after the film's release, she was arrested and accused of "abusing the arts as a tool for supporting counter-revolutionary groups." In prison for a week, she was released after an unprecedented intervention by President Khatami. The arrest "shouldn't have happened," he told a news conference, adding that if the film had been passed by the ministry it was a matter for the ministry alone and not the judiciary.

The one thing Milani would like to be able to include in her films is touch. "You can't show touching, even a mother touching her son, so you can't go for certain topics and you can't speak out bravely about what you believe." She also mentioned teenage life, where any talk about boyfriends or sex would be banned, and finally religion itself. The rules on covering

7. Godfrey Cheshire, "The Iranian Cinema," reprinted in *PBS Online.*

Iranian cinema poster for the controversial movie,
Two Women, *directed by Tahmineh Milani.*

Movie director Rakhshan Bani-Etemad

PHOTO BY ALI KHALIGH

women's hair mean that even in bedroom scenes, actresses have to keep on their headscarf and coat. "I feel that it's very funny and comical that a woman has to be covered up even with her husband. We try to avoid intimate scenes, but in a certain sense it's unavoidable. But I feel that this will improve with the times," she said.

Milani had always wanted to go into movies, but before the revolution her family discouraged her from going to film school on the grounds that the movies of the time were cheap and nasty imitations of Hollywood, and not the kind of business they wanted their daughter involved in. Afterwards, when the universities were closed, she worked as a set designer for a well-known director, at a time when many of the producers who are world famous today came to prominence. "These directors were not made overnight," she said. "The educated people who came up at the time of the revolution were set free. They didn't have the space before because of these filmmaking cartels. These directors couldn't talk about sex, they couldn't show fights, so they looked for areas of interest and they found their way."

The first Iranian movie I saw was *Bashu, the Little Stranger,* by a male director, Bahram Beyzaie. It tells the story of a small, dark-skinned boy from the south of Iran who flees from the chaos and horror of the war with Iraq and takes refuge in a northern village. A village woman takes pity on the child and cares for him in the face of prejudice from her neighbors. Publisher Shahla Lahiji has written a book on the image of women in Beyzaie's films. "I wanted to publish his scripts because he gives women good roles, not sexy-hexy ones or women as housewives," she explained. My Iranian friends had trouble following the dialogue, much of it in the northern dialect of Gilaki. The same friends struggled to follow the plot in *Gabbeh,* a story set among Qashqa'i nomads, where a love story in an idyllic landscape is woven metaphorically into a tribal rug, or *gabbeh.* The storyline in Iranian films often takes second place, but the movies are visually breathtaking, one reason, perhaps, they are so accessible to a world audience. In *Gabbeh,* director Mohsen Makhmalbaf uses the vivid colors of wild flowers to represent different emotions. Black, not surprisingly, is represented as the color of death, and speculation ran rife after its release that it was some kind of comment on the Islamic regime, with its ubiquitous black chadors and obsession with mourning. So it should have come as no surprise that critics looked for allegorical meanings when his precocious seventeen-year-old daughter, Samira, took her first feature film, *The Apple,* to the Cannes Film Festival.

The Apple tells the extraordinary true story of two twelve-year-old girls who were kept locked up by their father until finally released by a social worker. The film was shot in eleven days soon after the girls' release and most of the characters in the drama-documentary play themselves. It shows their delight at discovering the world outside in the narrow alleyways around their house. After being confined behind bars for so long, they can barely walk. They speak through grunts and moans. Their half-blind, religious father and blind mother are reluctant to set them free. They say they are scared their daughters will get lost, run away or become corrupted. More than one critic was haunted with the question: "Was Iran a country that imprisoned girls in their homes or a country that set them free to make films of international repute?"[8] Legendary French filmmaker Jean-Luc Godard expressed no such reservations, telling *Le Figaro:* "It's a wonderful film....And one can be hopeful that cinema is still alive."[9]

Samira's next film, *Blackboard,* won the prestigious Jury Prize at Cannes with a story of traveling literacy teachers trekking through the mountains of Kordestan. While male directors such as Abbas Kiarostami and Majid Majidi have often chosen to make lyrical idylls featuring children, as a way of evading the censors' glare, women directors have shown little such inclination. *Blackboard,* like *The Apple,* is based on a true story, and is a mixture of gritty realism and fantasy.

Iran's leading woman director, Rakhshan Bani-Etemad, began her career by making documentaries, and her films tackle stark social issues such as poverty and the problems of youth. One of her earlier works, *Narges,* tells the story of a manipulative female criminal involved in a love triangle with a ne'er-do-well thief and his virtuous bride. I watched the film sentence by sentence in my Persian lessons, fascinated by the unconventional portrayal of women and the rare glimpse of a seamy underworld. Some time later, when I met Bani-Etemad, she told me how she came to get permission for such a bleak subject. President Khatami had been Minister of Guidance, and directors were allowed to vet each other's scripts. "We called that period the golden time," she said. But even so, *Narges,* released in 1991, was a tricky subject. "Political conditions were so closed, it was not so easy. The main thing was that it highlighted love, which no film had done since the revolution. At that time, no film had been made about an ordinary love relationship." Afterwards, Khatami let her know indirectly that he was pleased that such a "dangerous" script had come out well.

Her next film, *Rusari-e Abi,* or "The Blue Headscarf," combines social realism with a sensitively told love story about a factory owner who falls in love with one of his farm workers. The romance is beautifully shot

---

8. Jasmin Darznik, *The Iranian,* March 1999; Kate Durbin, *Mirabella,* January 1999, "From Tehran With Love."
9. *Le Figaro,* 10 October 1998, quoted by *Iran News,* 2 June 2000.

alongside shocking scenes of poverty and drug abuse. In *Banu-ye Ordibehesht,* or the "May Lady," Bani-Etemad switches to a more middle-class setting for a wonderful film about a divorced woman making a documentary about the perfect mother. We see the heroine, Forough, cutting real interview material from real women such as Faezeh Hashemi and Shahla Lahiji, who discuss their idea of motherhood. Meanwhile she herself is struggling with the everyday grind of being a single mother with a teenage son. Moreover, she is having an affair with her boss, who never once appears in the film. "I'm one of the avant-garde," laughed Bani-Etemad. "The most I could do was to show the son putting a shawl around his mother's shoulders or putting out his mother's shoes....If I wanted to show the relationship between Dr. Rahbar [the boss] and Forough, it would not have got any further than sitting around a table talking about the sky. It would have been very boring." The film was notable for its groundbreaking treatment of young people's problems, where socializing is difficult and parties are danger zones. The young audience at the cinema near my house, where I saw the film, openly cheered when they saw images of a police raid on a birthday party. The mother goes to the police station to bail the teenager out. "This was the first time that a police raid was shown, and I showed the relationship between the mother and the law enforcement forces," said Bani-Etemad. "It was a first, but since then, many others have done it."

In Iranian films there is a kind of code that cinemagoers understand. When the son gives his mother a pair of earrings for her birthday, she tries them on and asks how they look. "Lovely," he replies, and the audience bursts out laughing, for they can see nothing but the mother's head cover— a shot of a woman's ear might attract the attention of the censor. The woman and her lover read poetry by Forough Farrokhzad to each other over the phone in what is a symbolic expression of freedom, also part of the code. The choice of the name Forough for the main character was not accidental. "Every filmmaker has to take a step to push filmmaking a bit further to make the environment a bit more open. Choosing the name Forough, or showing the relationship with her son, makes the atmosphere a bit more open for the rest," said Bani-Etemad.

Bani-Etemad has been invited to make films abroad but has always declined, feeling she is inextricably linked to Iran. She does not like to be labeled as a women's director but finds it interesting that although her movies are about Iran, women from other parts of the world tell her they can relate to them. The general reaction abroad, where many people she meets are surprised to find that a woman can work in Iran, let alone make movies, bothers her. "Because the image of Iranian women abroad is some-one who's just sitting at home and under a lot of pressure. And it's a fact that Iranian women are under a lot of pressure, but you can see that in spite of all this pressure they are still operating in every profession except as judges."

When I met Rakhshan Bani-Etemad she had just completed a new movie, *Under the Skin of the City.* She had had to wait fifteen years to feel the time was right to get permission to make it. The film is about a poor family, whose life never seems to get any better in spite of the promises of the revolution. The main character wants to leave to find a job abroad. She rewrote the script and set it during the 2000 parliamentary elections, when reformers took control of the parliament. "I think this time is a turning point in our history. This time for the people of Iran is a time of fear and hope. They don't know what to expect, what will happen." She invited me to a private screening but would not tell me how the plot ended so as not to spoil the suspense. For while Bani-Etemad is optimistic for the future of her country, that particular script ends in tragedy.

10

Making Your Own Freedom

Outside the Gandhi mall a small crowd had gathered. A young man was trying to maneuver a tiny, shiny Daewoo bubble car out of a tight corner. Two leggy girls, with scarves pushed back, looked on, and I realized the car belonged to them. Both heavily made up, one girl wore fancy, high-heeled flip-flops with daring mauve nail polish on her toes. The driver sawed to and fro, then, to his embarrassment, a group of youths came along and simply lifted the car out of the parking spot. The girls got in gracefully and drove off. They were going cruising, a favorite occupation of rich, young north Tehranis. Inside the mall is a gallery with a string of newly opened cafés. This is one of the few venues for young people to hang out. There are no bars, no discos, no dancing, few concerts, few plays—even a walk in the park is liable to be controlled by the Morals Police. But young people make their own fun, so that even going for a coffee can be trendy and exciting.

Social life in Iran has always been centered on family parties—birthdays, weddings, funerals, New Year's holidays and religious feast days. But there's still an urge to get out and about, to meet new people, to "go out" at night. Before arriving in Iran, I asked a diplomat's wife, "But what do you *do* all day?" You don't feel like jogging in a long raincoat and scarf, and even going out to a restaurant feels wrong when you have to keep your coat on. Moreover, following the conversation is a strain with your ears covered. If you go out with male friends or colleagues, there is always the possibility, however slight, that you might be arrested. Ever since the revolution, men and women, boys and girls not related by family or by marriage have been forbidden from meeting together, in public or in private. However, the laws on association are widely flouted, especially in the cities.

socializing

My friend Elaheh was a regular at the Gandhi shopping mall. We sat down and ordered a cappuccino, only the second one I had tasted in four years in Iran. Also on the menu were peanut butter coffee, and banana and butterscotch milkshakes, but Elaheh, in her early twenties, said she was on a diet. We looked around the tables, starting to fill up with teenagers and college students. Most were in single-sex groups, but some tables were mixed, and there was a buzz of excitement. This was a place to see and be seen. Elaheh told me she had been in this café a few weeks before when a policeman and a female official in a chador had marched in. They had gone straight up to a table where three boys and a girl were sitting and begun to question them. Elaheh and her friends did not wait to see if the young people were arrested but slid out of the back door surreptitiously. Outside they saw a minibus parked, ready to take groups away for a stiff reprimand or, in the worst-case scenario, a court appearance and lashes. "During the war, we wouldn't dare come to these places with a guy," she said. "You wouldn't see mixed tables like that with women and men barely related."

By around 7 P.M. the cafés were becoming crowded. I chose a table at random and we asked two young women if we could join them for coffee. Azadeh, twenty-three, was very pretty with long eyelashes, and Samira, twenty, was tall with silver highlights in a dark fringe. Dressed in black, they looked very chic while lingering over tea and sponge cake. Azadeh had just graduated with a degree in microbiology, and she told me she wanted to work abroad. "I don't want to live in Iran forever. I love Iran, but there are a lot of restrictions on young people." I asked her what she meant and what she did with her leisure time. "Honestly? I go driving around on the roads to meet boys and new people. I don't think this happens in other countries, but it happens here because of the limitations society puts on you." On most evenings, certain roads in north Tehran become clogged with bright young things driving round and round, "talent-spotting." Youths shout out their phone numbers to attractive girls or pass them their addresses on scraps of paper. Then it's left to the girls to take the initiative. "It's not necessarily fun," said Samira. "There is always a deep fear of being caught [by the police]. I've been stopped more than once for wearing makeup, but we usually manage to lose them; we speed off. I'd never like to think that I have got to live by other people's standards, like wearing a chador, so I try to resist it. This is the only resistance that I can show."

Samira and Azadeh, like most young Iranians, complained of the lack of opportunity to socialize outside their immediate families. "There's no good place in Iran to meet other people," said Azadeh. "When I went to university it was not a very good place for that—the atmosphere was very bad. There were different entrances for men and women, with three or four women sitting at the door criticizing your dress. Sometimes students get together and complain about the atmosphere and I've seen people in tears," she said. That year, an Iranian-made movie, *Born under Libra,* set a love story against just such an atmosphere, where a group of fanatical students had put pressure on the others to support even greater segregation.

Events for young people, such as pop concerts, were few and far between and left something to be desired, said Samira, who confessed to having dated a pop singer. "These pop concerts, these 'legal' pop concerts—we always get bothered at the door for what we're wearing. At pop concerts you get excited, but here you're not allowed to—you just sit there and if you do get excited there's usually a big fight or the Komiteh arrest you." Restaurants frequented by young people are often closed down, temporarily or permanently. One of the café owners told me he was worried about the increasing numbers of young people among his clientele. Before, when his bar was purely a haunt of intellectuals, there was little cause for concern.

Parents and young people told me many times they believed the restrictions were counterproductive, and these girls were no exception. "In my opinion these restrictions definitely have the opposite effect because young people can't get together in public so they meet at home," said Samira. "I think there's as much corruption—what they call *'fesad'*—happening in people's houses as there is in public places." Samira and Azadeh then launched into a tirade about double standards. They complained that their male friends did not want to get married to the girls they had been involved with. They both knew of girls who had needed to get their virginity surgically "fixed" before marrying.

Research done for the Leader's office in the early 1990s reportedly showed that far more students had boyfriends or girlfriends than had been the case before the revolution. One social scientist told me the survey of ten thousand students showed that around half of all girls questioned said they had a boyfriend, whereas in the 1970s the figure was a mere eight percent. "Girls and boys are too afraid to talk in the street, so boys generally encourage girls to come to their house to have a more secure area to talk," he said.

Pressure on young people to conform to traditional Islamic values comes not just from the state, but from families, who wish to control their children's movements through adolescence and beyond. Some want to keep their girls at home for reasons of religion, others want no distractions from the fierce competition at school, many fear brushes with the law. For some, the pressures at home become too much. Over the summer of 2000, a spate of news articles appeared about the problem of runaways. The Iranian news agency reported the opening by the mayor of Tehran of a new shelter for girls who had left home. It said that one such center, Reyhaneh House, had taken in 450 girls in its first year of work. Around half of them had been picked up wandering around railway stations and bus terminals. The mayor said such centers were urgently needed and called for runaways to be treated more sympathetically.[1] Azadeh said she believed she knew why many such girls left home. "A lot of these runaway girls have really strict fathers who force them to wear their hejab. They run away and they are basically homeless. A lot of them end up in boys' homes." Samira added: "We saw one just now—you can tell. She was here for hours and a lot of different men came up to her table before she went off with one."

run — away (handwritten note in left margin)

The girls, seated at a table with an optimum view of the entrance, were at pains to stress that they still managed to enjoy life. "Even though it does sound depressing, I've never regretted the fact that I'm a woman," said Samira. "I'd have liked to have been born somewhere else, but I'm not unhappy....Because we make our own freedom for ourselves, we do what we want." They said they often received invitations to wild parties, or "bad" parties, as they put it, but they rarely went. Large gatherings with loud music are most at risk from police raids, often as a result of a vindictive neighbor calling the authorities. Several young friends of mine, including Elaheh, seemed to lurch from one scrape to another without ever running into serious trouble. But another friend, Sousan, who turned up at the café later, told me of one particular party with tragic consequences.

Ali Reza wanted to celebrate his twenty-second birthday in style. He borrowed his sister's apartment on the eighteenth floor of a tower block in the western suburb of Shahrak-e Qods. The party was in full swing when, just before midnight, things started to go horribly wrong. The police arrived, tied up the guard downstairs so he could not alert the partygoers, then raided the flat. Girls scattered in all directions, reaching for their headscarves. In the confusion, three boys climbed over the balcony to the floor below. The police separated the boys from the girls and searched the apartment. They found no alcohol—there had only been one bottle, and it had already been disposed of. Then one girl appeared to have an epileptic fit. While everyone's attention was diverted, Ali Reza slipped out onto the balcony, followed by members of the police. It is not clear if he was trying to escape, but suddenly the young people realized he was no longer

---

1. *IRNA*, 17 September 2000.

there. He had fallen to his death from the eighteenth floor. The partygoers rushed downstairs and found his body on the pavement. Fighting broke out between the youngsters and the security forces in a near riot. Sousan ran to a nearby apartment in hysterics and called her mother.

In the next few days, the police arrested all those at the party plus the guard and the apartment block manager, an architect. They also arrested my friend Elaheh and other youngsters who had not even been present. In the hours of interrogation that followed, Sousan argued that she had been a close family friend who had known Ali Reza since childhood, but this cut no ice with the judge. "How is it that you go to his house now that he's grown up?" he said. "I don't allow my daughter even to visit the house of her married sister." Sousan was told she would be sentenced to twenty lashes suspended for five years, but after much argument this was commuted to a fine of two million rials. Her parents had to scratch around to raise the money, equivalent to about a month's salary for her father, a university professor.

While waiting outside the courtroom for one of the hearings, the apartment block manager died of a heart attack. The gruesome ramifications and the number of young people involved gave this case notoriety. Happening, as it did, not long before the presidential election of 1997, it became a focus for young people's discontent and demands for more personal freedom. Yet Sousan assured me she had other stories to tell—of being at an all-girls' birthday party broken up by eight law enforcement officers who came over the wall, or of how her sister was detained as part of a sweep on a café. Dozens of girls were arrested. Her mother asked the police if the youngsters had been sitting together. "No, but you know what they get up to" was the answer. It turned out that Sousan had also been present at the party in the street next to my house where the guests had been flogged. She had hid in the kitchen, and although a young conscript had seen her, he had let her escape.

The whole idea of parties and socializing before marriage is more prevalent in the upper and middle classes of north Tehran than in working-class or bazaar districts. "In the middle and higher classes, young people have more contact before marriage, but in lower or religious circles, this contact is very little," said Nahid Motiee, a lecturer in social sciences at Azad University. Another sociologist, Shahla Ezazi, of Allameh Tabatabaie University, highlighted the importance of phone relationships. "I'm the mother of a son and every day there are at least five or six girls who call him," she laughed.

For many young people, social life is confined to family parties, weddings and funerals, and even these are often segregated. I attended a women-only marriage party in the northern city of Tabriz where around two hundred guests had dressed up to enjoy tea, fruit and cakes in the afternoon in a public hall. One teenage girl put on an impromptu display of traditional dancing that to my mind enlivened the tedium. But when I began to film her with my camcorder, I realized that several well-dressed guests in the background were hiding their faces behind their handbags. They felt uncomfortable being recorded without being covered, and they asked me and another, Iranian, guest, who had had the same idea, to stop. I was surprised, as the bride and groom were educated—he was living abroad—and the guests were clearly well off. When the groom arrived to put in a twenty-minute appearance with his new bride, the same women dived under the table to grab their chadors out of plastic bags and cover up now that a male was present.

Funerals, too, have traditions that date back long before the revolution. When someone dies, it is the custom for family, friends and colleagues to visit the house to pay condolences. When the sister of a maid I knew well died in mysterious circumstances, I visited the house with my neighbor. The maid was distraught with grief, and for the first and last time I saw her in a chador. She clutched it around her for comfort as tears rolled down her cheeks. Female relatives sat with her and explained to me what had happened. They said it had been a tragic car accident. I was puzzled, as the maid herself had told me her sister had gone missing and had been sought by the police. Weeks afterwards, she told us her sister had been murdered by a gruesome serial killer known as the Night Bat of Tehran. The conventions of protecting the family honor made it inappropriate to tell the truth at such a time.

I once attended a mosque ceremony when my gynecologist friend, Shokrou Ghorbani, died. Women mourners were directed to an upstairs room that was entirely curtained off from the main ceremony. This would have been the case even before the revolution. We sat with our backs to the preacher, facing the family, which I found rather disconcerting. Tradition has it that this way the relatives can assess the quantity of tears shed by the various mourners, and vice versa. Some mourners stopped by for just a few minutes then left, but we stayed the course. Afterwards, the friend who was with me wondered if Dr. Ghorbani's sons, both of whom were living in the United States, were present. The only way we could find out was to ask outside, when the male mourners began to spill out onto the pavement. The answer, when it came, astounded me: "Nobody has told them yet" Iranians appear to believe that ignorance, in such cases, is bliss—and, of course, no one likes to be the bearer of bad news. One of my husband's colleagues returned home from a posting in China to be told that her grandmother had been dead for two years. After the burial, there are ceremonies at the mosque and elaborate gatherings after three days, one week, forty days and one year. In the later gatherings, the guests sit around the edge of the room and are served with a large meal or fruit and sweetmeats as they would be at New Year's parties.

There are times when young men and women are allowed to spend time together. During the stylized ritual of khastegari, or asking for the hand of someone in marriage, relatives or friends propose possible matches, and the courtship is then supervised by the family elders. In the vast majority of cases, the girl or boy is allowed to say yes or no to prospective partners. This period is crucial for young people, said Nahid Motiee. "In these 'negotiations,' they can see each other as normal people and not with hejab or official clothes, so these gatherings are important for socializing," she said. Increasingly, however, young people are marrying later. The limited opportunities for meeting people are a great source of frustration, said Motiee. "It's true that apart from khastegari there's no other leisure interest," she said. "People have their parties, they choose to have big parties and big family outings, and the community gets together and gets the news."

Picnics and visits to shrines are popular, especially on the thirteenth day of Persian New Year, or *Sizdeh Bedar,* when families load up with pots, pans and cooler boxes and head out into the countryside. They often drive off with a little pot of sprouts of wheat or lentils, known as *sabzeh, or* "greenery," balanced precariously on the car hood. The sabzeh has been growing for several weeks, on each family's *haft sin,* or "seven s" table, a display of seven goodies beginning with the letter "s" and other elements symbolizing rebirth and renewal. The little pot is then taken to the picnic spot and thrown into a river or creek. Each person makes a wish, hoping for good luck in the New Year. Single girls who want to find a husband tie a knot in the seedlings before they throw them into the water. Heaps of food, such as *baghali polow,* rice with fava beans and dill, are heated up over a campfire. This was one of my favorite times in Iran, with the weather miraculously picking up just in time for the annual picnic. It is considered bad luck to stay indoors on that day, so that city-dwellers with no opportunity to get out of town could be seen picnicking in parks and even in the middle of intersections.

For girls from traditional families, rules are rigidly enforced. Roya, the ward of my elderly gardener, Ali Agha, was a carefree child who occasionally came to play with my two young sons. A pretty little thing, with a gift for drawing, she would draw fashion sketches of ladies in floppy hats on

City girls out in the country. Young women visiting the
waterfall near Hamedan let their hair down a little.

Men and women on a family outing smoke the water pipe
side by side in a teahouse in central Tehran's City Park.

The Alborz Mountains north of Tehran are a magnet for courting couples seeking an escape from the beady eyes of the authorities.

A first time paraglider, wearing a maqna'eh under her helmet, receives last-minute advice.

Thomas and Sasha's blackboard. Roya was the daughter of the gardener's sister-in-law. He had taken her in when her mother died and her father was crippled in an accident. But since then his own wife had died, and after a while Ali Agha began to worry that it was not right for a young girl to be living under the same roof as his son. The son was some ten years older and not considered a relative under religious law; he could, technically, be married to her. But Ali Agha, although gruff and rather simple, was kindness itself, and he allowed Roya to stay. As she became a teenager, however, she became a handful. One day, my neighbor told me how Roya, now aged thirteen, had called her in tears. She had stayed out of the house till midnight, chatting to a boy on the street. When she returned, Ali Agha called the police and marched her off to take a virginity test. Fortunately, the test, carried out by a midwife, showed that nothing untoward had happened. The police were not interested, and Ali Agha threatened he would put her in an orphanage if she ever strayed again. Not long afterwards, he died, and Roya went to live with another relative.

In villages, the code of behavior is even stricter. In the award-winning movie *The Day I Became a Woman,* written by Mohsen Makhmalbaf and directed by his wife, Marzieh Meshkini, an eight-year-old girl's grandmother forbids her from playing with boys on the street on her ninth birthday as she is about to "become a woman." Set in a conservative community on the Persian Gulf, the film depicts the girl's final hours of freedom. While the little girl goes out in search of an ice cream to share with her playmate, her mother is sewing her a new chador, which she will now be expected to wear, marking her passage into puberty. When my maid Soghra's daughter, Nazanin, had her first period, she suddenly began to wear black and keep her coat on whenever my husband, Laurens, was in the house.

The Education Ministry's women's affairs adviser, Fatemeh Tondguyan, caused a stir when she blamed the lack of public sports and recreation facilities for women for rising rates of depression. "If seventy-three percent of our girls spend most of their time sleeping, or feeling drowsy, this is an alarm, and a warning sign. Because we have very few gyms, or sports centers for females, how do we expect Islamic society to keep Islamic values such as chastity or hejab intact?" she asked.[2] Her views proved controversial, and for a while, she gave no more interviews on the subject. "I didn't mean that depression is a kind of prevalent disease among female students," she told me some months later. "I was talking in a meeting of principals in Tehran city, and I wanted to make them aware of the changes which are being encountered in the world and I just wanted to

---

2. *Zanan,* November 1999.

make them pay more attention to the problem. What I said at that meeting was that statistics related to depression and suicide have been increasing and the rate is higher among females than males and that is because of the lack of cultural and sports facilities in the country and a discriminatory approach to females, which results in a kind of mental and spiritual damage." The ministry had established a new directorate of physical education for girls and was now allocating more resources for sports facilities.

Her comments coincided with a flurry of reports on female depression that appeared during a brief period of burgeoning press freedom. The head of the Center for Women's Participation, Zahra Shoja'i, described the results of a survey among women aged seventeen to twenty-two. Press reports in 1999 highlighted the situation in the conservative holy city of Qom, where young women were said to be more depressed than in Tehran. Mrs. Shoja'i reportedly laid the blame at the door of tough social and cultural restrictions and suppression of girls' interests.[3] A leading psychologist, Dr. Jafar Bolhar, said that women were three times more likely to be depressed than men. The greater the economic hardship, the bigger the risk of depression, he said.[4] He has also pointed out that the highest rate of suicides are to be found in the most traditional provinces, where arranged marriages are still forced on youngsters.[5] The debate continued the following year, when the authorities suggested for the first time that schoolgirls should be allowed to wear light-colored school uniforms, rather than the ubiquitous navy blue, bottle green and black. A criminologist even went so far as to suggest that black was a health risk and could contribute to depression, *Iran Daily* reported.[6] He advised a bright-colored scarf and coat.

At my aerobics class I was always struck by the contrast of the racks of black coats in the changing rooms and the vivid Lycra outfits in the gym. This was a private class in a well-heeled part of the city, yet several regulars turned up in chadors. The entrance to the club was concealed by a series of curtains to keep out prying eyes. Inside, however, you could see sexy sportswear, makeup and toes adorned with scarlet and silver nail polish. During the summer months, the class was taught by Soraya, the wife of a surgeon. In a roomful of a hundred women all moving as one, Soraya stood out for her sheer wild vitality. Her mop of dark, curly hair flying all over, she would whoop for joy while the rest of us grimaced and flagged. She seemed to be always there. In fact, she told me, she exercised about

women & depression

---

3. *Reuters*, 21 November 1999.
4. *Peyam-e Hajar*, 16 November 1999.
5. *ANSA*, 18 May 1999.
6. *AFP*, 25 September 2000.

fifteen hours a week. "Exercise for me is something which fills me up inside," she said. "It's not just for filling my time." Soraya started up her own exercise class at the age of seventeen, holding it in a sports club that was still under construction. She was doing postgraduate work in psychology when the revolution intervened. "I'd have made a good doctor, if someone had guided me, helped me in my career," she said. "Unfortunately the revolution changed my life, and now I feel that my life is very, very useless." Now she was concentrating on looking after her children, and charity work.

Mostly, however, the class was taught by a Danish woman married to an Iranian. Hanne Thomsen first came to Iran in 1962, and in the early days, she taught swimming. "Most of the village women had never seen a swimming pool before; they'd never done sports. When they showed up for the first classes, they didn't know what to wear; some of them had clothes on and a scarf." She had to ask the male lifeguard to leave. When the aerobics craze reached Iran in the 1980s, Hanne set up her class at a gym in the posh Farmaniyeh part of the city. The 58-year-old goes to Denmark every summer and takes advanced classes to keep up to date. She also updates her music collection, which includes techno, salsa and all the latest "dance" numbers, none of which would generally be heard in public. "Music is very important when you work out," she said. "Music like this is forbidden, and in the past they've come here and closed the place down for two or three weeks because we're not allowed to use this music. We're only supposed to use instrumental music," said Hanne. "But I'm very stubborn, and I just carry on."

Not all sports require facilities, and not all pastimes are organized. On one Friday morning on the Shahran Hills, overlooking a hazy, polluted Tehran, walkers were already heading up the bare, rocky mountainside. Couples, families and single figures strode out up craggy ravines in search of fresh air and a spectacular view. I passed one woman with her face totally swathed in a scarf, revealing nothing but a pair of designer sunglasses. This was not to protect her modesty, but to protect her skin against the incredible dryness and dust of the semidesert climate. I had worried that my coat was too short, but then I realized that some women were wearing daringly ordinary, bulky anoraks. Hiking is one of the few sports that can be enjoyed by all—men, women, rich and poor alike. It's a popular pastime that requires only a good pair of shoes and a lift to the edge of the mountains.

Fatemeh Dehqanpur, however, was perched on the edge of a cliff with another sport in mind. She's one of an exclusive band of paragliding enthusiasts who spend their free time throwing themselves off precipices with nothing but a billowing parachute to support them. Dressed in a black hood, regulation black coat and stout shoes, she wore a harness and a motorcycle-type crash helmet on top. As I stood at the bottom, a crowd of beginners watched in admiration as Fatemeh glided effortlessly down the hillside, controlling the descent with slight movements of her body. "It's flying," said one. "It's freedom," said another. "Men and women are both interested in this sport in Iran, but the women are more passionate about it," said Fatemeh. "The only difference is that women have more responsibilities such as housework, looking after children, etcetera, so maybe they have less time for it," she said. We were interrupted as she took a call on her mobile phone, then she continued: "Anyone taking up this sport will learn to rely on themselves because when you're up there, you are on your own."

Fatemeh's niece, Linda, is an old hand at the sport, even though she's only seventeen. "It's something you can't imagine, when you see that you are actually flying. That feeling of fear is always there, but it's mixed with excitement," she said. "It's all in men's heads, that we are restricted to certain kinds of sport," she continued. "Us women paragliders—especially wearing these clothes, like the manteau—we want to prove we can still do the same exercise that they are doing and we want this idea that we can't do certain sports to vanish from their heads." Her big bag of imported equipment was embroidered with the manufacturers' slogan: "Wings of Change."

Not far away, on the dusty plain south of the city, a women's show-jumping competition was under way. Here the women wore long jackets and velvet riding caps on top of black hoods. A succession of well-groomed young women careered round the ring, clearing high fences on big powerful horses. Several looked distinctly out of control. Nahid, one of the competitors, finished her round beaming, with a time of thirty-two seconds, putting her into the lead. She came and sat next to me, and we watched the rest of the competition. Minutes later, a nine-year-old boy on a neat little pony glided calmly around the course and beat her time to win the main trophy. I was a little puzzled about how he could have entered the women's competition, but Nahid explained it was the "novice ladies and under nines."

When I started riding again at a club outside of Tehran, the riding school was at first unwilling to allow us to form a mixed group. Any contravention of the laws prohibiting free association of men and women could, in theory, lead to the whole school being closed down. "It's dangerous," said the secretary, only half-joking. The management relented,

A woman paraglider soars over the Shahran Hills, just outside of Tehran.

Regulation gear for show-jumping competitions.

however, when they discovered that the single male in our group was a middle-aged ambassador. Perhaps this placed him above reproach, or, more likely, they thought a diplomatic clientele would be good for the club's reputation. In fact, the ambassador never had the time to come to the lessons, so it turned out to be an all-female group. The fact that we had a male instructor did not seem to bother anyone, nor did the fact that my short legs meant that, practically every time, he had to manhandle me onto my horse with a leg up.

Similarly with skiing, in Shemshak and Dizin, only an hour's drive away from the smog of the capital, male instructors could be seen guiding their female pupils down the mountainside with an unmistakably hands-on approach. In theory there was an all-female ski school, but in practice there were never enough women instructors to go around. In theory the ski lifts were segregated, but in practice a beginner like myself had to be physically lifted on to the *poma* button and hauled to my feet by a tanned male instructor when I fell off halfway up. After a while, I realized that only a fraction of the day-trippers sunning themselves in deck chairs halfway up the mountain were actually skiing. Most, especially young people, came to socialize in glitzy outfits and mirror shades. Every now and then there would be a clampdown on women in *bad hejab*, but the girls would argue that it was sunscreen, not makeup that they were wearing, anti-ultraviolet lip salve, not violently colored lipstick. However, politics was never very far from the ski slopes. The entrance to the slopes was emblazoned with a slogan from the Leader, urging the masses to develop a healthy body and a healthy mind. But an instructor might point out the Shah's private chalet complex and helicopter landing pad, recalling, with nostalgia, the old days. For while skiing was clearly the province of the middle and upper classes from north Tehran, it provided much-needed income for the surrounding villages.

While village women have few facilities and simply no time for leisure, city dwellers also seem to regard sport as a luxury. A special sports edition of *Zanan* magazine reported that seventy-nine percent of women surveyed took no part in athletic activities because they could not afford the time. More than half believed that housework was a kind of exercise. In an editorial, the magazine's editor, Shahla Sherkat, commented dryly on the decision to allow a woman to carry the Iranian team's flag at the 1996 Atlanta Olympics—she was the only Iranian female competitor: "On the one hand, a woman athlete was challenging the propaganda about the state of women in Iran. On the other hand, it showed up the weak presence of Iranian women in the sporting domain." The magazine noted that the budget devoted to women's sports was one-tenth that allocated to men.[7]

---

7. *Zanan* 30 October 1996.

The leading campaigner for women's sports is the ubiquitous Faezeh Hashemi. She studied sports at college, and worked as a physical education teacher and sports club manager for several years before entering politics. "I don't see sports just as sports," she told me. "I think sports have a great influence on personality and women's roles. For example, a sportswoman or sportsman has got more confidence and self esteem." As vice president of the Iranian Olympic Committee, she championed women's right to compete abroad. Hejab, however, strictly limits the sports in which Iranian women can compete. "First we tried to find how we could expand the possibilities for doing sports with hejab," she said. "We started with shooting, and now we have increased to thirteen, including rowing, riding, ski, chess, karate, archery and sports for handicapped people. Then for those kind of sports which you can't do in hejab, like volleyball, swimming, etcetera, we have created an Islamic atmosphere, and Islamic courts, so that more people can participate in this activity."

For Islamic courts, read single sex and heavily screened. Segregation is, of course, strictly enforced for men's sports, too. During my time in Iran, there was much debate over whether women should be able to play soccer, to which the answer seemed to be yes, so long as there were no men in the stadium. My Italian friend Nadia Pizzuti was the only woman journalist who managed to talk her way in to watch Iran play Australia in a 1998 World Cup qualifying match in front of 120,000 male fans. Guards brought her tea and sweets during the match but reminded her to cover her hair. With the success of the Iranian national team in Melbourne, girls danced in the street, even on the roofs of cars, in unprecedented victory celebrations. I was stuck in traffic for six hours, that night, as fans clogged every street of the capital, but it was difficult to feel angry amid the euphoria. The Khatami presidency reveled in a feel-good factor that boosted national pride. Pressure mounted for women to be able to watch their soccer stars in the flesh, not just on television. On the triumphant team's return, a crowd of five thousand delirious female fans literally pushed their way into the massive Azadi stadium to welcome back their heroes.

Nadia once played volleyball against a team captained by Faezeh Hashemi and recalls that the press team was trounced unceremoniously. Faezeh told me that volleyball was her favorite sport, although she also swam and played table tennis at home. But in traditional circles there was, and still is, resistance to the idea of women playing sports in public. "Religious families were not sending their daughters to sports clubs before the revolution," she said. "And even afterwards, when they could send their girls there [because they were segregated] they didn't have a very good impression of them. So when I joined a club, I went to break the ice, to say that it's not so bad, that I'm from a religious family and I go…"

Faezeh has a knack for attracting controversy, and one of her better-known exploits was supporting women cyclists who wanted to be able to ride freely along the paths of Chitgar Park on the western edge of Tehran. However, the cyclists' attempts were broken up by fanatics. When my friend Catherine Squire visited the park some years later, she hired bikes for herself and her family but was told that women and girls were only allowed to ride in a velodrome concealed behind high walls. Husbands and sons were free to pedal through the park along leafy purpose-built cycleways. Catherine had to run off after her six-year-old son, who had zoomed off with his pal, and she was duly chased by the guards, who flapped at her to get back into the corral.

The idea of women's legs straddling a saddle, whether on a bicycle or on a horse, seems to be particularly offensive to Islamic sensibilities. In 1999, the district governor of the Caspian Sea resort of Ramsar reportedly outlawed women cyclists altogether, saying, "Women cyclists cannot protect their chastity even if they are fully covered, so they should avoid this altogether or they will be dealt with."[8] Months later, the extreme right-wing weekly *Jebheh* carried a fascinating feature article which suggested that decadent activities were persisting.[9] "Girls with heavy make-up, tight blouses and trousers (!) [their emphasis] are riding bicycles together with their boyfriends….Somewhere else, you see girls and women riding rented horses, and in order to mount the animals, they have entirely unbuttoned their gowns! Which reminds you of a saying by Imam Sadegh about the signs of the apocalypse: 'These women wear the clothes of pagans, their appearance is like that of tyrants, they mount saddles and do not abide by their husbands, and do not confine themselves to their husband's house.'" The article's author, Soheil Karimi, laments the passing of the days when Ramsar was renowned for "martyr-breeding." He tries to escape such "satanic scenes" by going for a walk on the beach. But even there, he is shocked to see "naked" youngsters swimming, evidence of beer drinking and, not least, a boy cuddling a dog. He quotes the Ramsar Friday prayer leader as giving a warning that the moral security of the country is endangered.

The Caspian Sea is a good place to go to see the curious spectacle of women swimming in headscarves, coats and/or chadors. The main problem on public beaches is how to change, once you emerge from the water,

---

8. *Keyhan,* quoted by *Reuters,* 2 May 1999.
9. *Jebheh,* 25 April 2000, translated and carried on the *Payvand* website.

dripping and weighed down by sodden clothes. I once stayed at a privately run Armenian resort, where, in theory, swimming was allowed. In practice, we were asked to be discreet, and wear shorts and T-shirts rather than bathing suits. But it never tempted me, as the sea was generally gray and the beaches disappointing. Lake Orumiych, in the northwestern corner of the country near the border with Turkey, was another matter, however. The huge salt lake is a dazzling, light turquoise blue surrounded by spectacular scenery. I was traveling with my Iranian friends, Pari and Bijan, and we were planning to visit their family. After a long, dusty drive, we checked into a brand new hotel on the shores of the lake. We had heard there was a pool, so we made plans to take the children swimming. Unfortunately, the receptionist told us, the pool was open to men only until three o'clock. At three we went to the pool, only to be told that there had been a misunderstanding, it was open for men until six. Angrily, we decided to take the kids to the women's beach and we piled into the car. It was a short trip, but it was not at all clear where exactly the beach was, as it was hidden behind a railway line. My husband Laurens dropped us off, but Pari and I ended up walking, loaded down with picnic, windbreak and four children, down in the blazing sun.

When we got there, paid the man sitting at a dirty curtain and entered the "family" section, we realized we had made a big mistake. It was a Friday, the Muslim holy day, and the resort was crowded with day-trippers. A stretch of shingle beach no more than five hundred yards long was jam-packed with white, flabby bodies. My three-year-old's first words as we picked our way through the crowds were "Mommy, I smell pooh." The entrance was next to the toilet block and we appeared to be crossing rivulets of raw sewage. The scene on the beach was like Michelangelo's vision of hell. Fat women in their underwear were covering their entire bodies with handfuls of gray mud or frantically trying to scrub themselves clean. Only later did I discover that the mud is famous for its health-giving properties. The foul smell was probably due to the high sulfur content. Even the children did not want to stay, so we turned on our heels and fled. But as we got to the entrance we saw Laurens and the Landcruiser pulling away into the distance. Pari tried to hail a taxi. Holding her sixteen-month-old daughter in her arms, and dressed in a light coat and a turquoise scarf, she stood out among the locals, all clad in black. To my utter amazement, someone among the sullen crowd of onlookers threw a stone at her. We found a taxi and returned to the hotel in a state of shock.

The following day, we had practically the opposite experience. Bijan's family welcomed us with open arms, fed us with fabulous regional dishes, then took us to another part of the lake. First we made a little tour of some Armenian villages where we saw several women outside, on the street, with their heads uncovered. One woman showed us around a church and explained that, by and large, the local authorities in this area allowed the Christian communities to maintain their own traditions.

Then we headed for another beach on the western side of the lake. It was miles from anywhere, near a rocky outcrop that formed a spectacularly beautiful natural bay. A handful of other bathers were swimming. The men and children of our party stripped down and plunged in. The high salt content of the lake makes it practically impossible to sink, and the kids found this captivating. Before long, however, they were in tears, as they swallowed mouthfuls of brine, or even worse, rubbed their eyes. Bijan, who swam in the lake as a child, had come prepared. He handed them each two peeled cucumbers. They stuck one in each eye and it instantly took away the sting. Our husbands and friends urged us to join them. The place was so secluded, there was no risk, they said. But with the slightly sulfurous odor of the lake lingering in our nostrils, reminding us of the previous day's experience, Pari and I declined, and stayed on the shore.

11

The Nomad's Life and Journey's End

On the dusty road north of Shiraz a sudden flash of kingfisher blue lit up the landscape. "Nomads!" someone cried. A woman in vivid tribal dress was riding on a donkey alongside a flock of sheep and goats. As we traveled on through the Zagros Mountains, I counted forty-two herds in the space of two hours. These were Qashqa'i nomads migrating to summer pastures. The men go on ahead with the herds, often setting off before dawn to avoid the heat. The women and children follow with pack animals, laden with tents, tentpoles, kilims and mattresses. Some ride, others walk, making sure the animals don't trample crops by the roadside or grab mouthfuls of fodder as they pass. Wealthier groups are accompanied by a few camels. Small children are strapped to the back of donkeys. The gawky legs of a baby donkey were straddled over the saddle in front of one woman. Another girl held a young sheep, perhaps it was sick, in front of her.

Their progress is steady but fraught with difficulty. I saw three dead sheepdogs on the road and there must have been other casualties. Some families hire a truck to carry the heaviest gear, others have acquired jeeps or pickups. "We're Kashkuli Qashqa'is on our way from Gachsaran. It was getting so hot down there," one woman told me from the cab of a truck. She held a one-year-old baby in her lap, and a four-year-old boy peered out curiously. She had the distinctive long face and high cheekbones of her tribe, with Central Asian features rather than classical Persian features. The family had stopped to drink water from a spring. Behind them in the open truck were a handful of goats and chickens in front of piles and piles of bedding, pots, pans and tent poles. Every now and then we passed a tent encampment. The dark brown tents woven from goats' hair are pitched low with a ridge in the winter, when the mountains are covered in snow, and high and box-like in the summer, when the heat becomes overpowering. A low reed screen serves for privacy. Sometimes the nomads erect battered canvas tents if they are just staying for a night or making repairs to the traditional material. The women can be seen cooking outside over a campfire and looking after the livestock.[1]

The trip to Boyer Ahmad and Kohkiloyeh, the heartland of the Zagros tribes, was something special right from the start. The province is barely mentioned in the handful of Western guidebooks that cover Iran, and with such an unpronounceable name, even asking for information about the region was difficult. I jumped at the chance of accompanying members of an Iranian NGO involved in a health and development project on a visit to some of the remotest villages. We arrived in the southern city of Shiraz at 7 A.M. and breakfasted with the aunt of one of the group. Mrs. Hekmat, aged eighty, served us homemade cheese, honey and a preserve she had made from *narenj*, or bitter oranges, growing in her garden. There was flat *lavash* bread, watermelon, tomatoes and cucumbers. She bustled around her kitchen, fretting that we had not brought the driver in. Then, someone asked half-jokingly, "Why don't you come with us on the trip too, *Khanum?*" She paused, put her head to one side, and then said "When are you going?" We planned to leave in half an hour. "All right, I'll get my things," she said. Five minutes later, she came back into the kitchen with a large supermarket carrier bag stuffed with clothes. "I'm ready," she said.

The craggy Zagros Mountains form an impenetrable series of high ridges running alongside the Persian Gulf. The narrow river valley bottoms are often fertile, and used to grow wheat, barley and the famous Shiraz grape. But the uplands are bare and rocky, dotted with stunted oak trees. We headed first for the provincial capital, Yasuj. Estimates for how many nomads live in Iran vary from 1.5 million to 2.5 million. To be counted as nomads in the census figures you have to migrate, be dependent on livestock and recognize the authority of a tribal chief.[2] The nomads move from pasture to pasture, scratching a living from their animals, dairy products and the striking, woven textiles produced by women. There are dozens of different tribes and sub-tribes, including Qashqa'is, Bakhtiaris and Lurs, with a wide variety of different backgrounds. The Qashqa'is, for example, speak a Turkish-based language and have their own traditional political grouping. The tribes have repeatedly challenged the authority

---

1. See Beck, *Nomad*.
2. I am indebted to Dr. Jeremy Swift, of Sussex University, for introducing me to the subject.

of central government in the past and at times have been accused of siding with foreign powers, including Britain.

Contacts with the authorities seemed different, here. After calling in at the Health Ministry offices, our first meeting with officials was at a local spot, complete with waterfalls and a picnic site. Then we set off for the small Qashqa'i village of Amirabad, where the population had only recently settled. We drove along a high river valley. On our left was a prosperous strip of land farmed by Lurs who had lived there for years. On the right was a rocky mountainside with nothing but large thistles and sparse grass. On this side, various Qashqa'i families had settled, in small, box-like stone houses. "Look how the houses are built on the same layout as the tents," said Catherine Razavi, of the Cenesta NGO. There was a central porch and a room on either side, and many had the traditional reed screens around them. One or two were still only half-finished, and a waist-high stone wall had been covered with a woven tent. On the group's previous visit, a separate tent had been erected for a wedding.

Here and there, the red, white and green Iranian flag was flying on a yellowish brick-built building, signaling a school or health center. Successive governments have tried to settle the troublesome tribes by force. Nowadays, they are given an offer that's hard to refuse, as British anthropologist Jeremy Swift had told me: "They've gone back into 'Let's settle them' mode," he said. "Everybody who wants will receive agricultural land, a house built for them, etcetera." Stories abound, however, about the nomads having it both ways. Rather than give up their flocks, brothers from the same family will take houses in both the summer and winter pastures, for example, and while part of the community settles, another part continues to migrate. This was the case in Amirabad, where houses were waiting, empty, for other villagers to arrive.

We were invited into a villager's house to receive a report on how the Cenesta project was going. Dressed in long, green floral skirts, with a full-length turquoise pinafore over the top, a royal-blue shawl and a turquoise bandanna, Hatun Hekmatiyanzadeh first offered us cold spring water in metal beakers, then tea. She was expecting the rest of her family to arrive in around ten days' time. She had small children with her, but her older daughters were away at school in the nearby town of Yasuj. During the school year they lived with their uncle, as there was no secondary school in the village. Hatun herself had managed two years at school; the rest of her lessons had been in the white tent-schools set up in the 1960s to follow nomadic communities. She had lived in a house for around five years but still dreamed of her old lifestyle.

missing
traditional
way
of
life

"I miss the old life a lot," she said. "It was wonderful. You know, it's funny, now I have a better life, electricity and everything, but we lost something, too. Now it's more stressful—I'm worried about how to pay my electricity bill. But at that time, my life just carried on." We sat on the floor in the traditional Iranian way. The room was empty of furniture, with bare walls and factory-made carpets. At one end, cotton mattresses were neatly folded up for the night. We leaned against cylindrical cushions covered in gaudy velvet with a brightly embroidered panel in the middle. Hatun talked easily and openly, and was just getting into her stride, when there was a noise outside. A donkey had got among the chickens, was my first thought. But our hostess jumped to her feet. "Somebody's died." We peered out of the small window and saw women running in from the fields, wailing in a high-pitched way. Before I realized what was happening, Hatun ran outside. The dead man was her ninety-year-old father. She ran to find one particular shawl, then walked swiftly into the fields, ahead of the other women. Outside, we found her niece, clutching a gold lace wrap over a bright pink dress. She was waiting for her father to come out of the house next door. He had been entertaining the men of the party, and when the news broke, he insisted that they finish their tea.

The dead man was lying in a meadow by the river. He had been repairing a pump in a field next to a poplar grove. A ministry official tried mouth-to-mouth resuscitation, but it was no use. A small crowd gathered around the body, the men crying, the women keening. There was a strong scent of wild herbs, and occasionally a woman would uproot a handful of aromatic plants and lay them under the old man's head. There was some discussion about whether the coroner would have to be informed or whether they could proceed straight away with the funeral. Minutes later, some of the men cut down a few poplar saplings and strapped together a rough frame to carry the body away. This was then loaded onto the back of a small pickup truck. Hatun climbed in, too, and the dead man was taken back to the village. The rest of the community followed on foot. Cenesta could do no more work and left the villagers to their grief. "*Une belle mort,*" remarked Catherine, who's half-French. We took Hatun's husband with us in the minibus, stopping every time he saw a farmer in the field or a woman outside a house. He had to notify the clan of the death.

That night we visited a much more prosperous village, Servak, on the hillside outside Yasuj. There we drank tea with the Askeri family, sitting on their terrace on hand-woven carpets laid down on our arrival by the daughters of the house. Their parents were away with the flocks, higher up the mountain. They offered us local delicacies and the sweetest watermelon I have ever tasted. Dried curds, made from ewes' milk and flavored with mountain herbs, tasted not unlike Parmesan cheese. It lasts up to a year and can be reconstituted to make the sauce for *Kashk-e Bademjun,* or eggplant with curds. Iranians regard this as a special treat, but with its animal-like smell and slimy texture, it's not one I have ever been able to appreciate. Catherine told me the protein content of kashk was exceptionally high. Assessing nutrition for the UNICEF-sponsored project was made difficult by the great variations in local diet, she said. The girls brought out a bowl of green vegetables, which looked like elongated, juicy gooseberries but tasted unmistakably of peas. "The shepherds in this area carry a bag full of these instead of a water-bottle and chew one when they get thirsty," she said. Even the representative from the women's department of the Ministry of Agriculture in Yasuj, who was with us, did not know exactly what they were. "Mountain plants," she said.

The girls, one of whom was training to be an accountant, discussed the cost of the medicinal herb fumitory on the Tehran market and whether they could make a viable business from growing herbs. This family grew its own vegetables and had retained all the traditional skills of the region. One sister showed me how she spun wool from their own sheep using a small metal spindle with prongs. She had worked on the carpet we were sitting on. Another proudly showed off the woolen kilims her mother had woven to cover up the bedding, stashed away for the night. They were gaily decorated with tassels and fringes.

A village woman has a host of demands on her time. At a seminar for villagers conducted by Cenesta near Mount Damavand, east of Tehran, female participants, when asked to define their role, listed twenty-four tasks usually carried out by women.[3] Male participants at the same session listed twenty-nine jobs for themselves and up to thirty-five for women. Women felt their jobs as included raising the children, milking the cows, washing and feeding animals, snow removal, planting potatoes, diagnosing sick children and what was described as "being present in society." Men added that women should manage the household, make the home comfortable, provide for their daughters' trousseaus, take food to the men in the fields and establish a family based on compassion and friendship. Their list had a more flowery tone: "Women are the lights of any house," for example.

The seminar was run in conjunction with the Ministry of Jihad as part of a UN-sponsored pilot project to encourage what Cenesta called "participatory decision-making." *Jihad,* in this case, meant a revolutionary

---

3. Leila Pesaran, who helped organize the seminar, kindly lent me her notes of the proceedings.

*Qashqa'i tribeswomen in bright costumes trek to summer
pastures north of Shiraz on the annual spring migration.*

*Wealthier Qashqa'i nomad families now hire trucks
to transport heavy tents, women and children.*

*The author pictured in the remote Boyer Ahmad and Kohkiloyeh
mountains, home to the Qashqa'i and Lur tribes.*

*Lur tribeswomen in traditional dress sport orange hennaed hair and
henna tattoos. These two were invited in to the village meeting
but preferred to sit outside and smoke a water pipe.*

campaign to improve village life rather than the Holy War that Westerners might imagine. The list of "women's issues" pinned up on the wall began with "No exercise facilities" and ended, not surprisingly, with "Too many things expected of women." The men were noisier during discussion, but they listened respectfully whenever a woman made a contribution. During a tea break, the women told me they raised problems that men wouldn't appreciate, such as "problems in the family, carpet-weaving and embroidery." I asked one woman with a long, sallow face how she had been chosen to come. "They had a big meeting in the village, and I think they chose me because I'm used to getting out of the house and meeting people," she said. "I go to Koran classes and things like that." I realized that Koran classes and pilgrimages were an important opportunity for girls to broaden their horizons. "Every year we go on a pilgrimage to Mashhad or Qom. My Dad lets us because we have family there." Others said they attended *rowzeh,* all-women prayer meetings led by a mullah or one of the women themselves.

On the second day of the Boyer Ahmad trip, we got up at five to go to another village, four hours' drive away. There we were hoping to see village decision-making in action. We drove over ridge after ridge, then along fertile river bottoms as we approached the coastal plain. There were few tractors or other signs of mechanization. These river valleys were formerly plagued with malaria, and the population is sparse. Men and women worked side by side in the occasional rice paddies, but there were far fewer women than I had seen on my trip to the north, where rice cultivation is virtually an all-female occupation. I was curious to know why this was. I asked Mrs. Azar Shoja'i, a Ministry of Agriculture adviser who was accompanying us. "It's not very well thought of here, to have women working shoulder to shoulder with men," she said. "The more devout they are, the less likely they are to want their daughters working outside the house." Some of the girls she taught worked in the fields to earn their own dowry, she said. Mrs. Shoja'i also commented that in this province, second marriages were more frequent than in other parts of the country. "When a man gets a certain amount of money, he takes another wife," she said, disapprovingly.

We left Mrs. Hekmat in the town of Deh Dasht at the house of a Lur tribal chief, thinking the journey that day might be too much for her. Tribal chiefs often live in towns nowadays, but they continue to command respect from members of the clan.[4] Mr. Taheri, a colorful character, had a shock of gray hair and strong features. It was said that he had two wives, but when I asked him as tactfully as I could, he carefully evaded the question

4. Shahshahani, *The Four Seasons of the Sun.*

and implied that his first wife had died. Local people, however, pointed out the apartment next door where the co-wife was said to live. Moreover, Mrs. Hekmat reported afterwards that she had been entertained in our absence by his first wife, who had boasted that *her* children had been much more successful than those of the second marriage. Indeed, Mr. Taheri proudly showed me a delightful collection of drawings and poems about nomadic life published by a daughter now living in Tehran.

The road wound up and up into the mountains, getting steadily worse. Here and there, farmers with sickles were harvesting straggly wheat growing on the hillside. At the village of Qal'eh Dokhtar, or "Girl's Castle," we had to abandon the minibus for four-wheel-drive vehicles. Sure enough, there was a ruined castle, overlooking a most spectacular river valley. Mr. Taheri, who was accompanying us, said the name probably originated in the worship of the pre-Islamic goddess, Anahita, revered as the source of all waters. There were many Zoroastrian remains in the area. After bumping up a track paved with boulders, we came to the hamlet of Baraftab. It was perched on a rocky hillside on top of a steep cliff with a stunning view of the turquoise River Marun below. There, the villagers (Lurs who settled twenty years or so ago) had been taking part in a exercise aimed at developing civil society. The idea was that the local people get together to identify and analyze their own particular problems instead of having grandiose development projects thrust upon them. One man, in this case a farmer named Ali Gholam Tandpur, had been chosen to present the villagers' findings. We were shown into the house of the schoolteacher, who was married to the village health volunteer, or behvarz. Theirs was the only building with a color television and air conditioning. We sat down on the floor and waited as the men of the village arrived for the meeting. One or two were wearing a traditional felt skullcap. Several of them had film-star good looks. An elderly woman in Lur costume with bright-colored skirts, a black headdress and bright orange hennaed hair put her head inside the door. The men respectfully invited her in, but she declined, and went to sit outside to smoke a water pipe.

Mr. Tandpur got out big rolls of paper on which the villagers had drawn up their plans. On one they had made a map, marking every house, water source and electricity line. On another was a list of problems, and on another, a list putting them in order of priority. Possible projects proposed to improve the standard of living included a public bath, or *hammam,* a sports field, a library, classes in animal husbandry, carpet-making and dress-making. But it seemed that the main problem of the village was poverty and the poor water supply. The best way the villagers could think to improve their situation was to pump up more water from the river below.

The meeting went on for several hours, so I went for a wander in the village. There were many women around, doing household chores and sitting outside their small stone houses. They were all in colorful traditional dress, with the exception of the health worker, who wore a beige coat and hood, the Islamic uniform of government office workers. Each time I went past a house, someone would try to usher me inside. But when I tried to talk to them in basic Persian, they laughed and trilled: "*Na, Na Lurrri.*" Many of the older women only spoke Lur. One woman took me to her vegetable patch, and showed me some drooping onions and green herbs. She said she'd been without water for ten days; others said they only had supplies two days out of three. Next to her tiny garden, however, was a healthy looking willow and some small fig trees. Two Women from the ministry gave her advice on what would thrive better. Most families grew only a few cucumbers and tomatoes, and the officials were trying to persuade them to plant a greater variety of vegetables to improve their diet. They called an impromptu meeting of the women, again held on a carpet on the ground outside a house, and agreed to help them start up gardening classes. Back in the teacher's house, the meeting was coming to a close. The Cenesta people were delighted with the work the villagers had done. I looked at the signatures on the final plans. Out of around twenty-five names, almost half of the signatures were the pink thumbprints of people who could not write. I asked how many of the names were women's. There was a pause, then Mr. Tandpur confessed that none of the women had taken part in the exercise: "It was in my mind to do it with the women as well, but I forgot," he said.

We drove back to Yasuj late that night, to get back for a meeting at the provincial governor's office in the morning. Most of us got about three hours' sleep, but when I asked Mrs. Shoja'i if she had slept well, she answered that she had not gone to bed, as she had had to prepare that day's lunch for her three children. The session was chaired by the deputy governor for social affairs, a clergyman named Mir Mohammadi. His black turban marked him out as a *seyyed,* or descendant of the Prophet, and his smiling, easy manner put him in the same mold as President Khatami. Mr. Tandpur gave a confident presentation. With his flip charts and maps he looked more like a PR man than a farmer, as the officials listened intently. Then, the regional water expert was asked to comment. I watched to see his reaction. He kept consulting a map in front of him. A good sign, I thought. But then I saw that Mr. Tandpur looked more nervous now than he had done at the time of his presentation. "What's going on?" I asked an Iranian-Canadian scientist sitting next to me. "He says there's a project to build a dam and that it's possible this village may be totally under water. They may have to relocate them," he said. "It's going to be one of the biggest dams in the region, and the first phase is already completed."

I tried to take this in, amazed that no one had raised their voice, no one had launched into recriminations. Mr. Tandpur later admitted he wanted the ground to swallow him up. "I nearly collapsed when I heard the news about the dam," he told Catherine later. "All I could think of was, 'What am I going to tell them when I get back to the village? I'm a dead man.'" I was not all that surprised that the villagers had not known about the project, but what about all the other officials we had met? But the discussions continued with utmost politeness. The officials were clearly impressed by the exercise, and they proposed the formation of a committee to find a short-term solution to the village's water problems. Mr. Tandpur was then introduced to the governor, who promised to send a television crew around so that other communities could learn about this kind of exercise, and he presented him with a blanket as a token of his appreciation.

When the meeting ended, a representative from the Health Ministry asked if I would like to meet the governor's adviser on women's affairs. I hesitated, as I had met a couple of women in similar positions before who had turned out to be dry-as-dust political appointees. Moreover, I had observed the woman in question during the meeting, and noted that her hejab was very severe, with a hood as tight as a chinstrap. As this was one of the signs of a zealot, I feared it did not augur well for a friendly chat. But out of courtesy I agreed and went to her office. I wanted to ask something about the lifestyles of the different tribes and about how they adapt to being settled. Women's lives in tribal communities are clearly very different to the lives they lead in villages and towns, and most anthropologists agree that women are reluctant to give up their old lifestyle. This was something that Jeremy Swift had pointed out to me confirmed by anthropologist Soheila Shahshahani who studied a newly settled Lur clan.

"As nomads you share the public domain with your husband. Women who migrate to the towns have a difficult time. They are separated suddenly from their husbands, and they do not understand what their husband does outside the house," said Dr. Shahshahani, a professor at Shahid Beheshti University. "She was expecting to get more economic gains, but the workplace is completely alien to her. She feels left out, she loses her status and always looks forward to going back to take back her place in her kinship structure."

The governor's adviser, Kokab Hatamie, sitting in her own office, told me that she herself was from the Bakhtiari tribe further north. While the lifestyle of the various tribes was similar, based on raising animals and small-scale farming, differences did, indeed, she said, exist. "In general, in Luristan, men have almost absolute power over women, whereas in Qashqa'i communities, the women have a more assertive attitude. Here, we say that Lur men are like the mountains," she laughed. "They look like mountains, beautiful from a distance, but rocks and gravel close up." I commented that the area was poor compared to the rest of Iran, and worlds apart from the northern province of Gilan, which I had just visited. There, women are known for being independent and active in agriculture. "This place is under snow for more than six months of the year, so there's not much happening in agriculture," she said. "Gilan is next to the former Soviet Union and has been influenced by more progressive ideas, whereas here they have a lot of old beliefs. Women are kept more suppressed here, there's more polygamy, girls are sometimes given away as brides very young, and sometimes there are feuds between the clans," she said. "Some men have as many as four or five wives, and it's usually related to their need to get a son. They keep on trying again."

Getting into her stride, she talked enthusiastically about the reforms since Khatami's election, about the need for women to be more visible and play a greater role in public life. "Women had a very active role in the local council elections here," she said. "It shows that women are tired of their present lives and they want change. And now there's the message from the government that we should be more active. It's like in the revolution, when women participated in mass demonstrations and fought for change." I tried not to look surprised at her feminist slant, and indeed it wasn't the first time that I'd heard an enthusiastic Islamic feminist. I asked about adaptation—in villages, surely, women felt less free to get out and about. Ms. Hatamie, however, said that on the whole women were adapting well. Some, however, became dependent on aid from the government or religious foundations. "There's a confusion which exists now, economically and socially," she said. "Before, they used to be a free society moving around wherever they wanted. But I'm very hopeful that things are improving and the situation of women is improving."

I thought we were about to end on an optimistic note, but then she dropped a small bombshell. "I think our suicide rate among women must be the highest in the country," she remarked. "Two hundred suicide attempts in the last five years, in this province." She suggested that because women's lives were so controlled, they sometimes felt there was no other way out. "It's the complete control men have over women, here," she said.

"They say they even have to get permission from their husband to drink a glass of water. And at some point, the glass just smashes"

I asked if the men's suicide rate was also high. For men, she said, the more likely reasons for suicide were economic. Abandoning the nomadic life meant losing traditional roles, and in the villages, unemployment was high. This seemed to me to be a more reasonable explanation for psychological suffering among the women, too, but I was so bowled over by her radical thinking that I just listened. She was at pains to point out that the small tribal province did not have other social problems of the kind seen elsewhere, such as drug addiction or prostitution. But at that point a man suddenly banged on the office door and loudly demanded her attention. She called to him that she was busy and would be along later. Then she changed the subject, and asked me a couple of questions about myself and my "motivations" for writing a book. I answered that I had previously worked for the BBC and the *Guardian* but had been unable to work as a regular journalist in Iran because my husband's diplomatic status made it hard for me to get permission for a press card from the government. Moreover, I had two young children to look after. With a flourish, Ms. Hatamie produced a photocopy of a handwritten poem. "This is a strange city, this is a prison for a strange woman," it began. It was highly political and critical of the Lur tribe. "I circulated this among the men in the office," she said, laughing. "And look, it came back with some comments from the security services." A note on the corner read: "Sister Hatamie, with the greatest respect, these poems and these issues provoke tribal conflicts. In our society we need unity. This is unhealthy."

"How do you get away with it?" I asked. It seemed amazing enough that she had written the poem and circulated it, let alone handed it, with additions, to a British journalist. "Oh, by having connections with the governor general's wife. I can still get things done. It's a kind of women's networking. We're not in disagreement with the men, we don't talk about male supremacy, we say it's God's supremacy."

I left, after checking if she was sure I should use the material she had given me. I was scared she would get into trouble. At the Health Ministry I met the official who had suggested the interview. "I thought you would find her interesting," he said with a twinkle. "You may not realize this, but that woman spent ten years in jail for opposing the Shah." He added that she was tortured so much she could hardly speak. Not easily frightened, she would not be cowed into silence.

Theological students in Kashan.

12

Not without My Children

"Today we have a program to commemorate the death of Shahid Malcolm," said Ayesheh, a black American Muslim, addressing a roomful of women theological students in the desert city of Qom. "One of the many, many reasons I have for being thankful to the Iranian nation is that during the Iran-Iraq war I learned the value of shahids, or martyrs," she continued. "We have begun to refer to him—rightfully—by the honorable title of Shahid Malcolm." Suffering and martyrdom lie at the heart of the Shiite branch of Islam. Most foreign women living in Iran come to the country by chance, having married Iranians abroad. But some are attracted by the power of Islam.

Ayesheh organizes annual meetings in Qom to keep alive the memory of Malcolm X, the black civil rights leader and Muslim activist, who was murdered in 1965. Black and white pictures and posters about his life, one framed with plastic pink roses, adorned the walls. The students, around thirty of them, mostly young women, told me they came from all over the world, from the Philippines, Albania, Denmark, Congo, Guyana, Canada, Barbados and Britain. Most of them were studying at the Jame'at Al-Zahra, a women-only theological school in this dusty city of 12,000 students and more than a million inhabitants.

Ayesheh began by speaking of her conversion to Islam twenty-five years ago, when her aunt introduced her to the teachings of Malcolm X. She first came to Iran, "this strange land," partly out of fascination with the figure of Ayatollah Khomeini. Now, she said, Islam was the fastest-growing religion "in, of all places, the *Sheytan-e Bozorg*," the "Great Satan," as the revolutionaries dubbed the United States. Dressed in a long black skirt with a Malcolm X sweatshirt, Ayesheh put on a black scarf to pray. The majority of the audience remained covered for the whole ceremony, even though not a man was in sight. As I had arrived, two other guests ringing the doorbell were wearing full hejab including face veils and delicate black gloves, something I had never seen before in Iran. Next, a striking "sister" spoke. She came to Iran because her husband wanted to study in Qom, the center of Shiite learning. Holding her three-month-old daughter, Fatemeh, on her shoulder, she spoke about black anger, slavery and the importance of history. She wore a black coat but left her head uncovered. Later she led the gathering in a slow, musical chant commemorating the death of Hossein at the battle of Karbala. Hossein, Ali's son and a key Shiite martyr, is mourned every year in Iran on the day of Ashura. The rhythmic chant was a familiar anthem at the time of the revolution, but it was strange to hear it in English:

> Every day is Ashura
> Every place is Karbala
> Hossein, Hossein, Hossein, Hossein

Many of the audience beat their breasts and several cried. There were other prayers, spoken and sung, but this had more Western cadences, recalling gospel music.

Finally, sister Ziba gave a polished talk in excellent English. One of the few Iranians present, she teaches at the women's theological school and has traveled widely, spreading the message of Islam. She has lived in Canada, but her slight Arabic accent had come from studying so many Islamic texts, she said. Ziba is often invited to talk at women's prayer meetings, *rowzeh* or *jaleseh,* traditional gatherings that also serve as social gatherings.[1] On this day, however, Ziba set out to dispel the idea that martyrdom was only for men. She spoke about Zeinab, the Prophet's granddaughter and Hossein's sister, who was given the political role of spreading the word after the battle of Karbala. Dressed conservatively in a black maqna'eh and chador, she spoke like a professional teacher, with a clock by her side. As her talk reached a climax, a small black girl came around offering tissues, and, as if on cue, several of the audience began to cry. Ziba's own four-year-old daughter, wearing a smart black and white dress with red buttons, sat quietly next to her as she spoke. With the rhythmic chanting in Arabic and English, her eyes began to close, and she dozed on her mother's knee. A handful of other children were also

---

1. See Adelkhah, *La Revolution Sous le Voile,* 115, for an assessment of the importance of religious meetings for women.

present. One little girl stole my car keys and wouldn't give them back, but I didn't dare disrupt the meeting.

Afterwards, juice and sandwiches were served and I recovered my keys. The students were curious to find I was not a Muslim and wondered why I was there, but they answered my questions willingly. I asked the women why they had chosen to study in Qom. "I got this kind of spiritual hunger when I was eleven," said one young British Muslim from Lancashire. "So I decided to come here. My mother didn't like it too much at first, but I was the youngest of four, so they let me do what I wanted." I guessed that her parents were Pakistani, so I asked wasn't she brought up a Sunni, not a Shiite? "My parents had lived in Britain so long I don't think they were anything, really," she said.

The young women at Jame'at al-Zahra lived in student dormitories. But Ayesheh no longer attends college. She is an *azad* student, a freelance, having lived in Iran off and on for eleven years. Her husband and five out of her seven children were now living in the U.S., mostly in Philadelphia. I asked what kept her in Qom. "Have you ever lived in America?" she laughed. She told me it was for the future of her younger children, to avoid the horror stories of bringing up teenagers in Western society. There were no black role models in the U.S. anymore, she said, and she didn't want her children imitating Michael Jackson. Moreover, she said, she wanted her daughters to be "active" and committed to the Muslim faith.

Not far from Qom, in the city of Kashan, on the edge of Iran's great Salt Desert, I met another foreign woman who could not have been more different than Ayesheh, yet she, too, believed that Iran was a good place to raise children. "Wellcome," [sic] said the sign for the restaurant. We walked apprehensively past wilting potted palms and a shabby carpet down a flight of stairs to the basement. Once inside, however, everything was pink and white, brightly lit and spotlessly clean. A woman in a black hood and beige coat stepped forward to show us to our seats. Women rarely wait tables in Iran, but this was Jane, a British-trained chef married to an Iranian for twenty years, now running one of the best restaurants in the country. "What can I get you to drink?" she asked. The choice of water, cola, orangeade or "Islamic" beer [nonalcoholic] was not exactly sparkling, but the menu was something else. Jane's kababs were the most tender I ever ate in Iran, and the rest of the menu covered all the homemade specialties that most tourists only read about: *fesenjan,* a dark stew made with pomegranate juice and ground walnuts; *zereshk polow,* chicken and rice with saffron and tangy red barberries; various *khoresh,* or "stews" made with dried lemons, celery, lady fingers, orange peel—all depending on the season. The desserts departed from Persian cuisine, and Jane's husband Reza, also known as Ray, urged us to try the mud pie.

Kashan is about a three hour drive from Tehran. The bazaar, famous for its carpets, has a mud-domed roof typical of desert architecture, and the town is studded with shrines, mosques, old houses and an historic garden. It is the location of one of the oldest and richest prehistoric sites in Iran: Tepe Siyalk. Yet the hotels are cockroach-ridden, and it's hard even to find a teahouse to rest your weary feet. Since Jane and her family opened the Delpazir restaurant, they have done a booming business, but they didn't return to Iran to do business. "We came to Iran for the kids," explained Jane. Her children at that time were eleven, thirteen and eighteen. Her daughter, thirteen, comes to the restaurant straight from school, wearing her sober school uniform of black hood, coat and trousers. "We had been living in London for many years, but I thought it was safer for them to grow up here," said Jane. Family ties are given priority in Iran, and many parents feel there's less temptation in the shape of wild parties, drugs and crime. "You can keep more control of them here," she said.

They came for a quiet life, or "semiretirement," as Reza put it. But after a while, they got fed up with eating out at mediocre kabab houses and decided to open their own place. Each time I visited, it was doing a roaring trade. A group of European restoration experts was eating lunch at one table and at another was a large tour group. The regulars consisted of office workers and families, many of whom Jane greeted by name. She would have liked more help. Staff have to be trained from scratch, and employing women is tricky in Kashan, a conservative, provincial town. "I wanted to get a girl to help me, but so far we haven't been able to. Their families wouldn't allow it."

As we finished our meal, Jane sat down at our table to chat, and Reza brought her a lighted cigarette. She has no regrets about her decision to come to Iran. The couple married twenty years ago after meeting when Reza was a student in Britain. Now they take turns in making twice-yearly trips to Mitcham, south of London, where they still own a restaurant. Jane, however, prefers to stay in Kashan. "I like the people here, they are very kind, very nice and very polite," she said. She knows of only three other foreign wives in the city of almost half a million people. "Perhaps because I'm virtually the only foreigner in Kashan, I do get a lot of respect, even though they call me the 'mad Englishwoman.'" She recalls an incident in her Mitcham restaurant on her last trip back, when a drunken Irishman got into an argument with her over change for the phone. He ended up throwing a beer can at her and smashing a dish. "That would never happen in Iran," she said.

Within the walls of their comfortable, rented house, with its Kashan carpets, comfy sofas, television and pictures of pop stars on the kids' bedroom walls, Jane's home life has not changed much. She sometimes feels isolated, but her in-laws are easygoing and supportive. She knows of women for whom it has not worked out so well. "A lot of women who marry Iranians find their men change when they come back to Iran. I had an American friend who came over here about six years ago whose husband completely changed. He didn't prepare her for it at all—when she arrived she had no headscarf and no coat. Then when she arrived they took her passport away. They lived in his mother's house in Kashan, which was very old and crumbling and, to be honest, the family were not very nice people."

Many people's view of foreign women in Iran has been shaped by a single book, *Not without My Daughter*, subsequently made into a movie. It tells the story of Betty Mahmoody, an American who married an Iranian and then later battled to leave the country with their child. She tells one gruesome story after another about dirt in the kitchen and weevils in the rice, and about the pressures from her husband's family. The book is universally detested in Iran, even among women who knew Mahmoody personally. But the trouble with Iran's image problem is that a substantial number of horror stories are true. While the book in question may be exaggerated—one woman's account of a personal nightmare—it is an accurate reflection of the legal situation. Custody is almost always given to the father, and a woman needs her husband's permission to take a child out of the country. This is true for foreigners and Iranians alike.

What press reports rarely reflect is that women have developed ways of coping and, in some cases, beating the system. While the legal framework gives little room to maneuver, it is not that uncommon to hear of understanding judges, supportive families and lawyers who waive their fees. Jennifer (not her real name) fought her way through the Iranian divorce courts, family pressure and state bureaucracy to win custody of her three children from her opium-addicted husband. She told me her story in England, where she is trying to build a new life. "I met him when I was sixteen. I was working as a Saturday girl in Boots (the pharmacists'), and he was a student. He'd been in the country for two weeks. "We really had a wonderful marriage for twenty-three years. It was a wonderful marriage till we went to Iran. After a year of living there, I realized things were very different. He wouldn't let me go out; I couldn't have friends at the house in Tehran. I was just in all the time. I led the life of a typical Iranian woman. I wasn't allowed to answer the telephone. I had to put on my scarf if visitors came and when I brought tea to them I had to knock on the door."

A tourist perched on the balcony of a restored merchant's house in Kashan.

Nineteenth-century Agha Bozorg mosque and theological college at Kashan.

Rooftop view of Kashan.

Jennifer's lifestyle is probably only typical of a minority of families. Certainly, in my experience, women, including those from traditional backgrounds, chat endlessly on the phone without their husband's permission. But Jennifer's husband became more and more possessive, and increasingly morose. There was a reason for it, as she finally discovered. "There was an awful smell in the house. I found him smoking opium in the kitchen." Opium smoking is a traditional pastime among Iranian men, but it frequently leads to health problems and addiction. Jennifer's husband became increasingly withdrawn and depressed. "After a year, he started being violent toward me," she said. Then, he threw the family out. She took the children to stay in the north at her brother-in-law's house. A family argument broke out between this branch of the family, which was very supportive, and her mother-in-law and a second brother-in-law, living in the very religious town of Mashhad.

Desperate, she had all three children put on her British passport and tried to leave the country. But, she said, the embassy was slow to process the application, and in the meantime, her husband had alerted passport control. "They refused to allow us to go through. They let the elder one and the middle one, but when it came to the third, they said: 'He's not to go through. We have got his name down on the passport control computer saying that he can't go without his father.'"

Now running out of money, Jennifer left Iran overland through Turkey with the two teenagers, made her way to England, and left them with her parents. She then returned on her own to bring out her youngest son, only two and a half. Undaunted, she took her husband to court, demanded a divorce and persuaded the judge to give her custody of the toddler. "My husband wouldn't let me keep the youngest boy. I had a five-hour bus journey on a rickety old bus to come to the court in Tehran, and I did that about once a week. It was an absolutely awful experience. I haven't spoken about it to anybody, even my parents don't know how it was."

She presented her own case with very little Persian. It took months. A friend's father, a lawyer, helped her out and refused to take any money. "I went through an awful time to win this child back. I came away from the courts with nothing, just an agreement that I couldn't have anything: clothes, dowry, gold, maintenance—I just agreed to everything. The judge read the agreement that my husband wrote. He wanted this, he wanted that. He read it and looked at me and said, 'Do you agree with this?' Of course he was speaking in Persian, and he said again, 'Do you understand what I'm saying—do you agree with what your husband has written?' I hesitated and then said, 'Yes, I'm sure.' He said, '*Chera*?' 'Why?' And all I

could say was *'Man faqat bacheha-mo mikham'*—'I just want my children.'
He was very nice. He signed and then he said, 'Congratulations, I hope
God is with you.'" The stress took its toll. Back in the U.K. she was treated
for insomnia and depression, and for months she could barely speak. "They
say I'm very strong to have survived," she said. "I have just come off anti-
depressants and we're just starting a new life," she told me. "I'll never forget
him; I loved him a lot. But it's ruined me as a person."

I first heard about Jennifer's case at the British Wives' Library, a lending
library that serves as a meeting point for the many foreign women living in
Iran who feel isolated and a long way from home. Jennifer had attended a
few Sunday morning meetings, until her husband had stopped her. The library
is housed in the beautiful surroundings of the British Embassy's summer com-
pound at Gholhak in northern Tehran, just around the corner from our house.
Over instant coffee and homemade cakes, the women swap stories and tips
for surviving life in Iran. A visiting journalist once asked me to introduce her
to some of these women, whom, she said, she imagined must be sitting by a
pool drinking gin and tonic. The reality could not be farther from the truth.
The sale of alcohol is strictly forbidden, and the only time I tried to obtain
gin in Iran, it turned out to be illicitly brewed *arak*, or hooch, on which the
mothers at the playgroup choked. Moreover, many women married penni-
less students in Europe or the U.S., and on arrival in Iran live in a precarious
financial situation. At these gatherings there is generally a lot of talk about
legal problems and bureaucracy, and not only with regard to the Iranian government. Some complain about a lack of support from their home countries.
"The embassy makes it clear to us that they will do nothing special to help
us because as far as they are concerned we are Iranian citizens," one told me.
Under Iranian law, a woman automatically becomes Iranian upon marrying
an Iranian. This does not apply to foreign men marrying Iranian women.

Several British women told me they objected to paying up to $200 for
a certificate of entitlement to health care in Britain. To obtain the same
document in London would cost a fraction of that sum, they assured me.
"I finally got mine last year, but by the time I got it, I couldn't afford the
ticket," said one. "Now I'm starting to save up again. I haven't been home
in five years." At this point a plainly dressed, rather overweight woman
with an East European accent interrupted: "You're lucky you can go home
when you want to." This was Anna. I had seen her before at another informal meeting group of foreign wives when she had consulted a lawyer on
questions of inheritance.

Anna's problems began when her much-loved Iranian husband died. A
Christian wife cannot inherit from a Muslim husband. Her brother-in-law

intervened to prevent her from leaving the country with her three children. The law was on his side, as guardianship in such cases goes to the nearest male relative, rather than to the mother. When she managed to win custody, after four years of legal work—mostly carried out behind her brother-in-law's back—it was too late. Her in-laws had been at work on the children and persuaded them they should stay in Iran. The youngsters were convinced and they handed over power of attorney to their uncle, thus blocking her efforts. He became responsible for their financial affairs, as well as major decisions regarding education, travel and accommodations.

Most of my friends in Iran were women who had married into less religious, Westernized families. They carried on with a similar lifestyle to the one they had in London or Los Angeles. But Anna had married into traditional bazaari society, where the family was comfortably off and highly religious. She met her husband at UCLA at the time of anti-Vietnam war protests and sit-ins in the late 1960s. She was studying languages, he was doing a chemistry degree. But I believed her when she said she was not a hippy. Anna, now forty-seven, comes from a family of practicing Roman Catholics who escaped from Hungary at the time of the 1956 uprising. An icon of Christ hangs on the wall of her Tehran apartment, and she holds strong religious beliefs. "They have very strong family ties and because I came from a religious background, I could understand that," she said. She did not find it strange when her mother-in-law bought her a chador on their first shopping trip. But gradually she realized the family was uncomfortable with her Christian faith and wanted her to convert.

"I noticed that my husband's family would let me bring the dishes into the kitchen but wouldn't let me wash them," she recalled. "I realized that they had a problem." They considered her unclean—even though they knew she was meticulous about housework and personal hygiene. After Anna had her first child, her mother-in-law took advice from a mullah. "She said, 'My daughter-in-law's cleaner than me, but when I want to take my little granddaughter into my arms, her spit will be unclean.'" The mullah advised that a sigheh, temporary marriage under Islamic law, would suffice, and Anna agreed to it. "I thought, God will solve this and he's the one who cares," she said. "That made my daughter clean and everybody clean and that made everybody happy."

More tension surfaced when Anna developed cancer and needed a hysterectomy. While her husband nursed her throughout her illness and manfully looked after the children, her in-laws pressured her to get a divorce, the implication being that she was now "damaged goods." I would scarcely have believed her story, if I had not just seen a movie by the award-winning director Dariush Mehrjui in which the heroine, Leila, discovers she cannot have children. In the film, set in middle-class north Tehran, the husband's family puts immense pressure on her to leave their son to make way for a wife who is fertile. Ultimately, they persuade Leila to let him take a second wife. Although he goes through with the marriage, the arrangement does not work out, and the message of the film is clear. Anna told me that the prospect of a co-wife was a very real fear for her, too.

At the time of the revolution, amid the massive religious revival, Anna considered becoming a Muslim. She read a lot and attended prayer meetings for a while but decided on balance that she would rather stay as she was. She feels the family found this particularly difficult to accept. But her eldest daughter has become Islamic—and Iranian—in a big way. "My eldest daughter is very much like them. She's very religious and there was a time when she would not sit in a chair if a foreigner had sat on it, although that eased off when she went to university." When Anna visited the U.S. in 1989, the daughter, Mona, hesitated to come because she did not want to take off her headscarf. Soon afterwards, she decided to marry her cousin. "She had other suitors, but she really wanted to marry him. They think it's made in heaven to marry within the family." Worried that the children of such a marriage would run a higher risk of birth defects, Anna arranged for genetic counseling. The doctor told them that in Iran the marriage of first cousins was generally considered permissible. A young medical student sitting in on the consultation admitted that he himself, given the same set of circumstances, would not marry.

The wedding was a family affair. When it came to drawing up the marriage contract, it was agreed that Mona should have the right to continue her education written in. But the family opposed allowing her to specify her right to seek a divorce. The wedding reception was big, with a special room for the more traditional chadoris. Even so, some guests left, because they felt the music was "un-Islamic." Mona, beautifully made up, covered herself with a chador to preserve her modesty. "They had a woman making a movie there, and Mona had it put on a CD. She said she wanted it for posterity, but she wouldn't give my mother a copy," said Anna. "She wouldn't let her grandmother take a picture until she put on a rupush and scarf over her wedding dress." The eighty-year-old woman had come over specially from America, but afterwards, her granddaughter declined to give her a set of wedding photos taken without hejab on the grounds that she might show them to men who were not relatives.

As we chatted, Anna's eldest son was watching an American movie on VCR in the next room. Mother's Day flowers decorated the apartment, which was otherwise rather bare. She had just moved in, after her brother-in-law sold the villa with the swimming pool that was her previous home. She was not terribly happy with the move but pointed out that her in-laws had always been generous and protective in the typical Iranian way. When her husband was alive, his brother provided him with a car when cash was scarce. Now that he was dead, he felt it was his duty to provide for his widow. Indeed, at one point, Anna suspected that her husband's brother was building up to a marriage proposal, to make his "protection" complete in traditional fashion. He turned up repeatedly to eat with them in the evenings. Other members of the family tipped her off about his possible intentions, however, and she convinced them she was happy to live on her own.

While some women struggle with overwhelming family pressure, others thrive on close and supportive family ties. While some cling to their Christian beliefs, others are attracted to the clear, all-encompassing message of Islam. Pam was instantly recognizable at my son's international kindergarten as the only teacher who wore the scarf inside the school premises. I knew she attended Koran classes. I talked to her in the computer room, where she was typing out carols for the annual Christmas party. Pam was brought up in a large family in the American Midwest. She had six brothers and sisters, and what she called a "stepfather situation" that led to her going to another town for her high-school education. There she lodged with a Palestinian family, who took her under their wing.

"They were not practicing Muslims but were very warm and close knit," she said. "That society I found lacking at home, they had there, and of course the first thing that popped up was Islam, and I thought 'This is what I want.'" She began to learn Arabic. Later she moved back to her hometown and found herself seeking out the company of foreign students. She fell in love with her husband-to-be, an Iranian computer engineering student, in what she laughingly called "a typical American romance." The courtship was more typically Iranian. In spite of opposition from his brother-in-law, who did not want him to marry an American, Mahmud sent his sister to sound her out. "His sister proposed marriage—it was very strange," she recalled. He was thinking Iranian-style and he would have been too embarrassed to ask me himself. She was coming to do a *khastegari*, but of course I was not familiar with Iranian customs at all."

Pam's conversion to Islam was gradual, she said. Mahmud was deeply religious, it was the 1979 revolution, and it seemed the natural thing to do. She began to wear long-sleeved shirts, longish skirts and a headscarf. For her wedding she wore an ordinary dress at a civil ceremony in a

Methodist chapel in the United States, then changed into a white satin wedding dress with a maqna'eh, or hood, for a traditional Iranian ceremony. They asked her to read something in Persian, and only afterwards did she realize that it was the Islamic creed. "There was this thing I had to say and I didn't realize what they were saying, and afterwards they all said, 'Now you've become a Muslim.' I was rather aggravated when I found out." I know other women who read out the same phrases at Iranian consulates around the world. They are generally told they do not absolutely have to convert but that they are unlikely to get a visa for the Islamic Republic if they do not.

Pam and her husband stayed in the U.S. for several years before returning to Iran. They were welcomed with open arms, literally. While Pam was shaking from fatigue at the airport, one of her in-laws scooped up the baby from her arms, before she even realized who it was. It seemed a good beginning. But this was at the time of the Iran-Iraq war, a time of great hardship and fear. They stayed with Mahmud's parents in a small apartment packed with thirteen people. "We came to realize that living in Iran was not going to be as easy as we'd thought," she said. "It was overcrowded because everyone was living together because of the war....I was treated as a guest and after a year I felt I was beginning to wear on them." Every morning she went out to buy milk from a man with a donkey then brought it back to boil before drinking. This was her main outing for the day. She would have liked to get out and about, but the other women preferred to stay at home, partly for fear of the bombing.

Since then, Pam and her husband have traveled back and forth to the U.S. Things became easier when they built their own house in Tehran. She found a job teaching English at a theological college, and later at the kindergarten. Wearing a rust-colored scarf over a baggy sweatshirt adorned with cartoon characters, she says she feels at ease in both worlds. She is not so keen on the Iranian official dress code, however. "I've never had a personal problem with hejab," she said. "I have become very angry, though, about the way it is imposed on people here. This is not religion, this is not Islam."

When I spoke to Pam, the family was planning to go back to America, mainly for the sake of her four daughters' education. "The education system sucks. All these exams are hateful," she declared. She said her children were particularly bored by history, which is presented as a series of dates and kings to recite by heart. Each year, they learned the same period over and over again in slightly more detail. Now her eldest daughter, seventeen, had left Iranian school and was studying over the Internet in the evenings. She had already been accepted at an American university and was helping out at the kindergarten. I wondered if she was concerned that her daughters would abandon Islam if they moved back. "I don't think that they will drift away from Islam," she said. "They will drift away from the food and start going to McDonald's, and they may drift away from hejab. But that doesn't worry me so long as I feel their ideals are Islamic.... I do worry about the stress, the adaptation, that the social pressure will be too much—for them to come to the bars on Friday nights and dress this way or that way."

Coming to terms with an extended family is clearly one of the key issues for foreign women living in Iran. Marianne, another long-term resident who works at a Western European embassy, did not enjoy the endless round of traditional family parties. They reach their peak at Nowruz, when they are known as *Did o baz did,* to see and see again (your friends and relatives). "This visiting in groups killed me, because I can't cook," she said. "A friend of mine was leaving so I decided to take over her dog. I thought this was a good way of keeping big groups away." The strategy worked, as many Iranians not only consider dogs unclean, they are afraid of them.

With closer family, however, she had a rather stormy relationship. Lighting up a cigarette, she recalls getting to know her father-in-law, a traditional Iranian landowner with two wives. She would smoke in front of him, something even his son did not dare to do. Moreover, she preferred to join the company of the men at mealtimes. And it was not just for the conversation that she joined the men. The food was better: "After the gentlemen had eaten, what was left over was brought down to the kitchen, rearranged on plates and given to the ladies. So one time I made some kind of sarcastic remark, saying I thought human beings ate chicken, not chicken bones, and after that he used to ask me to join them."

This was the time of miniskirts and hippy clothes, yet traditional customs existed side by side with new Western trends. On one occasion, Marianne was invited to go to Qom on a pilgrimage to the famous shrine of the blessed Massumeh, a ninth-century female Shiite saint. Her relatives provided her with a chador and thick stockings, and suggested she take off her gold hoop earrings. As they left the shrine, she noticed they were giggling among themselves. "The wife of my husband's uncle was chubby and beautiful, and one of the mullahs had actually come up to her and proposed sigheh with her," she said. "They were all kind of proud that she had received a proposal from a mullah, but I was shocked that she hadn't slapped his face."

Marianne found herself naturally taking sides with her husband's mother, who had led a difficult, long-suffering life. She had been married off at the age of twelve, lost status when her husband took a co-wife and was humiliated by having to put up with various sigheh affairs. "We formed a united front," she said. For Marianne, things came to a head with her father-in-law in an argument about the chador. "My father-in-law told me that if I wanted to come to his house, I should put on a chador or not come at all. 'I said who the hell are you to tell me you're a good Muslim. Just look how you treat your two wives.' I got up and said I wouldn't put a chador on and I never went back to his house. I didn't even go to his funeral."

With her striking looks and strong personality, Marianne never had any trouble getting what she wanted. Because she and her husband have good jobs, she is able to travel to Europe on a regular basis. "I do need to go once a year to Europe," she said. "I need the freedom to wear shorts or jump on my bike and go to the shopping center." Her three sons are grown up now, but like Jane in Kashan, she valued the "control" that Iranian society expects during the problems of adolescence.

Yet Iranian society has changed immensely in the last thirty years, and the nuclear family is increasingly the norm. For Mary, an Irish woman who moved here long before the revolution, that's a relief. "The good thing is that my husband is not one of those Iranians who come back to the bosom of their family," she laughed. "He's a second son so there's not so much pressure on him. We were invited for dinner and lunch at the beginning, but when we didn't reciprocate, they dropped us, thank God!"

Mary has a different view on the strict rules society sets for young people, however. There may be a more old-fashioned approach, and in one sense the streets are more secure, but risks do exist in the form of drugs and wild parties. Mary saw her two daughters get into scrape after scrape as they rebelled against the suffocating restrictions on social life. While her daughters have been successful at university, she is not sure what kind of a future they will have in Iran. "I'd be very happy if my children left," she said. "I feel as if they have missed out on so much. They are not free to talk to people, there are people checking up on them all the time at university. I must say I admire the resilience of these kids. You have some kids picked up at a party on Thursday and then they're back at another party on Saturday. They do their best to beat the system just with the way they leave a little bit of hair out or the way they walk." She remembers one day during the war when her eldest daughter was shaking with terror as the bombs fell. "On several occasions I have thought: 'Have I made a terrible mistake staying in Iran, has it been fair to them?'"

Mary came in the 1960s when the oil boom was just beginning, and the supermarket shelves (there were more supermarkets then, she says) were stocked with whisky. Her university professor husband earned ten times his present salary in real terms, and she taught English to Iranian air force personnel. Like many observers, she was puzzled at how easily the country accepted the drastic measures brought in by the revolutionary regime. "One thing that surprised me then, which I understand more now, is the ease with which they could bring in the hejab. I saw friends wearing stockings and scarves, saying, 'What can I do?' But don't forget that their grandmothers and mothers wore this. It is not something alien for them to wear. I saw that middle-class women had a chador to put on when they went to the door. This Westernization was just a veneer. When I look back now I realize that it was only in the north of Tehran that we were free to wear what we wanted. When we went to the country I'd say fifty percent were wearing chadors, and in small towns it was up to ninety percent."

The revolutionary fervor was particularly strong at school. One time Mary was called to school to be told that her younger daughter had pulled a girl's maqna'eh off her head. On another occasion the same child was reprimanded for having a handful of dried plums in her pocket during the holy month of Ramadan, when devout Muslims are expected to fast. Yet Mary takes it all philosophically: "I never had any real problems with the school. And I always think if I survived an Irish Catholic education, they can survive this." Mary sometimes thinks of moving back to Ireland but knows it would be difficult for her husband to adapt. "I could get a job, but then I'd have a depressed husband." Men at the top of their fields in Iran are rarely able to find a job that provides them with similar status in the West. An additional tie is elderly relatives. I know many couples who feel they cannot leave Iran while their parents, grandparents or in-laws are alive.

Yet many women choose to stay when others around them leave. I met Helga, a beaming, well-groomed seventy-year-old, at a smart diplomatic coffee morning. She told me she had been here for forty-five years and wouldn't dream of leaving. A children's nurse working in Germany, she married an Iranian engineer and came to Tehran in 1954. "We came out of the plane, and most of the family were wearing the chador. I was dressed in a gray suit. My father-in-law came forward and spoke to me in French, then he just grabbed me and hugged me so nicely, I felt so secure." He was a widower, so Helga had no rivals in the house. "My father-in-law told the servants: 'Let her do what she wants,' so I made the furniture shine and the house became nice." He defended her against the curiosity of friends and relatives. "The first thing they would ask me was 'Did you become a Muslim?' But my father-in-law always told them: 'Leave her alone, it's none of your business.' He used to say that religion was not like a dress you change."

In her comfortable, airy apartment, Helga's eyes shone as she remembered a trip to the tailor—accompanied by her father-in-law. She called him *"Aghajun,"* a term of respect and endearment. They were occasionally invited to the palace of the Shah, and he insisted that she have a new dress made. He chose a strappy décolleté model, much to Helga's amazement, as she was from a strict, conventional German family. "With your white skin, you'll look like a princess," he told her.

From the beginning, Helga worked, first in an orphanage, then in an international kindergarten that she set up herself. In the meantime, she had two daughters and nursed her father-in-law through a long illness from which he finally died. Her husband was a senior civil servant. When the revolution came, the family's closeness to the Shah meant that he and his brother had to flee the country. She stayed behind. "He went to Germany the day the Shah left," she said. "I stayed here. I had the kindergarten and in the beginning it wasn't that bad." However, she was practically on her own for more than four years. During that time the Komiteh searched the house and closed down the kindergarten, and the war with Iraq began. She supported her husband with her own savings. It is a time she does not like to remember: "I was so scared," she said.

When the political climate eased and her husband was able to come back, there were different problems. He could not expect to find employment. "When he came back he suffered from very severe depression. Every day he'd dress himself in his gray suit and black shoes then sit in the kitchen. He started to recover but he wasn't his old self. A hundred times he told me, 'Darling, come and join me in Germany; but I said, 'I'm not going to leave this house.'" Some years later, her husband died of cancer.

Helga has a modern apartment in central Tehran. One of her daughters lives in the apartment upstairs, Iranian-style. Another daughter lives in Düsseldorf, but she is not tempted to go and join her. "I couldn't live there anymore," she said. "The way I think, the way I take life, is so different." In Germany, her daughter has little contact with her neighbors. In Tehran, the grocer worries if she misses two days' shopping, and the street sweeper greets her when she's been away. "When I come back, he tells me, 'The street is bright again.'" She doesn't like having to cover up, but she makes the best of it, wearing a smart raincoat and a Dior headscarf.

Helga loves the Persian traditions of hospitality, serving guests the best sweets and fruit in a certain way. Yet she maintains German traditions, baking cookies at Christmas that last all the way through to Nowruz. She starred in an Iranian documentary film about foreign women in Tehran in which I also took part. Her sheer enjoyment of life shines through, as she repeatedly insists: "I'm a very happy girl." In my chat with her, she kept on describing life as "wonderful": "I had a most wonderful life in this country, and I could not just throw it away like that."

Helga has the choice. She can leave, stay or take a holiday whenever she likes. My time in Iran was limited to a UN posting. It passed in a whirl of playgroups, dinner parties and weekend breaks. The general frustration with everyday life here, the petty restrictions of the dress code and the restrictions on freedom of speech are tempered with the warmth and hospitality of Iranians. For me, it was a fascinating experience and a lot of fun. But for some women, not just foreigners, Iran sometimes feels like a life sentence from which they cannot escape. Only those who live here have the power to understand that and to change women's lives.

Epilogue

I met many remarkable women in my time in Iran, none more so than Mary Gharagozlou, who died in September 2001. Daughter of a tribal chief and an American librarian, she spent her last days surrounded by horses at a traditionally built house in the foothills west of Tehran. A gifted raconteur, she told me endless stories over tea and cakes. She recalled how, as a twelve-year-old, she'd galloped past Reza Shah, riding so well that he thought she was a boy. He was so impressed that he had her trained to be an Olympic show jumper—the only girl at the military academy. Mary became a legendary figure in the Bakhtiari tribe. She married a tribesman and, with knowledge from agricultural college, saved thousands of dying sheep by buying them and treating them herself. After the revolution she was thrown in jail on suspicion of fomenting unrest among the nomads, but she confounded her jailers by translating Shiite texts in her cell. She was an odd figure, in baggy black Kurdish men's trousers and a pink polo-neck sweater. She had no phone, but she was extremely well informed, and spent most of her time compiling a studbook of Arab horses in Iran. After a delightful afternoon, I told her apologetically that my book was about ordinary people's lives and I really didn't know where to fit her in since she had such an extraordinary life story. She laughed and we said goodbye.

Yet looking back, I met many extraordinary women in Iran, battling their way through the bizarre legal framework and everyday rules and regulations with energy and humor. Since I left Iran in 2000, their lives have continued, and so have their battles. The life of women's rights lawyer Mehrangiz Kar has turned into a struggle of epic proportions. She was jailed after the Berlin Conference, when she and other leading reformists were accused of insulting Islamic sanctities. She discovered she was suffering from breast cancer. She described her experiences in the notorious Evin Prison, which included weeks in solitary confinement. "I got used to the doctors visiting us at night....They were scared of heart attacks, in case someone should be blamed. But they didn't know that cancerous cells were developing and spreading in the body of this new prisoner and that the tumor was growing rapidly due to psychological pressure."[1] Her thoughts were published in a pro-reform monthly, *Payam-e Emruz*, along with those of other prisoners. After a trial held in secret, Kar, and her publisher friend, Shahla Lahiji, were given four-year sentences, but this was commuted to a fine of five million rials (around $600). Kar, however, was faced with additional charges of not wearing a headscarf at other functions she attended while in Germany, and at the time of writing, she still had these hanging over her—two years after the actual event.

The authorities at first banned her from travelling abroad for treatment. She underwent chemotherapy in Tehran and at my leaving party wore a fur hat to conceal her hair loss. Later, with the help of the Dutch embassy, Kar was allowed to leave on medical grounds, and she went to stay with one of her daughters in the United States. Then, in November 2001, her seventy-two-year-old husband, Siamak Pourzand, disappeared. The manager of a cultural center, he was missing for some time before he turned up—in jail. His sister was asked to take him a change of clothes, but when she inquired what he had been charged with, she was told it was none of her business. "It was a really scary time," their daughter, Lily, told me. The family had reason to be scared. In previous years writers who disappeared in mysterious circumstances were found murdered, in some cases by government agents. The following spring, Pourzand was charged with spying and threatening national security and put on trial behind closed doors. Newspaper reports carried "confessions" which his family believe were made under duress. Human Rights Watch accused the judiciary of making a mockery of the rule of law. The evidence against Pourzand was not made public, but in May he was sentenced to at least eight years' imprisonment. Around the same time, his family received word that he had suffered a heart attack in jail. This ordeal, combined with the stress of Kar's own detention, court case and the threat of ongoing proceedings, raised concerns about the effect on her own health. Yet she has responded with quiet courage, vowing to make a book out of it. "I hope that my cancer will not progress too quickly so I will have the time to write about these experiences and disappointments," she told one interviewer.[2]

1. *Iran Reporter*, 21 July 2001.
2. *Bad Jens*, "Settling the Score," 1 November 2000.

In the battle for freedom of expression and the continuing power struggle between the reformers and hard-line conservatives, women were again in the front line. A parliamentarian, Fatemeh Haghighatjou was sentenced to twenty-two months in jail for "plotting against the Islamic system." She had made a speech in a parliamentary debate defending a woman journalist who was reportedly subject to a violent arrest. Haghighatjou, an outspoken former student leader, is a devout Muslim with immaculate hejab. She was one of several deputies taken to court for remarks made under cover of parliamentary immunity, a crisis which finally led to a walk-out of parliament and a climb-down by the Supreme Leader. It is an example of how women's rights are inextricably bound up with the bigger political picture in Iran. It is no coincidence that the most serious court case arising from Berlin was that of Hasan Yousefi Eshkevari, a reformist cleric who has defended women's rights and individual freedoms, saying openly that the Islamic dress code should be a matter of choice. At a secret trial he was convicted of apostasy, a "crime" that carries the death sentence. After the intervention of President Khatami and an international outcry, it was thought unlikely he would be executed, but he remains in jail.

Iran remains full of paradoxes. The blind singer Pari Zanganeh, a star at the time of the Shah, was invited to perform at the opening of a concert for the third Muslim Women's Games in October 2001. Previously, women had only been officially permitted to perform in front of women-only audiences. The ceremony was open to men and women, but male spectators were restricted to events such as chess and shooting, where the women competitors were suitably covered.

While hard-line courts close down magazines and newspapers by the dozen, filmmakers continue to expand the boundaries of what can be discussed in public. Many recent films focus on women's lives, and they portray them with gritty realism, breaking various taboos in the process. *Water and Fire* tells the story of a prostitute and a writer who have an affair and are caught by the police. *The Sunglasses* tackles the question of divorce and arranged marriages that do not work out. Rakhshan Bani-Etemad's *Our Times* was a two-part film, half drama, half documentary, portraying President Khatami's second election campaign and interviewing the forty-seven women who attempted to stand against him. After the success of their documentary about divorce, Ziba Mir-Hosseini and Kim Longinotto collaborated on a second film, *Runaway*, about girls fleeing abuse and domestic violence.

The fact that the media were given access to Reyhaneh House, where runaways can seek refuge, is testimony to a new openness on the part of the authorities. Officials spoke of the need to launch an emergency hotline and open shelters for battered women. Zahra Bonyanian, of the government-backed Center for Women's Participation, told *Iran Daily* that the hotline was in response to "increasing aggression against women at home."[3] She pulled no punches, spelling out what she meant: "Beatings, rape, abortions, financial and mental pressures, as well as verbal abuse from their husbands, brothers and even children." She added that no statistics on the problem were available because women were afraid to confess to being abused. Not so long ago, sociologists would say that there were no women's shelters in Iran because they were culturally inappropriate, as the subject of domestic violence was taboo and dealt with entirely by the family.

Prostitution, which clearly should have no place in the utopia envisioned by the Islamic Revolution, became a major public issue. "Two thousand prostitutes. Isn't this shameful?" lamented Tehran's chief justice, Abbasali Alizadeh.[4] And he was only talking about Tehran. In the holy city of Mashhad, it was the murder of at least sixteen prostitutes that grabbed the headlines. Women parliament members demanded an explanation from the intelligence minister as the killings continued. The killer—or killers—would have been caught in less than six months anywhere else, they said. Eventually, a religious fanatic, Saeed Hanaei, dubbed the "Spider Killer," confessed to strangling the prostitutes with their own headscarves and leaving their bodies wrapped in chadors. He said he acted alone, in the name of God, and that his victims were garbage, which needed to be eradicated.

Hanaei's trial turned out to be as controversial as the manhunt. His lawyer, Abdollah Farahani, claimed he had received 40,000 letters of support from sympathetic bazaaris, who were willing to pay blood money to the victims' families to spare the defendant's life. His initial line of argument outraged civil rights campaigners, for Farahani appealed to Article 226 of the penal code, which says that a killer can escape punishment if he can prove that his victims deserved to die. The criticism was led by veteran human rights lawyer Shirin Ebadi who said, "This is our law, but this is not Islam."[5] The defense counsel had to abandon his

---

3. Women standing up against physical, mental abuse at home, *Agence France Presse*, 3 July 2001.
4. "Iran justice chief bemoans Tehran vice," Reuters, 17 August 2001.
5. *Iran Reporter*, 22 October 2001.

approach when the defendant admitted to having had sex with some of the women before killing them, and Hanaei was sentenced to death and executed by hanging.

As the power struggle between the reformers and the conservative-controlled judiciary intensified, Iran's Islamic penal code increasingly came under the spotlight. Human Rights Watch found that the judiciary and security forces increasingly resorted to intimidatory tactics, with a sharp increase in public executions and floggings.[6] In 2001, two women were stoned to death in Evin jail in what were the first reported stonings since 1997.[7] One woman was an unnamed thirty-five-year-old convicted of acting in pornographic films, the other, thirty-year-old Maryam Ayubi, had been found guilty of murdering her husband with the help of her lover.

The periodic clampdowns on "un-Islamic" women (those who fail to conform to the dress code) continue unabated. Police issued warnings that women who showed their hair, smoked in public or wore tight clothing in public places would be dealt with severely.[8] One edict warned salesmen not to sell lingerie to single women or to display products which carried "Latin sentences and words carrying ugly meanings, images of immoral groups such as homosexuals, the Playboy rabbit and rap." The laws on social gatherings still make partygoing a risky business, for youngsters especially. In one incident, fifty Iranians aged 18 to 25 were whipped after attending a "depraved" Tehran party, which the judge did not believe was a simple birthday bash.[9] And while the press showed sympathy to runaways, the judiciary demonstrated little mercy. A twenty-year-old woman was given fifty lashes and four months imprisonment for staying away from home and living with a boyfriend. She had been living, unhappily, in her brother's house since the death of their parents, and it was he who reported her to the police.[10]

Attempts, however modest, to reform the laws relating to women were blocked by the conservative Guardian Council and the office of the Supreme Leader. President Khatami looked increasingly powerless, even though he won a second landslide in the June 2001 presidential elections. Once again, he played to the women's vote: "We have to try to increase the role of women in decision-making in politics and society," he declared in a message read to a women's election rally. "Women are not second-class, they are no less than men," he said.[11] Forty-seven women, an unprecedented

6. *Human Rights Watch World Report,* 2002.
7. Amnesty International spokesman, quoted on Radio Free Europe/ Radio Liberty, 4 July 2001.
8. *Agence France Presse,* 2 October 2001.
9. *Agence France Presse,* 4 July 2001.
10. IRNA, 16 June 2001.
11. "Iranian women aspire towards share of power," Reuters, 1 June 2001.

number, registered to run against him. The leading female candidate, Farah Khosravi, accused him of not being tough enough. "Mohammad Khatami has not kept his promises.... He has failed to keep his promises to the people, to the young and to the women." Khosravi, Secretary General of the conservative Iran-e Farda party, pulled out of the contest without explanation four days before the Guardian Council was due to give its decision on whether she was eligible to run. In the event, only ten candidates, all men, were deemed eligible to stand, and the long-running debate on whether women can actually hold the presidency remained unresolved.

Elected for a second term with seventy-seven percent of the vote, Khatami came under substantial pressure to appoint women ministers. In 1997 he had given two women cabinet status (Vice President Massoumeh Ebtekar and his advisor on women's affairs, Zahra Shoja'i), but no women had held a ministerial portfolio since before the revolution. Even among his allies, there was strong opposition to the idea. One supposedly reformist member declared it was "not dignified" for women to be put on display in government. The eleven women in parliament reacted angrily and circulated a petition with the names of 163 deputies, a majority of members, saying that women's time had come. When he finally announced his cabinet, Khatami was forced to defend his decision to pass over female ministerial candidates yet again. He said that women were long-time victims of "oppression," and should be given an important place in society. But positions should be given on merit and women needed to work their way up: "We do not want to use women as decorative elements," he told a news conference.[12] "It was a big disappointment," one seasoned women's rights campaigner told me. Others spoke of feeling insulted, especially as hopes had been high.

While women remain marginalized from politics, their voices continue to be heard. The Special Representative of the UN Human Rights Commission remarked in 2002 that although little progress had been made in reforming discriminatory laws, social pressure for change was steadily growing. Women's demands were now out in the open. He said he was confident that pressure inside Iran for change in the treatment of women would only increase. And within the establishment, there are positive signs that women's rights are being taken seriously. The Center for Women's Participation, established in the wake of the Beijing Conference on the status of women, has become increasingly active, holding workshops, among other things,

---

12. *Agence France Presse,* 22 August 2001.

on gender awareness and domestic violence. It backed a new Center for Women's Studies at Tehran University, which opened in 2001, after being given the go ahead by the Ministry of Education. Meanwhile graduate programs in women's studies were established in at least three other universities. The Tehran University center launched research projects into the presence of women in society and in the economy and set up a Master's degree program. One remarkable aspect was the choice of director, the outspoken sociologist Jaleh Shaditalab. A long-time civil servant, she has been highly critical of the government's record of promoting women to managerial roles. Recently she attacked what she called "obvious discrimination" in the state sector, where, she said, fifty-three percent of women employed in government have completed higher education yet only five percent have achieved managerial positions.[13]

[handwritten margin note: Current edu- cation]

On the surface, little has changed, but women's steady march towards education must surely mark one of the biggest social revolutions since 1979. Women's enrollment in higher education continued to increase, leading to worries about achievement among boys. "The reluctance of boys to enter universities can destabilize the social structure of the nation," Hosein Amiri, deputy head of parliament's education committee, told state television.[14] With engaging frankness, he said one reason boys were disinclined to study was the number of unemployed graduates.

When the September 11 attacks on Washington and New York put Iran's neighbor, Afghanistan, into the forefront of world news in 2001, I couldn't help remembering the Afghan girls I had met in Mashhad. In Iran, only a few percent of girls still fail to attend primary school. In Afghanistan, only a few had been able to go to school. In Iran, women voted in millions and took credit for electing the president of their choice. Yet they were rewarded with not a single minister, whereas the new Afghan administration found two suitably qualified women.

President Khatami won praise for his decisive condemnation of the attacks on the United States. Women led a candlelight vigil in Tehran's Mother Square in memory of the victims. Some reports said it was the first public demonstration of sympathy for America since the revolution. The mourners turned out for a second night but were dispersed by police. The earth-shattering events of 2001 could bring Iran closer to the West or alienate it still further. But women will be having their say and it could be decisive to the future of Iran.

---

13. *Zanan*, July 2001, Number 77.
14. *Agence France Presse*, 3 July 2001.

Leading reformers, lawyer Mehrangiz Kar (left) and publisher Shahla Lahiji, shortly after being released from jail. They were detained after speaking at a conference in Berlin.

Acknowledgements

I received overwhelming support from Iranians in all walks of life in the preparation of this book. Yet I cannot thank them all as publicly as I would like. In the shifting political climate of Iran, a special note of thanks from a British writer could still go down on a secret file.

Data on women's issues in Iran is sketchy, sometimes unreliable and often filtered through the eyes of Iranians living abroad. Yet there are many people in Iran who understand the situation and took the trouble to explain it to me during the five years I lived there. Many used personal connections to arrange interviews and meetings for me that would otherwise have been impossible to obtain. I would particularly like to thank the many government officials who stuck their neck out to help me. They include Ali Reza Shiravi at the Ministry of Culture and Islamic Guidance, Shayesteh Amiri at the president's office, Homayoun Teymurpour at the Ministry of Agriculture and Farhad Eftekharzadeh at the Ministry of Education.

I spent some time working for the office of the United Nations Resident Coordinator in Tehran, and I am grateful to all those UN staff members who helped me with documentation, introductions and valuable advice, especially Michael von der Schulenburg of UNDP, Gamal Ahmed of FAO, Sharareh Amirkhalili of UNFPA, Sharad Sapra and Foroogh Foyouzat of UNICEF, Afsaneh Ashrafi and Shabnam Besharat of UNHCR.

Many journalists helped and encouraged me, including Shahla Sherkat, Nadia Pizzuti, Christophe de Roquefeuil, Mehrdad Balali, Kaveh Golestan, Jim Muir, Gabriella Bianchi, Guy Dinmore, Geneive Abdo, Roger Hardy, David Hirst, Thomas Goltz and Hugh Pope. Academics such as Afsaneh Najmabadi, Ziba Mir-Hosseini, Nasrin Jazani and Jeremy Swift were generous with their time. The staff of Cenesta NGO, especially Catherine Razavi, opened my eyes to village life outside of Tehran. Translators

Ameneh Barzegar, Noushine, Maryam and Afshan arranged interviews that were difficult to obtain.

Friends such as Pari Namazie, Bijan Khajehpour, Hedieh Rouhani, Guita Rezakhanlou, Mamak Nourbakhsh, and Hosein and Nevine Mahdavi introduced me simultaneously to Iranian family life and current affairs. Pari Momen Nassiri and Mary James opened the door to many meetings with the fascinating guests at their Professional Women's Group. They included Mehrangiz Kar, Shahla Lahiji, Jaleh Shaditalab, Soheila Shahshahani and Mansoureh Ettehadiyeh. Nastaran Musavy, Mahsa Shekarloo and Nooshin Ahmady alerted me to happenings in the women's movement. The British Wives' Library and the British Institute for Persian Studies, just around the corner from my house, were always welcoming.

A special mention goes to my friend and neighbor, Catherine Squire, who made me feel part of her Iranian family and made many helpful suggestions on the manuscript. I was lucky to have an incisive editor in Mohammad Batmanglij at Mage.

My husband, Laurens, fell in love with Iran long before his job with UNHCR brought us to Tehran. It was he who urged me to write this book and nagged me to finish it when we left. Our children, Sasha and Thomas, grew up with it. They did not pester me too much, so I did not, unlike Shirin Ebadi, have to lock myself into the bathroom to write.

Finally I would like to thank my mother and father, who gave me the curiosity and confidence to go out into the world and believe in myself.

Jane Howard
Geneva, 2002

Bibliography

Abrahamian, Ervand. *Khomeinism*. Berkeley: University of California Press, 1993.

Adelkhah, Fariba. *Etre Moderne en Iran*. Paris: Editions Karthala, 1998.

———. *La Revolution Sous le Voile*. Paris: Editions Karthala, 1991.

Afkhami, Mahnaz. "Introduction." In *Faith and Freedom: Women's Human Rights in the Muslim World*. New York: Syracuse University Press, 1995.

——— and Erika Friedl. *In the Eye of the Storm: Women in Post-Revolutionary Iran*. New York: Syracuse University Press, 1994.

Afshar, Haleh. *Islam and Feminisms: An Iranian Case-Study*. New York: Palgrave, 1998.

Ahmed, Leila. *Women and Gender in Islam: Historical Roots of a Modern Debate*. New Haven: Yale University Press, 1992.

Al-Saltana, Taj. *Crowning Anguish: Memoirs of a Persian Princess from the Harem to Modernity*. Edited with introduction and notes by Abbas Amanat. Washington: Mage Publishers, 1993.

Bahrampour, Tara. *To See and See Again: A Life in Iran and America*. New York: Farrar, Straus and Giroux, 1999.

Bakhash, Shaul. *The Reign of the Ayatollahs*. New York: Basic Books, 1985.

Batmanglij, Najmieh. *New Food of Life: Ancient Persian and Modern Iranian Cooking and Ceremonies*. Washington: Mage Publishers, 1994.

Beck, Lois. *Nomad: A Year in the Life of a Qashqa'i Tribesman in Iran*. London: I.B. Tauris, 1991.

Bird, Isabella. *Journeys through Persia and Kurdistan*. London: Virago, 1989.

Brooks, Geraldine. *Nine Parts of Desire: The Hidden World of Islamic Women*. New York: Anchor Books, 1996.

Cameron, Averil, and A. Kuhrt, eds. *Images of Women in Antiquity.*
London and Canberra: Croom Helm, 1983.

Daneshvar, Simin. *Savushun.* Translated by M. Ghanoonparvar.
Washington: Mage Publishers, 1990.

Deonna, Laurence. *Persianeries.* Geneva: Editions Zoe, 1998.

Diba, Layla S., with Maryam Ekhtiar, eds. *Royal Persian Paintings: The
Qajar Epoch 1785–1925.* New York: Brooklyn Museum of Art, 1998.

Dorry, Getrude Nye. *45 Years in Iran: A Memoir.* Wareham,
Massachusetts: 1998.

Ebadi, Shirin. *The Rights of the Child: A Study on Legal Aspects of
Children's Rights in Iran.* Tehran: Roshangaran, 1992. Reprint, translated by M. Zaimaran, UNICEF, 1994.

Esfandiari, Haleh. *Reconstructed Lives: Women and Iran's Islamic
Revolution.* Baltimore: Johns Hopkins University Press, 1997.

Falk, S. J. *Qajar Paintings.* London: Sotheby Publications, 1972.

Faramarzi, Mohammad T. *A Travel Guide to Iran.* Tehran: Yassaman
Publications, 1997.

Farman Farmaian, Sattareh. *Daughter of Persia.* New York: Anchor
Books, 1992.

Farrokhzad, Forugh. *Another Birth: Selected Poems of Forugh Farrokhzad.*
Translated by Hasan Javadi and Susan Sallee. California: Albany Press, 1981.

Fernea, Elizabeth Warnock. *Women and the Family in the Middle East:
New Voices of Change.* Austin, University of Texas Press, 1985.

Friedl, Erika. *Children of Deh Koh.* New York: Syracuse University
Press, 1997.

———. *Women of Deh Koh.* London: Penguin, Smithsonian Institution 1989.

Frye, Richard. *The Golden Age of Persia.* London: Weidenfeld, 1993.

Ghirshman, R. *Iran.* London: Penguin, 1954.

Guppy, Shusha. *The Blindfold Horse: Memories of a Persian Childhood.*
London: Heinemann, 1988.

Haeri, Shahla. *Law of Desire: Temporary Marriage in Iran.* New York:
Syracuse University Press, 1989.

Harney, Desmond. *The Priest and the King: An Eyewitness Account of the
Iranian Revolution.* London: I.B. Tauris, 1998.

Hinnells, John R. *Persian Mythology.* London: Hamlyn, 1973.

Hiro, Dilip. *Iran under the Ayatollahs.* London: Routledge & Kegan Paul,
1985.

Jerome, Carole. *The Man in the Mirror.* London: Unwin Hyman, 1988.

Kandiyoti, Deniz, ed. *Gendering the Middle East.* New York: Syracuse
University Press, 1996.

Keddie, Nikki R., ed. *Religion and Politics in Iran: Shi'ism from Quietism to Revolution*. New Haven, Connecticut: Yale University Press, 1983.

Lahiji, Shahla and Mehrangiz Kar. *The Quest for Identity: The Image of Iranian Women in Prehistory and History*. Tehran: Roshangaran Publishers, 1993 (in Persian).

Leonie Picard, Barbara. *Tales of Ancient Persia*. Oxford: Oxford University Press, 1972.

Mabro, Judy. *Veiled Half-Truths: Western Travellers' Perceptions of Middle Eastern Women*. London: I.B. Tauris, 1991.

Matheson, Sylvia A. *Persia: An Archaeological Guide*. New Jersey: Noyes Press, 1973.

Mernissi, Fatima. *Beyond the Veil*. Revised edition. Indiana: University Press, 1987.

Milani, Farzaneh. *Veils and Words: The Emerging Voices of Iranian Women Writers*. New York: Syracuse University Press, 1992.

Mir-Hosseini, Ziba. *Islam and Gender: The Religious Debate in Contemporary Iran*. Princeton: Princeton University Press 1999.

———. *Marriage on Trial: A Study of Islamic Family Law*. London: I.B. Tauris, 1993.

Moghadam, Valentine M. *Modernizing Women: Gender and Social Change in the Middle East*. Boulder and London: Lynne Rienner Publishers, 1993.

Moghissi, Haideh. *Populism and Feminism in Iran: Women's Struggle in a Male-Defined Revolutionary Movement*. London: Macmillan, 1994.

Mottahedeh, Roy. *The Mantle of the Prophet*. London: Chatto and Windus, 1988.

Najmabadi, Afsaneh. "Power, Morality, and the New Muslim Womanhood." In *The Politics of Social Transformation in Afghanistan, Iran and Pakistan*. New York: Syracuse University Press, 1994.

---, ed. *Women's Autobiographies in Contemporary Iran*. Cambridge: Harvard University Press, 1990.

---. *The Story of the Daughters of Quchan*. New York: Syracuse University Press, 1998.

Paidar, Parvin. *Women and the Political Process in Twentieth-Century Iran*. Cambridge: Cambridge University Press, 1995.

Perrin, Jean-Pierre. *L'Iran Sous le Voile*. Paris: Editions de l'Aube, 1996.

Poya, Maryam. *Women, Work and Islamism: Ideology and Resistance in Iran*. London and New York: Zed Books, 1999.

Raby, Julian, ed. *Qajar Portraits*. London: Azimuth Editions, with the Iran Heritage Foundation, 1999.

Sciolino, Elaine. *Persian Mirrors*. New York: The Free Press, 2000.

Shahshahani, Soheila. *The Four Seasons of the Sun: an Ethnography of the Sedentarized village of the Mamasani Pastoral Nomads of Iran*. Ann Arbor: University Microfilms International, 1982.

Shawcross, William. *The Shah's Last Ride*. London: Chatto and Windus, 1989.

Simpson, John. *Behind Iranian Lines*. London: Fontana/Collins, 1989.

———. *Under the Veil*. London: Coronet, 1995.

St. Vincent, David. *Iran: A Travel Survival Kit*. Hawthorn, Australia: Lonely Planet Publications, 1992.

Stark, Freya. *Valleys of the Assassins*. First published in 1934 by John Murray. Reprint, Los Angeles: J. P. Tarcher, 1983.

Stevens, Roger. *The Land of the Great Sophy*. London: Methuen, 1971.

UNICEF. *The State of the Young*. Islamic Republic of Iran. Tehran: UNICEF, 1998.

———. *The State of Women*. Islamic Republic of Iran. Tehran: UNICEF, 1998.

United Nations Development Program and Plan and Budget Organization. *Human Development Report of the Islamic Republic of Iran, 1999*. Tehran: United Nations Development Program and Plan Budget Organization, 1999.

United Nations Population Fund. *Country Population Assessment*. Tehran: UNFPA, 2000.

Wiesehöfer, Josef. *Ancient Persia*. London and New York: I.B. Tauris, 1996.

Wright, Robin. *Sacred Rage: The Crusade of Modern Islam*. London: Andre Deutsch, 1986.

———. *The Last Great Revolution*. New York: Alfred A. Knopf, 2000.

About the Author

Jane Howard is a freelance journalist living in Geneva. A graduate of Cambridge University, she worked as a foreign correspondent for BBC World Service and The *Guardian*, reporting from Turkey, Yugoslavia and Eastern Europe. She covered the fall of Communism in Bulgaria and the war in Croatia and Bosnia. From the beginning of 1996 to the end of 2000, she lived in Iran where her husband was working for the United Nations. She has two sons.